TOM DOUGLAS, Chef/owner, Seattle's Dahlia Lounge and Etta's Seafood, 1994 Winner of the James Beard Award: "Beautifully insightful and concise! Revive the art of cooking and bring the family meal (one you can eat!) back to its rightful place of prominence in the home."

MARY GARLAND SCHAUPP, Management Consultant, married with two babies, travels often: "When I'm home I want dinner to be a cozy family time. Because of this book I don't waste time wandering through the market trying to think of what to cook. I can play with the kids, pull a few things out of my 'pantry,' and produce a wonderful dinner in less than an hour. This author knows what it's like to be a working mom."

LEE BRILLHART, CEO, father of two, the family cook: "For me, cooking is easy. I just follow the recipe. But choosing what to make and serve can be a chore. With this book, Heidi puts the joy back in cooking. She offers dozens of expertly planned menus—and even lets you know how to make great meals with the leftovers. If you like to eat, you need this book."

MEG WESTBROOK, Mother of three, active in church, school, and home projects: "What terrific ideas! This book opens my mind to creative and easy ways I can use leftovers. A perfect gift for all of my 'Busy Mom' friends."

THE
WHAT TO FIX
FOR DINNER
COOKBOOK

Heidi Rabel

Silvyn HARA
PUBLISHING

Seattle, WA

Published by
Hara Publishing
P.O. Box 19732
Seattle, WA 98109

ISBN: 1-883697-91-3

Library of Congress Number: 95-79402

Design: Shaun Hubbard Graphic Design
Desktop Publisher: Paulette Eickman
Illustrator: Cheri Ryan
Editor: Cherie Tucker
Recipe Testing Coordinator: Shannon Conway

Dedication

In loving memory of my mother who ignited my life-long passion for cooking when I was five years old, inviting me to make the family's breakfast toast, "any way you think will make it special, dear."

My heartfelt thanks to John, Mari, Eric, Anna, Peter, Lance, Laura, and Stephanie for their unequivocal encouragement.

Acknowledgments

To the meticulous recipe testers and their families who ate the results, thank you: Shannon, Martha, Alison, Lisa, Phoebe, Patsy, Mary, Jan, Judy, Grace, Susan, and Wendy.

A portion of the proceeds from the sale of this book will be donated to the YWCA of Seattle-King County emergency shelter program.

How It Works: The Menus, The Recipes, The Suggestions

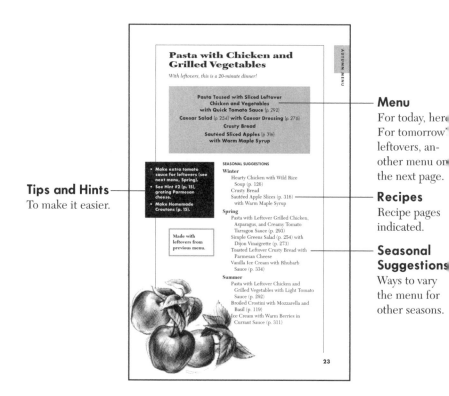

Menu
For today, here
For tomorrow'
leftovers, an-
other menu on
the next page.

Recipes
Recipe pages
indicated.

Seasonal Suggestions
Ways to vary
the menu for
other seasons.

Tips and Hints
To make it easier.

Pasta with Chicken and Grilled Vegetables

With leftovers, this is a 20-minute dinner!

Pasta Tossed with Sliced Leftover
Chicken and Vegetables
with Quick Tomato Sauce (p. 292)
Caesar Salad (p 254) with Caesar Dressing (p 276)
Crusty Bread
Sautéed Sliced Apples (p 316)
with Warm Maple Syrup

- Make extra tomato sauce for leftovers (see next menu, Spring).
- See Hint #2 (p. 15), grating Parmesan cheese.
- Make Homemade Croutons (p. 15).

Made with leftovers from previous menu.

SEASONAL SUGGESTIONS

Winter
Hearty Chicken with Wild Rice Soup (p. 126)
Crusty Bread
Sautéed Apple Slices (p. 316) with Warm Maple Syrup

Spring
Pasta with Leftover Grilled Chicken, Asparagus, and Creamy Tomato Tarragon Sauce (p. 293)
Simple Greens Salad (p. 254) with Dijon Vinaigrette (p. 273)
Toasted Leftover Crusty Bread with Parmesan Cheese
Vanilla Ice Cream with Rhubarb Sauce (p. 334)

Summer
Pasta with Leftover Chicken and Grilled Vegetables with Light Tomato Sauce (p. 292)
Broiled Crostini with Mozzarella and Basil (p. 119)
Ice Cream with Warm Berries in Currant Sauce (p. 311)

AUTUMN MENU

23

Decide what you want to cook by looking at menus in a particular season, or scan the index for ideas:

- By food types—pasta, vegetables, soups, etc.
- By a particular food—chicken, fish, etc.
- By a meal category—appetizer, dessert, salad, etc.

Table of Contents

Introduction

Dear Fellow Home Cook,

For just a moment, imagine yourself hard at work on a late afternoon as that Oh-God-what-will-I-cook-for-dinner realization hits. Stumped for an idea and feeling guilty about all the take-out cartons in your garbage, you quietly slip into Dinner Planning Denial and go on working, knowing that the first words you will hear at home are "What's for dinner?"—Another night of frozen pizza or pasta and spaghetti sauce from a jar.

How did something as important and supposedly comforting as dinner become such an onerous burden?

I love food and I love to cook; it's my profession. But somehow that and all those gorgeous food magazines at the checkstand don't relate to planning dinners for the family, night after night.

So when the kids grew up, and my life simplified, I decided to write that menu guide I had longed for so desperately during the more hectic years. Not a life restructuring home management system requiring family chore delegation, matching Tupperware® for leftovers, and cases of sticky notes. Just a straight-forward, easy-to-use book of inspiring, delicious sounding answers to that haunting question, What's for dinner? Something to look at once in awhile or every night, filled with complete dinners that seem really inviting.

So here it is, a year's supply of wholesome dinner menus presented by seasons, and recipes to go with them. And from beginning to end it is written with the assumption that time is one of your most precious, challenging commodities.

I hope you enjoy reading **The What To Fix For Dinner Cookbook** and that it helps simplify your life. You deserve it.

Heidi Rabel

A Word About Leftovers

Leftovers are a dying art in America.

While *leftover* may be a humble word, the concept has been the core of creative cooking since the first meat brought home from the hunt was too much to eat in one night, but not enough to provide a full meal the following day.

For generations, leftovers have kept people from starving and inspired creativity in millions of kitchens all over the world. Think about it. How did the ideas for chicken and dumplings or bread pudding or chili or turkey pot pie originate?

Americans seem to have put aside the leftover concept. We approach meals as single entities prepared from recipes so precisely that there is not a spoonful left for the next day. Instead of an economical, thrown-together-in-10 minutes, original and delicious use of things that might spoil, we buy noodles in a cup, risotto in a box, stew spices in an envelope, and spaghetti sauce in a jar. We spend as much as 40 percent of our grocery dollars on disposable packaging, and there are almost no pots of soup simmering on the backs of American stoves.

Sadly, while we are in the midst of a culinary renaissance, inundated with ideas and foods from all over the world, we are not producing inspired home cooks who can stretch a pork roast or four pounds of beets into three or four meals.

So this book is filled with real leftovers. My dream is that they will inspire you to experiment with taste so often that someday you will conjure up a dish as wonderful and new as meatloaf was 200 years ago.

The Well-Stocked Pantry— Investing Time Now To Save Lots Later

A well-stocked pantry allows you to cook really good food at the drop of a hat.

I first considered the concept as a parent of starving teenagers (I know that's redundant), who can devour a week's worth of ready-made foods in five minutes, but won't touch diced tomatoes in puree, flavored olive oil, uncooked arborio rice, minced garlic, frozen chicken stock, or capers.

Now, when I face cooking dinner at 7 p.m., exhausted from a full day at work and knowing I have laundry to do later, I really appreciate my well-stocked pantry, with all of its ingredients to make fabulous pasta sauce, pasta, and a salad with homemade dressing in twenty minutes.

Initial stocking takes about three hours because it involves creating your own list and shopping for it. From then on you're just picking up one or two items while you are at the store.

Following is my pantry list including many items called for in the menus. You might notice that mine doesn't include peanut butter, ice cream, popcorn, bacon, or chocolate chips. Add your own favorites so the list will work for you.

Heidi's Pantry List

Also see Resources, p. 340

Oils

Extra Virgin, Lite, and Flavored Olive Oil

Peanut Oil

Pure Sesame Oil

Spray Corn or Olive Oil

Vegetable Oil (Corn or Saffola)

Vinegars (refrigerated)

Apple Cider

Balsamic

Rice (unseasoned)

Mustards (refrigerated)

Dijon (biggest jar)

Dijon Glaze (p. 105)

Whole Grain

Capers

Olives

Pitted Calamata (Resources, p. 340) (refrigerated)

Pitted Black

Kosher Salt

Ground Pepper

Peppercorns

Crushed Red Pepper Flakes

Asian Black Bean Sauce
(Resources, p. 340) (refrigerated)

Nouc Mam, Asian Fish Sauce
(Resources, p. 340) (refrigerated)

Sesame Seeds (toasted)

Soy Sauce (refrigerated)

Dried Herbs

Basil

Ground Ancho Chilies

Garlic (fresh or dehydrated)

Green Onions (fresh) or Chives (dehydrated)

Onions (fresh or dehydrated)

Shallots (fresh or dehydrated)

Tarragon

Thyme

Legumes

Black Beans (can)

Garbanzo Beans (can)

White Beans (can)

Lentils (dry)

Cheese and Dairy (refrigerated)

Aged Parmesan (not the green tube kind)

Blue Cheese

Yogurt

Produce

Carrots (refrigerated)

Lemons (reconstituted or fresh)

Lettuce (refrigerated)

Limes (reconstituted or fresh)

Oranges or Frozen Orange Zest

Onions

Clam Nectar

Premium Diced Tomatoes In Purée

Canned Mild Chilies

Pasta

Linguini (dry)

Fettucine (dry)

Penne (dry)

Ravioli, Tortellini (frozen, fresh)

Grains

Arborio Rice

Mixed Rice (Basmati, wild, brown)

Pearl Barley

Baking Soda

Baking Powder

Brown, Granulated, and Superfine Sugar

All-Purpose and Cake Flour

Cornmeal

Scone Mix

Baking Mix

Flavorings (pure only)

Vanilla (Mexican and bourbon)

Almond

Spices

Cinnamon

Cloves (whole and ground)

Garam Masala Curry Paste® (Resources, p. 340)

Curry Powder

Nutmeg

Allspice (ground)

Ground Chili Pepper (not pure Cayenne)

Ground Cumin

Honey

Dried Fruits

Raisins

Currants

Chopped Dates

Minute Tapioca®

Chutneys (Unopened, they last indefinitely; opened and refrigerated, they last for months.)

Pesto

Basil (frozen or shelf-stable)

Sun-Dried Tomato (p. 284)

Boxed Lavosh, Melba, and Water Crackers

Cooking Brandy

California Dry Sherry

Wine (Take the time to build a stock of 3 cases of wine, balanced for different tastes, qualities, and varieties. Replenish when you use so you always have a good choice.)

Frozen Items

Butter (unsalted)

Doughs

Tart

Pie Crust

Puff Pastry

Pear Poaching Liquid (p. 313)

Raspberries and Blueberries

Berry Sauce (p. 333)

Stock (p. 108)

Chicken

Fish

Vegetable

The Magic Stock Bag

The most important hint I can pass along to you is how to make your own stock. It is unbelievably easy, uses trimmings you would otherwise throw away, recycles nutritious food waste, and provides you with fabulous stock to make risotto, sauces, soups, stews, gravies, and chowders. Homemade stock revolutionized my cooking because it is such a delicious flavor base. The only thing you need to buy for stock is a package of chicken necks and backs for chicken stock, a package of soup bones for beef stock, or a package of fish head and tail for fish stock. (You don't need anything for vegetable stock.) It almost takes longer to describe how to make stock than it does to prepare it. It is that simple.

Here's what you do. Put a plastic produce bag into the sink while you are cooking. Each time you work with produce, taking the tops and skins off onions, peeling carrots, taking leaves off fresh herbs, or cutting off the tired parts of stems, put all the waste into the bag. Close it with a twist tie and put it in the freezer. The only exceptions are: cabbage of all kinds, broccoli, lettuce, artichokes, beets—unless you like red stock—radishes, and mint.

When the bag is full, dump the frozen trimmings into a stock pot with 2 gallons of water, a little kosher salt, and 5 or 6 crushed red pepper flakes. Look in the refrigerator and pull out any tired produce that you would throw away, and add it to the pot. For chicken stock, add the frozen package of chicken necks and backs to the pot (for meat, add bones; for fish, add heads and tails). Also add 1 or 2 tbsp. of the oldest dried herbs in your cupboard (double that for vegetable stock).

Bring the water to a hard boil, turn the heat down to low and let the stock simmer until it is reduced to about 2 quarts of liquid (it's a little hard to tell through all the stuff; just guess).

You probably will want to turn on an exhaust fan to cut down steam, but you do not need to stir, watch, or do anything else to help the stock along. It cooks itself in about 3 - 4 hours.

After the stock has cooked down, strain it through a colander or strainer into a mixing bowl, cover it loosely with plastic wrap, and refrigerate it until the fat solidifies on the top (vegetable stock will not have fat). Remove the fat, throw it away (see box below), transfer the stock to recycled pint containers (cottage cheese, sour cream, salsa, etc.), and freeze it until you need it.

Here are some things I have learned:

•I almost always start stock at times when I know I will be around for four to five hours.

•If it's late afternoon after the stock cooks down, I let it sit in the pot until just before I go to bed, then put it into the colander and leave it draining over night. In the morning it goes into the refrigerator to set up during the day. The point is, **this is a very versatile process that will work around your schedule.** Except for boiling it dry, there is hardly anything you can do to wreck it.

•I buy carrots with stems and tops because they have such good flavor.

•Vegetable stock is wonderful with mushrooms and a couple of garlic cloves added.

Stock is a great way to use up old dried herbs!

When you make chicken stock, freeze some of the fat that you take off the chilled stock, and use it to fry chicken hash or potatoes, etc.

High Temperature Cooking

Did you ever wonder why, when you order stuffed breast of chicken in a restaurant, it can be at your table, obviously freshly cooked and delicious, in about 15 minutes? (We all know that chicken breasts take 30 minutes to cook . . . or do they?)

Restaurants cook chicken, fish, meat, and many other foods at very high temperatures, so that food can get to their customers in a reasonable length of time. You can too, as long as you are careful and protect the food from drying out.

Many of the recipes in this book call for high temperature cooking (450-500°) using Dijon Glaze (p. 105), a simple sauce that seals the pores of foods to protect against moisture loss, and adds a subtle base flavor.

With high temperature cooking you will produce crisp, moist chicken, meats, and fish as quickly as professional restaurant chefs do.

A Few Helpful Hints

These are things I have learned over the years that save me time and effort.
I hope you find them useful.

1 **If crusty French or Italian bread is not available** in your community, you can modify frozen bread dough. Thaw and reshape the dough into a round or baguette-shaped loaf; then let it rise according to the manufacturer's directions. Hard crusts are a result of steam added during the cooking process. While the oven is preheating to baking temperature, heat a 9 x 9 x 2" pan and place it on the rack below the one on which the bread will bake. Meanwhile, boil 2 cups of water. Just before putting the loaf in the oven, dust the top with a little flour and, with a sharp, serrated knife or razor blade, make 3 diagonal slits across the top of the loaf. When the oven is up to temperature, put in the bread and pour the boiling water into the other hot pan. Close the door immediately to trap the steam, and cook the loaf. You will be excited about the results.

2 **Good Parmesan cheese** is so firm that it is difficult to grate. If you heat it in the microwave for a few seconds, it softens enough to grate easily.

3 **Is this pear ripe?** Gently press a pear at the top next to the stem; if it just barely gives to the pressure, it is perfectly ripe. Like avocados and bananas, pears ripen quickly in a brown bag.

4 **Entertaining Hint:** Don't stuff the guests! If your guests are anything like mine, they will arrive hungry and ready to attack the first food they see, the hors d'oeuvres. Too many just squelch appetites for the dinner you have prepared. Polite guests eat everything bravely and end up moaning on the way home; others pick at their dinners, and you feel like a D+ cook. Try to plan hors d'oeuvres that are just a bite, a hint of what's to come. Think light, flavor, crunch, and color.

5 **When you make apple pie:** Make extra filling and freeze it. Then, in December, with refrigerated pie dough and a small jar of mincemeat, you can make bite-sized mince apple turnovers and really impress your mother-in-law.

6 **Save caper juice and brine-cured olive (Spanish, Sicilian, calamata) juice.** Use it to flavor mayonnaise, Dijon Glaze, tartar sauce, vinaigrettes, etc. It is flavorful and adds an interesting taste to lots of things.

7 **To slice vegetables**, lay them on a flat surface, and make a slice on one side to create a flat bottom. That way, the vegetables won't slip out from under the knife!

8 **Dried herbs**, once opened, lose flavor after a few months. (Did you say months? I have some in my cupboard that are 5 years old!) Don't throw them out; use them for stock.

9 **To grate citrus zest**, put a piece of plastic wrap over the zest grater surface, and grate away. Peel the wrap off the grater and scrape off the zest.

Keeping fresh ginger root: Freeze, then peel as much as you need and use a zester to remove the flesh from the frozen root. Or peel and grate the whole root, put extra into a zip-type bag (pressing out all air), and refrigerate for up to a month or freeze for up to two months.

For the Thanksgiving turkey, I buy one of those cards with trussing skewers and string. That way I won't have to think about where I left the string or hunt through the work bench for stainless steel nails. Other times of year, I use wooden skewers and, if I can't find string, I use dental floss (not mint flavored), the world's strongest, most versatile string.

The heat in chili peppers releases as it cooks, so food containing chilies tends to get hotter over time.

When you make chicken stock, freeze some of the fat that you take off the refrigerated stock and use it to fry chicken, hash, potatoes, etc.

Melting chocolate: Burned chocolate is ruined chocolate! Whether you use cheap chocolate chips or the finest Belgian chocolate, it should be melted over simmering water to obtain a silky smooth texture and to avoid burning it. If you use double boiler pans, make sure that the water touches the upper pan, because steam is hotter than simmering water, and chocolate burns very easily.

The fastest way to get skinless citrus fruit sections is to set the fruit upright on a cutting surface, and peel it from top to bottom with a sharp knife, cutting away any of the white pith. Pick up the skinned fruit and cut into it directly alongside the separating membranes until all the sections are removed.

Pasta can be precooked and held, refrigerated, for 2 or 3 days. Cook, rinse (in cool water to stop the cooking), and drain the pasta. Toss it with a little olive oil and put it into a zip-type plastic bag. Press the air out of the bag before sealing it. To reheat: Boil water in a saucepan, put the cold pasta in a strainer and plunge the strainer into the water for 1 minute. Remove the strainer, let the pasta drain, and serve immediately.

Make Dijon Glaze (p. 105) by the pint. Divide it among several smaller jars, add a different herb to each one, and leave one plain. That way, you will have several glazes on hand ready to go.

Beano®, a product available in most drug stores and many grocery stores, breaks down undigestible proteins before they reach the large intestine (where bacteria break them down, causing gas). A tasteless liquid, Beano® is added after legumes are cooked, just before they are eaten.

19 Tomato purée and tomato sauce are not the same. Tomato sauce is seasoned; tomato purée is 100% tomato.

20 Timing is critical when cooking fish, therefore, cook everything else first and let it wait for the fish. I would much rather eat warm vegetables with piping hot fish than piping hot vegetables with overdone, lukewarm fish.

21 Oil will not stick to wet greens, which is why so many salad dressings taste like they are just vinegar. If you like salad, use a lettuce spinner to dry the lettuce. You will need much less dressing, and it won't end up in the bottom of the salad bowl.

22 Swirls made in sauces add a special touch that makes you look like a pro. All you need is a plastic bottle with a 1/8" open tip lid (drug stores carry them for travel cosmetics). Suggestion: practice on a plain plate. Put the sauce into the container and squeeze swirls to your heart's content. For "bleeding hearts": squeeze dots about 1" apart on top of sauce. In one movement, pull the tip of a paring knife, skewer, or toothpick through and slightly beyond each dot. For fleur-de-lis, squeeze straight, horizontal lines across the sauce about 1" apart. Using the tip of a sharp paring knife, skewer, or toothpick, pull vertical lines through the horizontal lines, alternating from top to bottom, then from bottom to top.

23 Cooked fish for cold sandwiches or salads should be brought to room temperature before using. The cold fat is quite firm, and it creates a tough consistency. At room temperature, it is soft and delicate.

24 Shellfish cooks perfectly in a microwave (lobster might be too unwieldy); it also takes less time than steaming or poaching on top of the stove, and it cooks in its own juices. Place the shellfish in a single layer in the cooking dish. Crack crab or crayfish shells slightly before they are put into the dish to make sure that steam can escape as they cook. Cover the container tightly with plastic wrap, and cook on the highest temperature until done. Cooking time will depend upon the amount of shellfish. Check after 5 minutes and continue to cook if necessary.

25 Cornstarch is a wonderful thickener for sauces or soups, but there are a few tricks that make it work better. First, always add liquid to cornstarch, not the reverse. Second, the starch needs to cook to expand and thicken, and a little more to cook off the starchy (chalky) taste. But third, if it is cooked too long or too hot (more than simmering for 5 minutes), the cornstarch breaks down and the creamy thick sauce gets thin again. Sauces thickened with cornstarch get thicker when they are refrigerated, and thin slightly when they are reheated.

26 **If you love the flavor of wild mushrooms** as much as I do, this hint will make your day. Some specialty food companies produce powdered wild mushrooms to flavor sauces, soups, etc., but it is very expensive. I make my own by grinding packaged dried wild mushrooms into a fine powder. It stores perfectly in a darkened cupboard and is always ready.

27 **For grinding spices, seeds, etc.,** I use an inexpensive coffee grinder. I do not advise using the same grinder for coffee and spices, because coffee beans contain oil that is next to impossible to clean out of a grinder.

28 **This incredibly easy way to peel ripe tomatoes** was taught to me by Marcella Hazan, the gracious leading lady of Italian cooking. Hold the tomato stem side up, and using a sharp vegetable peeler in a side-to-side sawing motion, peel the tomato in strips from the stem to the bottom. If you don't apply pressure, the juice will stay in the tomato. Cut the peeled tomato into wedges and scoop the seeds out with your thumb or a spoon, then cut away the pith. (It takes longer to describe this process than it does to peel a tomato!) If the tomato has been oil sprayed by the grocer, wash it first so the peeler will work easily. Use the boiling water method for winter tomatoes (see next Hint).

29 **Tomato concasse**, a classic French garnish for sauces or finished food, is peeled, seeded, and chopped tomato. To make concasse, prepare an ice-water bath in a medium size mixing bowl, and boil water in a small saucepan. Cut two small, shallow cross slits in the bottom end of a tomato, and dip it into the boiling water for 30 seconds. With a slotted spoon, transfer it to the ice water to cool. Take it out and peel it starting at the slits. Cut the tomato in half horizontally (like a grapefruit), and squeeze out the juice and seeds (into the stock bag, with the tomato peel!). Press the halves flat onto a cutting board with the palm of your hand, dice the halves, and drain.

30 **A non-reactive container** is one that will not react chemically to the acid in fruit, peppers, vinegar, or salt. Stainless steel, plastic, and glass are non-reactive. Aluminum and copper are reactive.

What To Fix For Dinner?

The Menus

Autumn

Spectacular sky-filling sunsets, fog hovering over the wetlands, welcome afternoon rains, Trick or Treat, football, and leaves to kick. The beach fire has moved inside, a crackling beacon focusing inward. Everywhere the dazzling colors of Nature slowing down remind us to store the harvest for winter. Food thoughts turn to crusty breads hot from the oven, hand-warming mugs of rich tomato soup, buttery popcorn after a day of cleaning up the yard, and the smells of roasting chicken drifting through the house. Forty years later, I can still taste the juice of Mr. Anderson's crisp Jonathon apples my best friend and I picked on our way home from school.

Menus

Italian Grilled Chicken and Autumn Vegetables

Pasta with Chicken and Grilled Vegetables

Lamb Shanks with Barley

Homemade Scotch Broth, Bread and Cheese

Dijon-Glazed Swordfish with Fresh Tomato Sauce

Chilled Fish and Vegetable Salad

Chicken with Lentils, Caramelized Onion, and Wild Mushrooms

Homemade Chicken and Wild Mushroom Soup

Risotto with Winter Squash, Ham, Caramelized Onion, and Sage

Grilled Sandwiches with Curried Pumpkin Bisque

Pasta with Puttanesca Sauce and Grated Parmesan

Potato Leek Soup and Broiled Sandwiches

Italian Grilled Chicken and Autumn Vegetables

The grilled vegetable flavors really complement the chicken.

Grilled Chicken (p. 167) **with Garlic Rosemary Dijon Glaze** (p. 105)

Grilled Marinated Vegetables (p. 226)**: Bell Peppers, Sweet Onion, Japanese Eggplant, and Fennel**

Crusty Bread

Mixed Greens Salad (p. 254)

Tomato Vinaigrette (p. 273) **and Grated Parmesan Cheese**

Apple Crisp (p. 309)

- **Buy extra chicken, vegetables, and apples for leftovers (see next menu).**
- **Small, oblong Japanese eggplants do not need to be presalted.**
- **See Hint #1 (p. 15), crusty bread.**
- **See Hint #2 (p. 15), grating Parmesan cheese.**
- **Winter: Make extra caramelized onion, freeze for later. Time-starved? Buy pilaf in a box.**

SEASONAL SUGGESTIONS

Winter

Grilled Chicken with Dijon Demi-Glace (p. 105), Caramelized Onion (p. 231), and Cranberry

Frozen Peas with Chopped Mint

Wild Rice Pilaf (p. 248)

Cranberry Apple Crisp (p. 309)

Spring

Chicken with Tarragon Dijon Glaze (p. 105)

Oven-Roasted New Potatoes (p. 237)

Steamed Asparagus (p. 224) with Lemon Oil Drizzle (p. 283)

Salad with Orange Sections and Orange Shallot Vinaigrette (p. 274)

Strawberry Rhubarb Crisp (p. 309)

Summer

Chicken with Lemon Herb Dijon Glaze

Grilled Summer Vegetables with Greek Marinade (p. 285)

Cucumber, Yogurt, and Mint Salad (p. 256)

Ice Cream with Licorice Liqueur and Toasted Almonds

Pasta with Chicken and Grilled Vegetables

With leftovers, this is a 20-minute dinner!

> **Pasta Tossed with Sliced Leftover
> Chicken and Vegetables
> with Quick Tomato Sauce** (p. 292)
> **Caesar Salad** (p. 254) **with Caesar Dressing** (p. 276)
> **Crusty Bread**
> **Sautéed Sliced Apples** (p. 316)
> **with Warm Maple Syrup**

Make extra tomato sauce for leftovers (see next menu, Spring).

See Hint #2 (p. 15), grating Parmesan cheese.

Make Homemade Croutons (p. 118).

Made with leftovers from previous menu.

SEASONAL SUGGESTIONS

Winter

Hearty Chicken with Wild Rice
Soup (p. 131)
Crusty Bread
Sautéed Apple Slices (p. 316)
with Warm Maple Syrup

Spring

Pasta with Leftover Grilled Chicken,
Asparagus, and Creamy Tomato
Tarragon Sauce (p. 293)
Simple Greens Salad (p. 254) with
Dijon Vinaigrette (p. 273)
Toasted Leftover Crusty Bread with
Parmesan Cheese
Vanilla Ice Cream with Rhubarb
Sauce (p. 334)

Summer

Pasta with Leftover Chicken and
Grilled Vegetables with Light Tomato
Sauce (p. 292)
Broiled Crostini with Mozzarella and
Basil (p. 119)
Ice Cream with Warm Berries in
Currant Sauce (p. 311)

Lamb Shanks with Barley

A flavor-filled, comforting dinner topped off with the old favorite, bread pudding.

Easy Lamb Shanks with Garlic, Rosemary, Orange, and Barley (p. 211)

Steamed Carrots and Broccoli (p. 224) **Tossed with Lemon Oil Drizzle** (p. 283)

Simple Greens Salad (p. 254) **with Roasted Mexican Pumpkin Seeds** (p. 110) **or Sunflower Nuts**

Orange Shallot Vinaigrette (p. 274)

Bread Pudding (p. 319) **with Whiskey Sauce** (p. 336)

- Make extra for leftovers (see next menu).
- Buy toasted sunflower nuts ready-made.
- Carrot ends in Stock Bag (p. 12), not broccoli.
- Winter: Leftover rice pudding or vanilla ice cream with maple syrup.
- Spring: Use "just add water" cornbread mix.

SEASONAL SUGGESTIONS

Winter

Lamb Shanks with Lentils and Mushrooms (above)

Spinach Salad with Orange Sections and Honey Mustard Dressing (p. 277)

Crusty Bread

Honey Vanilla Ice Cream with Warm Maple Syrup

Spring

Lamb Shanks with Tomato, Carrots, Fennel, and Lentils (above)

Mixed Greens Salad (p. 254) with Celery, Apple, and Caesar Dressing (p. 276)

Cheese Cornbread Muffins

Ice Cream with Heated Apricot Preserves

Summer

Lamb Shanks with White Beans, Baby Carrots, Garlic, and Fresh Sage (above)

Sliced Tomato and Cucumber Salad with Dijon Vinaigrette (p. 273)

Warm Garlic Bread

Berries with Lemon Cream (p. 337)

Homemade Scotch Broth, Bread and Cheese

Don't let the idea of homemade soup intimidate you; it's easy, very creative, and hard to find these days.

Homemade Lamb Barley Soup (p. 131)
Crusty Bread and Aged Cheddar Cheese
Mixed Greens Salad (p. 254) **with Sliced Pear**
Dijon Vinaigrette (p. 273)
Reheated Bread Pudding (p. 319) **or**
Chocolate Brownies

See Hint #3 (p. 15), selecting pears.
Use brownie mix.

Made with leftovers from previous menu.

SEASONAL SUGGESTIONS

Winter
Lamb Soup with Mushrooms
and Lentils (above)
Crusty Bread
Mixed Greens Salad with Dijon
Vinaigrette (p. 273)
Poached Pears (p. 313) with Berry
Sauce (p. 333)

Spring
Lamb Soup (above)
Mixed Greens Salad (p. 254) with Sliced
Apple, Chevre, and Dijon Vinaigrette
(p. 273)
Cornbread Pudding (p. 319) with Dried
Cherries and Vanilla Sauce (p. 335)

Summer
Marinated White Bean Salad (p. 258)
Leftover Cold Lamb and Vegetables
over Chiffonade-Cut Steamed Chard
(p. 223) and Italian Vinaigrette (p. 273)
Sliced Tomato and Mozzarella Cheese
with Fresh Basil and Olive Oil
Crusty Bread
Fresh Melon and Berries

Dijon-Glazed Swordfish with Fresh Tomato Sauce

Frozen potatoes + ready-made pesto = pesto fries!

Dijon-Glazed Grilled or Oven-Cooked Swordfish (p. 182) **(or other firm white fish) with Salsa Cruda** (p. 291)

Pesto Fries (p. 238)

Steamed String Beans (p. 224) **Tossed with Lemon Oil Drizzle** (p. 283)

Mixed Greens Salad (p. 254)

Dijon Vinaigrette (p. 273)

Fresh Pears with Berry Sauce (p. 333)

- **Buy extra fish and vegetables for leftovers.**
- **See Hint #3 (p. 15), selecting pears.**
- **Spring: In a hurry? Try Quick Fruit Chutney (p. 287).**

SEASONAL SUGGESTIONS

Winter
Cod or Halibut with Caponata (p. 115)
Steamed New Potatoes with Parsley Sauce (p. 283)
Sautéed Chiffonade-Cut Chard (p. 223) with Cracked Pepper and Lemon Oil Drizzle (p. 283)
Ice Cream or Frozen Yogurt

Spring
Fish with Tropical Fruit Salsa (p. 290)
Jamaican Beans and Rice (p. 249)
Salad (above) with Honey Mustard Dressing (p. 277)
Crusty Bread
Fruit Sorbet and Cookies

Summer
Fish with Lemon Herb Dijon Glaze (p. 105)
Steamed Baby Summer Vegetables (p. 224) with Lemon Oil Drizzle (p. 283)
Simple Greens Salad (p. 254)
Blue Cheese Vinaigrette (p. 273)
Berries with Lemon Whipped Cream (p. 337)

Chilled Fish and Vegetable Salad

A light, Indian Summer dinner made with leftover grilled fish.

**Arranged Salad with Leftover Fish,
Marinated Steamed New Potatoes** (p. 224)**, String
Beans, Tomatoes, Capers, and Black Olives**

Dijon Vinaigrette (p. 273)

**Broiled French Bread
with Grated Parmesan Cheese**

Hot Fudge Sundaes

**See Hint #23 (p. 17),
about chilled fish.**

**If there is leftover Salsa
Cruda from day before,
add it to the salad.**

**See Hint #1 (p. 15),
crusty bread.**

**See Hint #2 (p. 15),
grating Parmesan
cheese.**

Buy fudge sauce.

**Winter: Save time
with refrigerated
biscuit dough.
Buy caramel sauce.**

Made with
leftovers from
previous menu.

SEASONAL SUGGESTIONS

Winter
Salad with Fish, Chard, New Potatoes
and Caponata (p. 115)
Fresh Warm Biscuits (p. 120) with
Sliced Fontina Cheese
Sautéed Apples (p. 316) with
Caramel Sauce

Spring
Salad (above) with Fish, Marinated
Leftover Beans and Rice,
Chilled Asparagus, Tomato Sections,
and Homemade Mayonnaise (p. 279)
Ice Cream with Hot Caramel Sauce

Summer
Salad (above) with Fish, Chilled Baby
Vegetables, New Potatoes, Tomato,
Black Olives, and Capers
Crusty Bread
Ice Cream with Fresh Berries

Chicken with Lentils, Caramelized Onion, and Wild Mushrooms

A hearty, first chilly Fall night dinner that sets up several leftover meals.

**Dijon-Glazed Roasted
Chicken Quarters** (p.167)

**Lentils with Caramelized Onion
and Wild Mushrooms** (p. 233)

Steamed Julienne-Cut Winter Vegetables (p. 224)
with Chopped Sage and Lemon Oil Drizzle (p. 283)

Simple Greens Salad (p. 254)

Dijon Vinaigrette (p. 273)

**Honey Vanilla Ice Cream with
Warm Plum Sauce** (p. 334)

- **Make extra for leftovers (see next menu). This menu will fill your Stock Bag (p. 12).**
- **See Hint #26 (p. 18), wild mushrooms.**
- **Extra plum sauce freezes beautifully.**
- **Spring: Pepperidge Farm® makes good frozen pound cake.**

SEASONAL SUGGESTIONS

Winter
> Roasted Chicken (above)
> Wide Egg Fettucini tossed with Roasted Garlic (p. 225), Olive Oil, and Thyme
> Steamed Broccoli and Carrots with Sage (p. 224) and Lemon Oil Drizzle (above)
> Poached Pears (p. 313) with Warm Plum Sauce (above)

Spring
> Roasted Chicken (above)
> White Beans with Caramelized Onion and Sage (p. 253)
> Steamed Asparagus with Lemon Oil Drizzle (above)
> Apricot Cream (p. 338) over Pound Cake

Summer
> Barbecued Dijon-Glazed Chicken (p. 167)
> Marinated Bean Salad (p. 258)
> Crusty Bread
> Fresh Berry Cobbler (p. 309)

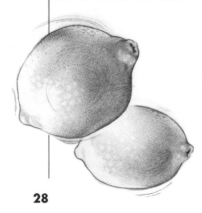

Homemade Chicken and Wild Mushroom Soup

Another easy, rib-sticking homemade soup. (Warning: they can become habit forming!)

Chicken, Wild Mushroom and Lentil Soup (p. 131)

Simple Greens Salad (p. 254)

Dijon Vinaigrette (p. 273)

Crusty French or Italian Bread

Rustic Pear Tart (p. 305) **with**
Quick Honey Vanilla Sauce (see box, p. 335)

Homemade stock from the freezer? Sound good? See p. 12.

See Hint #26 (p. 18), wild mushrooms.

See Hint #3 (p. 15), selecting pears.

With pre-made pie dough, this tart can be put together in 15 minutes.

Spring: Pepperidge Farm® makes good frozen pound cake.

Made with leftovers from previous menu.

SEASONAL SUGGESTIONS

Winter
> Homemade Chicken Noodle Soup (p. 122)
> Caesar Salad (p. 254) with Caesar Dressing (p. 276)
> Warm Herb Bread
> Rustic Pear Cranberry Tart (p. 305)

Spring
> Chicken, White Bean, and Onion Soup (p. 122)
> Simple Greens Salad with Italian Vinaigrette (p. 273)
> Caramel Sauce over Pound Cake

Summer
> Chicken Noodle Soup with Summer Vegetables (p. 122)
> Broiled French Bread with Pesto
> Ice Cream Cones

Risotto with Winter Squash, Ham, Caramelized Onion, and Sage

This dinner is as colorful as Autumn leaves.

Risotto (p. 151) **with Paper Thin Ham, Winter Squash, Caramelized Onion** (p. 231), **and Sage**

Mixed Greens Salad (p. 254) **with Sliced Red Apple and Crumbled Chevre**

Dijon Vinaigrette (p. 273)

Crusty Bread

Cranberry Sorbet and Snickerdoodle Cookies

- **If you haven't made a Stock Bag, see p. 12.**
- **Buy extra ham and apples for leftovers (see next menu).**
- **Buy the sorbet, cookies, and biscotti.**

SEASONAL SUGGESTIONS

Winter
> Risotto (above) with Chopped Chard, Ham, Red Onion, Diced Tomato in Purée, and Italian Herbs
> Sorbet and Biscotti

Spring
> Risotto (above) with Asparagus Tips, Julienne-Cut Carrots (p. 224), and Chopped Green Onion
> Spinach Salad with Apple, and Orange Shallot Vinaigrette (p. 274)
> Vanilla Ice Cream with Frozen Berry Sauce (p. 333)

Summer
> Leek Risotto (above) with Ham, Herbs and Chopped Summer Vegetables
> Crusty Bread
> Simple Greens Salad (p. 254)
> Dijon Vinaigrette (p. 273)
> Sliced Melon

Grilled Sandwiches with Curried Pumpkin Bisque

This sandwich combines wonderful Fall flavors.
A 30-minute dinner.

Grilled Ham, Jarlsberg Cheese, Caramelized Onion and Apple Sandwiches (p. 159) **on Sourdough Bread**

Quick Curried Pumpkin Bisque (p. 127)

Carrot Cake

- Buy the cake ready-made, frozen, or use a cake mix with added fresh carrots.
- Spring: Use brownie mix.

Made with leftovers from previous menu.

SEASONAL SUGGESTIONS

Winter
> Winter Root, Mushroom, Onion, and Prosciutto, and Rice Pasties (p. 161)
> Carrot Cake

Spring
> Grilled Sandwiches with Ham, Cheddar, Onion, Apple, and Curry Mayonnaise (p. 159)
> Chocolate Brownies

Summer
> Summer Vegetable and Ham Pasties (p. 161)
> Coleslaw (p. 255)
> Ice Cream with Fresh Sliced Peaches

31

Pasta with Puttanesca Sauce and Grated Parmesan

You only need a little of this tart, spicy sauce. For a heartier meal, serve grilled Italian sausage on the side.

Penne Pasta with Puttanesca Sauce (p. 294)
and Grated Parmesan Cheese

Crusty Bread

Mixed Greens Salad (p. 254)

Italian Vinaigrette (p. 273)

**Fresh Peach Halves with Berry
or Plum Sauce** (p. 333)

- **The cylinder shape of penne traps the sauce.**
- **See Hint #2 (p. 15), grating Parmesan cheese.**
- **See Hint #1 (p. 15), crusty bread.**
- **Spring: See Hint #3 (p. 15), selecting pears.**

SEASONAL SUGGESTIONS

Winter

Pasta with Quick Tomato Sauce (p. 292)
and Tuscan Meatballs (p. 208)

Caesar Salad (p. 254) with Caesar
Dressing (p. 276)

Rice Pudding with Almonds
and Raisins (p. 322)

Spring

Pasta Primavera (p. 147) with Creamy
Quick Tomato Sauce (p. 292)

Mixed Greens Salad (254)

Italian Vinaigrette (p. 273)

Fresh Pears with Rhubarb Sauce (p. 334)

Summer

Raddiatori Pasta with Puttanesca
Sauce (p. 294)

Sliced Tomatoes, Mozzarella Cheese,
and Chopped Basil

Crusty Bread

Strawberries with Brown Sugar and
Sour Cream (p. 312)

Potato Leek Soup and Broiled Sandwiches

If you want meat in the sandwiches, add cooked ham or Canadian bacon. Did you know that scallions are the white part of green onions? I just learned that!

Quick Potato Leek Soup (p. 133)

Broiled Open-Faced English Muffins with Quick Tomato Sauce (p. 292) **and Monterey Jack Cheese**

Mixed Greens Salad (p. 254) **with Sliced Apples**

Dijon Vinaigrette (p. 273)

Pumpkin or Rum Raisin Ice Cream with Sugar Cookies

- **Scallions may be substituted for leeks; provolone cheese will substitute for Monterey Jack.**
- **I love sugar cookies from refrigerated tube dough.**
- **Winter: Remember your Stock Bag (p. 12).**
- **Spring: Purée the peas and swirl them through the soup.**
- **I use brownie mix.**

SEASONAL SUGGESTIONS

Winter

Vegetable Chowder (p. 140) with Potato, Onion, and Winter Roots

Grilled Ham, Caramelized Onion, Swiss Cheese, and Apple Sandwiches (p. 159)

Simple Greens Salad (p. 254) with Dijon Vinaigrette (p. 273)

Leftover Rice Pudding (p. 322)

Spring

Potato Soup (p. 132) with Peas

Broiled Open-Faced English Muffins with Havarti Cheese

Chilled Leftover Steamed Asparagus (p. 224) and Chopped Nuts over Simple Greens with Dijon Vinaigrette (p. 273)

Chocolate Brownies

Summer

Vichyssoise (p. 133)

Marinated Summer Vegetables (p. 257) with Crumbled Blue Cheese

Crusty Bread

Sliced Melons with Lime and Fresh Berries

Winter

Holidays . . . those compelling rituals that rekindle magic memories one day and cause hissed arguments the next.

Real winter begins when the holidays are packed away for another year, and winds that gently cooled sun-baked summer days whine stark warnings of their raw power. Afternoons disappear into nights by 4 o'clock, snowfalls silence busy streets, mittens hang by the back door, and the labrador sleeps for hours in front of the fireplace.

Herbs hanging dormant in the shed come alive in soups and sauces. Content to linger awhile longer at the table, we rediscover roasted meats, hearty chowders, and stews resplendent with nutty root vegetables.

It's time to slip into cozy wool socks, throw another log on the fire, curl up with a good book, and smell the pot roast cooking itself into a soul-comforting dinner.

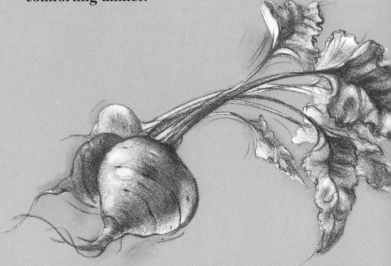

Menus

Pot Roast with Winter Root Vegetables

Pot Roast Ragu and Gnocchi

Red Chili Snapper with Santa Cruz Hominy

Broiled Fish Sandwiches and Winter Squash Soup

Moroccan Chicken Dinner

Moroccan Chicken and Couscous Soup

Southwest Black Bean Chili and Cheesy Cornbread

Chicken Quesadillas and Refried Black Beans

Cranberry Sage Pork Roast with Lentils and Caramelized Onion

Pork and Lentil Stew with Biscuits

Ham Loaf with Polenta

Warm Ham Loaf Sandwiches and Tomato Soup

Shrimp Curry

Pot Roast with Winter Root Vegetables

How do you spell Winter? P-O-T-R-O-A-S-T. In the oven, frozen solid at 7 a.m., its unbelievable fragrance greets you at 5 p.m. ready for an array of winter vegetables.

Pot Roast with Winter Root Vegetables: Onion, Carrot, Parsnip, and Potato (p. 201)

Mixed Greens Salad (p. 254) **with Tangerine Sections**

Dijon Vinaigrette (p. 273)

Crusty Bread

Cranberry Pudding (p. 321) **with Quick Honey Vanilla Sauce** (p. 335)

- Buy extra meat for leftovers (see next menu).
- Fill your Stock Bag (p. 12).
- See Hint #1 (p. 15), crusty bread.
- This simple cranberry pudding is unusual and delicious.
- Autumn: Pepperidge Farm® makes good frozen pound cake.
- Spring: Buy angel food cake.

SEASONAL SUGGESTIONS

Autumn
Pot Roast (above) with Cannellini Beans and Carrots
Spinach Salad with Honey Mustard Dressing (p. 277)
Ice Cream and Berry Sauce (p. 333) on Pound Cake

Spring
Pot Roast (above) with Spring Baby Onions, Red Potatoes, and Peas
Mixed Greens Salad (p. 254) with Apple Slices and Dijon Vinaigrette (p. 273)
Apricot Cream (p. 338) over Angel Food Cake

Summer
Barbecued Pot Roast (p. 204)
Marinated Summer Vegetable Salad (p. 257)
Old-Fashioned Potato Salad (p. 261)
Berry Cobbler (p. 309)

Pot Roast Ragu and Gnocchi

Pot roast ragu is the quintessential leftover comfort food. Gnocchi, tiny Italian potato dumplings, are available frozen in many supermarkets.

Pot Roast Ragu (p. 203) **over Gnocchi or Fresh Wide Fettuccine with Grated Parmesan Cheese**

Simple Greens Salad (p. 254)

Italian Vinaigrette (p. 273)

Broiled Crusty Bread with Pesto

Sautéed Tangerines, Bananas, and Cranberries (p. 316) **over Honey Vanilla Ice Cream**

• **Time-starved? Buy ready-made pesto.**

Made with leftovers from previous menu.

SEASONAL SUGGESTIONS

Autumn

Deep Dish Pot Roast Pie with Whipped Mashed Potato Crust (p. 213)

Mixed Greens Salad (p. 254) with Dijon Vinaigrette (p. 273)

Leftover Pound Cake Bread Pudding (p. 319) with Lemon Blueberry Sauce (p. 333)

Spring

Ragu (p. 203) over Rotini Pasta

Steamed Asparagus (p. 224) with Lemon Oil Drizzle (p. 283)

Leftover Angel Food Cake with Leftover Apricot Cream (p. 338)

Summer

Sliced Leftover Barbecued Pot Roast Sandwiches

Leftover Potato Salad (p. 261)

Sliced Melon with Berries and Lime

Red Chili Snapper with Santa Cruz Hominy

A little spice for a cold winter night. Any firm, white, deep-water fish will work with this glaze and sauce.

Dijon-Glazed Red Snapper (p. 182)
with Red Chili Sauce (p. 298)
Santa Cruz Hominy (p. 247)
Steamed Broccoli with Lemon Oil Drizzle (p. 283)
Simple Greens Salad (p. 254)
Lime Cumin Vinaigrette (p. 274)
Fresh or Poached Pear Halves (p. 313)
with Frozen Berry Sauce (p. 333)

- **Cook extra fish for tomorrow's sandwiches.**
- **If you haven't tasted hominy, try it.**
- **Summer: Alaska halibut is fresh all Summer. I use Krusteaz® scone mix for shortcake.**

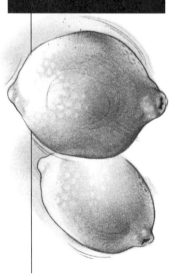

SEASONAL SUGGESTIONS

Autumn

Fish (above) with Lemon Herb Dijon Glaze (p. 105)

Corn Fritters (p. 165) with Quick Tomato Salsa (p. 287)

Sliced Tomatoes and Cucumber with Dijon Vinaigrette (p. 273)

Winter Fruit Compote (p. 315) and Cookies

Spring

Fish (above) with Quick Fruit Chutney (p. 287)

Frozen Peas with Tarragon

Simple Greens Salad (p. 254) with Dijon Vinaigrette (p. 273)

Berry Cobbler (p. 309)

Summer

Grilled Halibut (p. 182) with Lemon Herb Dijon Demi-Glaze (p. 107)

Summer Tomato Tart (p. 163)

Salad (above) with Dijon Vinaigrette

Strawberry Shortcake

Broiled Fish Sandwiches and Winter Squash Soup

If you haven't tasted a sandwich made with fresh fish, you are in for a fabulous surprise!

Broiled Fish Sandwich (p. 160) **with Sliced Red Onion, Monterey Jack Cheese, and Red Chili Mayonnaise** (p. 280)

Winter Squash Soup (p. 128) **with Cilantro Mock Crème Fraîche** (p. 282)

Waldorf Salad

Poached Pears in Port (p. 313)

- **Time-starved? Use canned pumpkin in soup.**
- **Waldorf Salad: Chopped apples and celery mixed with mayonnaise. Both red and green apples are especially colorful; Homemade Mayonnaise (p. 279) makes it taste fabulous!. Buy extra apples for next menu.**
- **Spring: For extra rich brownies see Easy Chocolate Frosting (p. 326).**

Made with leftovers from previous menu.

SEASONAL SUGGESTIONS

Autumn

Fish Sandwich (above) with Sliced Red Onion, Provolone Cheese, and Pesto Mayonnaise (p. 279)

Spicy Corn Chowder (p. 142)

Winter Fruit Compote (p. 315) over Ice Cream

Spring

Fish Sandwich (above) with Sliced Red Onion, Jarlsberg Cheese, and Fruit Chutney Mayonnaise (p. 279)

Green Pea Soup (p. 135)

Brownies

Summer

Fresh Fish Sandwich (p. 160) with Caper Mayonnaise, Shaved Red Onion, and Sliced Tomato on Sourdough Bread

New Potato Salad, French Style (p. 263)

Strawberries with Powdered Sugar and Sour Cream (p. 312)

Moroccan Chicken Dinner

Garam Masala Curry Paste® provides the distinct flavor for this colorful hearty casserole. It's worth getting (Resources, p. 340).

Moroccan Chicken with Couscous (p. 169)

Mixed Greens Salad (p. 254) **with Sliced Apple and Chopped Nuts**

Lime Cumin Vinaigrette (p. 274)

Warm Pita Bread

Honey Vanilla Ice Cream with Quick Ginger Sauce (p. 337)

- **Cook extra chicken and freeze it for menu, p. 43.**
- **Make extra casserole for leftovers (see next menu).**
- **Couscous is less expensive in bulk or 1 lb. bags.**

SEASONAL SUGGESTIONS

Autumn

Moroccan Chicken (above) with
Arborio Rice
Spinach Salad with Orange Sections
and Curried Honey Mustard
Dressing (p. 277)
Crusty Bread
Ice Cream with Shredded Coconut

Spring

Hungarian Chicken (p. 171) over
Steamed Rice
Steamed Asparagus (p. 224) with
Lemon Oil Drizzle (p. 283)
Simple Greens Salad (p. 254) with
Tomato Vinaigrette (p. 273)
Ice Cream with Rhubarb Sauce (p. 334)

Summer

Hungarian Chicken (p. 171) over
Steamed Rice
Marinated Summer Vegetable Salad
(p. 257)
Ice Cream with Sliced Strawberries

Moroccan Chicken and Couscous Soup

This is a classic "chop up the chicken, add stock and whatever to the pot" leftover soup. It can be as thick and hearty as you wish.

Moroccan Chicken Soup (p. 170)

Warm Pita Bread with Grated Cucumber and Yogurt Dip (p. 256)

Fresh Orange Sections with Warm Quick Ginger Sauce (p. 337)

SEASONAL SUGGESTIONS

• See Hint #15 (p. 16), peeling citrus.

Made with leftovers from previous menu.

Autumn

>   Moroccan Chicken Soup (above)
>   with Rice
>   Crusty Bread
>   Fresh Orange Sections with Warm
>   Currant Jelly and Sprinkled Coconut

Spring

>   Leftover Hungarian Chicken (p. 171)
>   and Rice as a Casserole
>   Mixed Greens Salad (p. 254) with
>   Marinated Asparagus (p. 257) and
>   Dijon Vinaigrette (p. 273)
>   Toasted Crusty Bread with Parmesan
>   Cheese
>   Lemon Bars (p. 330)

Summer

>   Leftover Hungarian Chicken (p. 171)
>   and Rice as a Casserole
>   Mixed Greens Salad (p. 254) with
>   Marinated Summer Vegetables (p. 257)
>   and Italian Vinaigrette (p. 273)
>   Lemon Bars (p. 330)

Southwest Black Bean Chili and Cheesy Cornbread

The fermented black beans used in Chinese black bean sauce give this chili a unique Southwestern flavor (Resources, p. 340). A great weekend cooking project. It freezes very well!

Black Bean Chili (p. 138) **Quick Tomato Salsa** (p. 287) **and Sour Cream**

Cornbread with Chilies and Cheddar Cheese

Simple Greens Salad (p. 254) **with Chopped Cranberries**

Lime Cumin Vinaigrette (p. 274)

Hot Caramel Sundae Sprinkled with Cinnamon

- **If you want meat, add cooked chorizo sausage.**
- **Buy "just add water" cornbread mix.**
- **Buy ready-made caramel sauce.**
- **Autumn: Salsa Verde is green chili salsa, available at most supermarkets.**

SEASONAL SUGGESTIONS

Autumn

Chili (above) with Salsa Verde

Warm Flour Tortillas with Cilantro Butter (p. 278)

Salad (above) with Pomegranate Seeds

Poached Pears (p. 313) with Caramel Sauce

Spring

Three Bean and Lentil Soup (p. 129)

Warm Flour Tortillas with Cumin Butter (p. 278)

Salad (above) with Roasted Pumpkin Seeds (p. 110) and Salsa Vinaigrette (p. 273)

Rhubarb Cinnamon Crisp (p. 309)

Summer

Black Bean Chili (p. 138)

Plain Cornbread

Watermelon, Radish, and Jicama Salad (p. 272) with Lime Cumin Vinaigrette (p. 274)

Fresh Berries and Leftover Lemon Bars (p. 330)

Chicken Quesadillas and Refried Black Beans

You don't need much leftover chicken to produce wonderful quesadillas. These refried beans are different and delicious.

Chicken Quesadillas (p. 176) **with Quick Tomato Salsa** (p. 287) **and Sour Cream**

Refried Black Beans (p. 251)

Mixed Greens Salad (p. 254) **with Chopped Cranberries**

Lime Cumin Vinaigrette (p. 274)

Poached Pears (p. 313) **with Hot Maple Syrup**

• **Better 2 smaller Quesadillas than 1 huge one.**

Made with leftovers from previous menu.

SEASONAL SUGGESTIONS

Autumn
Quesadillas and Refried Beans (above)
Salad (above) with Jicama and Sliced Apple and Vinaigrette (above)
Pear Crisp (p. 309)

Spring
Quesadillas (above)
Black Bean, Jicama, and Melon Salad with Lime Cumin Vinaigrette (above)
Leftover Rhubarb Cinnamon Crisp (p. 309)

Summer
Quesadillas and Refried Beans (above)
Marinated Summer Vegetables (p. 257) in Lime Cumin Vinaigrette (p. 274)
Sliced Melons with Fresh Lime Juice

Cranberry Sage Pork Roast with Lentils and Caramelized Onion

This dinner is easier to make than it sounds. The roast cooks while you fix the onions and vegetables.

Sage Dijon-Glazed Pork Roast (p. 105) **with Cranberry Demi-Glace** (p. 217)

Lentils with Mushrooms and Caramelized Onion (p. 233)

Sautéed Winter Root Vegetables and Chard (p. 225) **with Lemon Oil Drizzle** (p. 283)

Simple Greens Salad (p. 254)

Orange Shallot Vinaigrette (p. 274)

Gingerbread with Vanilla Sauce (p. 335)

- Make extra for leftovers (see next menu).
- Fill your Stock Bag (p. 12) with vegetable trimmings.
- For gingerbread, use a mix.
- See Hint #2 (p. 15), grating Parmesan cheese.
- Autumn: Pierce spaghetti squash with a sharp knife and cook it on high heat in the microwave. See Hint #1 (p. 15), crusty bread.

SEASONAL SUGGESTIONS

Autumn

Stuffed Pork Chops (p. 218)

Spaghetti Squash (see box at left) with Olive Oil and Parmesan Cheese

Mixed Greens Salad (p. 254) with Italian Vinaigrette (p. 273)

Crusty Bread

Blueberry Lemon Pudding Cake (p. 323)

Spring

Grilled Dijon-Glazed Pork Chops (p. 217)

Potato Sage Pancakes (p. 244)

Steamed Carrots and Broccoli (p. 224) with Lemon Oil Drizzle (p. 283)

Apple Ginger Upside-Down Cake (p. 327)

Summer

Barbecued Dijon-Glazed Pork Chops (p. 217)

German Potato Salad (p. 262)

Steamed Green Beans (p. 224) with Lemon Oil Drizzle (p. 283)

Lemon Berry Tart (p. 308)

Pork and Lentil Stew with Biscuits

Leftover pork, leftover lentils, a few vegetables, and a big pot. Classic Stew!

Pork, Lentil, Mushroom, and Winter Vegetable Stew (p. 220)

Biscuits (p. 120)

Spinach Salad with Grapefruit Sections

Honey Mustard Dressing (p. 277)

Leftover Gingerbread with Quick Honey Vanilla Bourbon Sauce (see box, p. 335) **or Ice Cream with Mocha Sauce**

If you have time, try the biscuit recipe (p. 120); if not, use a mix or refrigerated tube.

Made with leftovers from previous menu.

SEASONAL SUGGESTIONS

Autumn
Shredded Pork Ragu (p. 203) over Polenta (p. 245)
Broiled Crusty Pesto Bread
Mixed Greens Salad (p. 254) with Italian Vinaigrette (p. 273)
Leftover Pudding Cake or Biscotti with Fresh Fruit

Spring
Pork Hash from Leftovers (See Chicken Hash, p. 179) with Quick Tomato Salsa (p. 287)
Coleslaw (p. 255), with Coleslaw Dressing (p. 277)
Leftover Upside-Down Cake or Berry Sorbet

Summer
Warm Barbecued Pork Sandwiches on Sourdough Buns
Mixed Greens Salad (p. 254) with Blue Cheese Vinaigrette (p. 273)
Fresh Strawberries Dipped in Sour Cream and Powdered Sugar (p. 312)

Ham Loaf with Polenta

This dinner brings Mrs. Cleaver into the 90's!

Ham Loaf (p. 208)

Polenta (p. 245) **with Asiago or other
Sharp Italian Cheese**

Sautéed Chard and Spinach (p. 225) **with
Lemon Oil Drizzle** (p. 273)

Simple Greens Salad (p. 254)

Orange Shallot Vinaigrette (p. 274)

Ginger Tapioca Pudding

- **Make extra ham loaf, meatballs, sausage, or chicken loaf for leftovers (see next menu).**
- **Tapioca pudding: See recipe on box, add fruit or flavors.**
- **Summer: Fill your Stock Bag (p. 12).**

SEASONAL SUGGESTIONS

Autumn

    Tuscan Meatballs (p. 208)
    Polenta, Vegetable, and Salad (above)
    Apricot Almond Tapioca with
      Apricot Cream (p. 338)

Spring

    Grilled Italian Sausage
    Polenta, Vegetable, and Salad (above)
    Pear Tapioca with Fresh Pear Sauce
      (p. 334)

Summer

    Ground Chicken Loaf (p. 208) with
      Dijon Demi-Glace (p. 107)
    Steamed Baby Vegetables (p. 224) with
      Lemon Oil Drizzle (p. 283)
    Salad (above) with Tomato Vinaigrette
      (p. 273)
    Tapioca with Fresh Berries

Warm Ham Loaf Sandwiches and Tomato Soup

A quick, hearty dinner.

Warm Ham Loaf Sandwiches on Sourdough Bread
Quick Tomato Soup (p. 121)
Spinach Salad
Dijon Vinaigrette (p. 273)
Leftover Pudding or
Winter Fruit Compote (p. 315) **and Biscotti**

- Buy biscotti at your favorite bakery.
- Store-bought gingersnaps are fine as well.

Made with leftovers from previous menu.

SEASONAL SUGGESTIONS

Autumn
> Meatball Sandwiches
> Marinated String Beans (p. 257) with
> Crumbled Blue Cheese
> Leftover Pudding or Pumpkin Ice
> Cream and Gingersnaps

Spring
> Grilled Sausage Sandwiches
> Quick Tomato Soup (p. 121)
> Simple Greens Salad (p. 254)
> Leftover Pudding or Rhubarb Crisp
> (p. 309)

Summer
> Chicken Loaf Sandwiches with Cajun
> Tartar Sauce (p. 281)
> Summer Vegetable Soup (p. 123)
> Fresh Fruit and Cookies

Shrimp Curry

I love the creativity of condiments. Tradition calls for one per person with chutney as a given (there are wonderful ones available in most markets). With this curry you might try a fresh tropical fruit chutney with condiments such as: minced green onion and radish mixed together; dried cranberries or blueberries instead of raisins; broiled shaved coconut; pickled lime (Resources, p. 340).

Shrimp Curry over Asian Rice (p. 200)
Mixed Greens Salad (p. 254) **with Chopped Nuts**
Lime Cumin Vinaigrette (p. 274)
**Toasted Pita Bread with
Cream Cheese and Chutney**
Deep Dish Apple Pie (p. 302)

- **Frozen shrimp works fine in this curry. Make it as hot as you like.**
- **See Hint #1 (p. 15), crusty bread.**
- **Time-starved? Use refrigerated pie dough.**
- **Spring: Buy chocolate sauce.**
- **Summer: I use Krusteaz® scone mix for shortcake.**

SEASONAL SUGGESTIONS

Autumn
Curried Shrimp with Rice (p. 200)
Salad and Vinaigrette (above)
Crusty Bread
Apple Crisp (p. 309)

Spring
Cajun Shrimp Stew (p. 194)
Garlic Bread
Salad (above) with Dijon Vinaigrette
(p. 273)
Sautéed Bananas (p. 316) with
Chocolate Sauce

Summer
Paella (p. 155)
Salad (above) with Dijon Vinaigrette
(p. 273)
Crusty Bread
Peach Shortcake

Spring

Renewal. Tiny green buds dot every tree, flats of color-splashed primroses replace the woodpile at the grocery store, crocuses pop up in the flower beds, and soccer practice goes until 6 o'clock. Even those of us living hundreds of miles from the rhythms of the soil ritually respond to the promise of Spring. We see closets that need cleaning, lawnmowers that need sharpening, and windows that need washing. The backdoor, propped ajar for the first sunny afternoon, opens into the garden waiting patiently for its new plants.

Sometime during the first week of April, as the ethereal cherry blossoms burst into cascading pink and white umbrellas, I start to hunger for crunchy green asparagus, rosemary roasted lamb, grilled king salmon, and mouth-tingling lemon tarts.

Menus

Rosemary Roasted Spring Lamb

Shepherd's Pie

Risotto Primavera

Herb-Roasted Chicken and Vegetables

Chicken and Dumplings

Beans and Rice with Shrimp and Scallops

Tex-Mex Chicken Hash and Black Beans

Grilled Salmon and Artichokes

Salmon and Pasta with Creamy Tomato Sauce

Country Cheese Soufflé

Potato and Italian Sausage Tart

Pasta with Morel Mushrooms, Roasted Garlic, Tomato, and Chard

Rosemary Roasted Spring Lamb

The dinner that assures us it's Spring.

Leg or Rolled Roast of Spring Lamb (p. 210) **with Rosemary Dijon Demi-Glace** (p. 167)

Garlic Mashed Potatoes (p. 242)

Steamed Asparagus and Baby Carrots (p. 224) **with Lemon Oil Drizzle** (p. 283)

Mixed Greens Salad (p. 254) **with Chevre Tomato Vinaigrette** (p. 273)

Lemon Tarts (p. 308)

- **Lamb is expensive; let the butcher select your perfect piece.**
- **Buy for leftovers, and make extra demi-glace (see next menu).**
- **No shortcuts work for these yummy potatoes. No time? Substitute garlic roasted new potatoes. Cook extra potatoes for next menu but *don't mash them* until next day.**
- **Buy the lemon tarts, or whisk lemon curd into whipped cream and fill tart shells.**

SEASONAL SUGGESTIONS

Autumn

Lamb and Demi-Glace (above)
Steamed String Beans (p. 224) with Lemon Oil Drizzle (p. 283)
Rice Pilaf (p. 248)
Simple Greens Salad (p. 254) with Dijon Vinaigrette (p. 273)
Apple Pie (p. 302)

Winter

Lamb and Demi-Glace (above)
Couscous
Steamed Chard (p. 224) with Lemon Oil Drizzle (p. 283)
Stewed Tomatoes
Mixed Greens Salad (p. 254) with Orange, Roasted Pumpkin Seeds (p. 110), and Orange Shallot Vinaigrette (p. 274)
Apple Pie (p. 302)

Summer

Dijon-Glazed Barbecued Lamb (p. 210)
White Beans with Onion and Sage (p. 253)
Chilled Summer Vegetables with Tomato Vinaigrette (p. 273)
Berry Cobbler (p. 309)

Shepherd's Pie

Such a humble name for such a great dish—another ultimate leftover comfort food.

Shepherd's Pie (p. 213) **with Mashed Potato Crust**
Simple Greens Salad (p. 254) **with Sliced Tomato and Cucumber**
Italian Vinaigrette (p. 273)
Rhubarb Crisp (p. 309)

If you didn't make or you ate all the mashed potatoes, use instant.

Winter: Buy the cookies.

Summer: If barbecued leg of lamb was served the day before, serve it sliced and cold with Dijon caper mayonnaise, and make the tabbouleh meatless. Use your own favorite recipe or box mix for tabbouleh.

Made with leftovers from previous menu.

SEASONAL SUGGESTIONS

Autumn

Cheddar and Caramelized Onion Country Soufflé (p. 235) with Leftover Lamb Demi-Glace (p. 167)

Mixed Greens Salad (p. 254) with Dijon Vinaigrette (p. 274)

Leftover Apple Pie or Fresh Pears with Berry Sauce (p. 333)

Winter

Lamb Curry (p. 215) over Couscous

Spinach Salad with Citrus and Dijon Vinaigrette (p. 273)

Pita Chips with Cumin (p. 111)

Thin Ginger Cookies

Summer

Sliced Leftover Barbecued Lamb with Caper Dijon Mayonnaise (p. 279)

Tabbouleh with Mint

Chilled Cucumber Soup with Yogurt (p. 128)

Pita Bread

Leftover Cobbler (p. 309) or Quick Lemon Sauce (p. 337) over Blueberries

Risotto Primavera

This is one of the prettiest risottos you will ever see! If you want to, add smoked salmon, or grill Italian sausages and serve on the side.

Risotto (p. 151) **Primavera with Asparagus Tips, Tomato, Artichoke Hearts, Carrots, Spinach, ...whatever is fresh!**

Shaved Parmesan Cheese

Simple Greens Salad (p. 254)

Italian Vinaigrette (p. 273)

Crusty Bread

Chocolate Brownies

- Remember your Stock Bag (p. 12)!
- Buy extra vegetables for leftovers (see next 2 menus).
- See Hint #1 (p. 15), crusty bread.
- See Hint #2 (p. 15), grating Parmesan cheese.
- Make brownies with a mix or buy ready-made. See p. 326 for Easy Chocolate Frosting.
- For heartier risotto:
  Autumn: smoked chicken
  Winter: pancetta or pepper bacon
  Summer: julienne-cut summer sausage

SEASONAL SUGGESTIONS

Autumn
> Risotto (above) with Fresh Autumn Vegetables
> Salad and Bread (above)
> Oatmeal Fruit Bars (p. 331)

Winter
> Risotto (above) with Winter Root Vegetables and Caramelized Onions (p. 231)
> Salad and Bread (above)
> Winter Fruit Compote (p. 315)

Summer
> Risotto (above) with Garden Fresh Summer Vegetables
> Salad and Bread (above)
> Melon, Fresh Berries, and Cookies

Herb-Roasted Chicken and Vegetables

High temperature cooking makes this a 45-minute dinner. (See next 3 menus for chicken leftovers.)

Dijon-Glazed Oven-Roasted Chicken (p. 167) **and Vegetables, including Potatoes** (p. 224)

Mixed Greens Salad (p. 254) **with Orange Sections, Shaved Red Onion**

Orange Shallot Vinaigrette (p. 274)

Pound Cake with Chocolate Sauce

- **Buy and cook extra chicken and potatoes for upcoming menus (next and later Hash).**
- **Remember your Stock Bag (p. 12).**
- **See p. 14 for hints on high temperature cooking.**
- **Pepperidge Farm® makes good frozen pound cake. Buy chocolate sauce.**
- **Summer: No time? Substitute plain rice or boxed pilaf mix.**

SEASONAL SUGGESTIONS

Autumn

Chicken (above) with Roasted Seasonal Vegetables: Fennel, Yellow Fin Potatoes, Celery Root, Carrots

Salad (above) with Pomegranate and Roasted Mexican Pumpkin Seeds (p. 110) and Vinaigrette (above)

Pound Cake with Sautéed Apples (p. 316) and Quick Honey Vanilla Sauce (see box, p. 335)

Winter

Chicken (above) with Roasted Winter Root Vegetables: Turnip, Parsnip, Rutabaga, Carrots, Potato

Salad (above) with Tangerines, Feta Cheese, and Vinaigrette (above)

Leftover Fruit Compote (p. 315) over Pound Cake

Summer

Chicken (above) with Steamed Summer Vegetables (p. 224) and Lemon Oil Drizzle (p. 283)

Rice Pilaf (p. 248)

Ice Cream with Fresh Berries

Chicken and Dumplings

An old-fashioned family dinner.

Chicken and Herb Dumplings (p. 172)

Mixed Greens Salad (p. 254) **with Tomatoes and Peas**

Dijon Vinaigrette (p. 273)

Fruit Sorbet and Cookies

- I use biscuit mix to make dumplings and cobbler dough.
- Summer: See Hint #1 (p. 15), crusty bread.

Made with leftovers from previous menu.

SEASONAL SUGGESTIONS

Autumn

Chicken Cobbler (p. 174)
Salad and Vinaigrette (above)
Fresh Sliced Peaches with Blueberry
Sauce (p. 333)

Winter

Chicken Pot Pie (p. 174)
Salad (above) with Shaved Red
Onion, Grapefruit Sections, and
Tomato Vinaigrette (p. 273)
Cranberry Sorbet

Summer

Chicken Vegetable Chowder (p. 141)
Warm Biscuits (p. 120) or Broiled
Crusty Bread with Parmesan Cheese
Fresh Sliced Peaches over Ice Cream

Beans and Rice with Shrimp and Scallops

These flavors are inspired by the time I have spent on Exuma, in the Bahamas. Use at least three kinds of beans; try to find pigeon peas, a staple of the Bahamas.

Jamaican Beans and Rice (p. 249) **with Sautéed Prawns and Scallops** (p. 184)

Warm Flour Tortillas with Cream Cheese and Hot Mango Chutney

Mixed Greens Salad (p. 254) **with Thin Melon Slices**

Lime Cumin Vinaigrette (p. 274)

Grapes with Sour Cream and Brown Sugar (p. 312)

- **Beans: Include black beans and buy extra (see next menu).**
- **Buy extra tortillas also.**

SEASONAL SUGGESTIONS

Autumn
> Outdoor Grilled Shrimp and Scallops (p. 182), Marinated in Lime Cumin Vinaigrette (p. 274)
> Quick Fruit Chutney (p. 287)
> Beans and Rice (above)
> Parmesan Tortilla Chips (p. 111)
> Peaches with Sour Cream and Brown Sugar (p. 312)

Winter
> Cajun Shrimp and Scallop Stew (p. 194) or Gumbo (p. 196)
> Simple Greens Salad (p. 254) with Grapefruit, Avocado, and Dijon Vinaigrette (p. 273)
> Bread Pudding (p. 319) with Quick Honey Vanilla Sauce (p. 335)

Summer
> Outdoor Grilled Shrimp and Scallops (p. 182) with Spicy Caribbean Sauce (p. 297)
> Cold Beans and Rice Salad (p. 265) with Lime Cumin Vinaigrette (p. 274)
> Strawberries Dipped in Sour Cream and Brown Sugar (p. 312)

Tex-Mex Chicken Hash and Black Beans

Brand-new flavors for leftover chicken!

Chicken Hash (p. 179) **with
Quick Tomato Salsa** (p. 287)

Black Beans with Lime and Cilantro (p. 252)

Warm Flour Tortillas with Cumin Butter (p. 278)

Simple Greens Salad (p. 254) **with Chopped
Cilantro, Anaheim Pepper, Orange Sections,
Roasted Mexican Pumpkin Seeds** (p. 110)

Orange Shallot Vinaigrette (p. 274)

Chocolate Pudding Cake (p. 324)

- **Save time by chopping for the hash and salad at one time.**
- **The recipe for chocolate pudding cake is wonderful, but the mix variety with rich vanilla ice cream is fine if you are in a hurry.**
- **Autumn and Summer: Use "add water only" cornbread mix.**
- **Winter: See Hint #3 (p. 15), selecting pears.**

Made with leftovers from previous menu.

SEASONAL SUGGESTIONS

Autumn
    Chicken Hash (above)
    Cheddar Cornbread
    Salad (above) with Sliced Red Apple,
      Jicama, Shaved Red Onion,
      Chopped Anaheim Pepper, and
      Lime Cumin Vinaigrette (p. 274)
    Fresh Peaches with Frozen Blueberry
      Sauce (p. 333)

Winter
    Chicken Hash (above)
    Salad (above) with Grapefruit
      Sections, Avocado, Sliced Green
      Pepper, Shaved Red Onion, and
      Lime Cumin Vinaigrette (p. 274)
    Poached Pear (p. 313) with
      Caramel Sauce

Summer
    Chicken Hash (above)
    Traditional Cornbread
    Watermelon, Jicama, and Radish
      Salad (p. 272) with Lime Cumin
      Vinaigrette (p. 274)
    Lemon Pudding Cake (p. 323) with
      Fresh Blueberries

Grilled Salmon and Artichokes

If you haven't tried artichokes prepared this way, you are in for a treat! For a lighter meal, serve just artichokes, bread, and dessert (never skip dessert!).

Artichokes with Garlic, Fresh Basil, and Parmesan Cheese (p. 230)

Grilled Dijon-Glazed Alaska King Salmon (p. 182) **with Fresh Tomato Sauce** (p. 295)

Simple Greens Salad (p. 254)

Dijon Vinaigrette (p. 273)

Crusty Bread

Mocha Ice Cream with Sprinkled Instant Espresso and Grated Chocolate

- Cook extra salmon for leftovers (see next menu).
- The artichokes can be cooked ahead and reheated.
- Get the salmon all ready to cook, then serve and relish the artichokes. Take a break while the salmon cooks and enjoy the rest of your special Spring dinner.
- See Hint #1 (p. 15), crusty bread.
- See Hint #2 (p. 15), grating Parmesan cheese.
- Autumn: Sun-Dried Tomato Pesto is a cinch to make, and it is also available ready-made.
- Winter: Buy pesto. Make caponata ahead.

SEASONAL SUGGESTIONS

Autumn
> Salmon with Sun-Dried Tomato Pesto (p. 284)
> Artichokes (above)
> Salad and Vinaigrette (above)
> Crusty Bread
> Toffee Crunch Ice Cream

Winter
> Salmon with Pesto Dijon Glaze (p. 105)
> Caponata (p. 115)
> Crusty Bread
> Steamed Cauliflower with Lemon Caper Sauce (p. 283)
> Vanilla Ice Cream with Sautéed Poached Pears (p. 313)

Summer
> Salmon with Salsa Cruda (p. 291)
> Steamed Baby New Potatoes (p. 224) with Drizzled Olive Oil and Pepper
> Marinated Green, Yellow Wax and Italian White Beans (p. 257) with Italian Vinaigrette (p. 273) and Crumbled Feta Cheese
> Mixed Fresh Fruit and Cookies

59

Salmon and Pasta with Creamy Tomato Sauce

Use a simple pasta such as fettuccine, and toss the salmon in carefully so it won't break apart. A very quick dinner.

Pasta tossed with Creamy Tomato Sauce (p. 293),
Salmon, and Chopped, Blanched Spinach

Mixed Greens Salad (p. 254)

Dijon Vinaigrette (p. 273)

Broiled Pesto Bread

Angel Food Cake with Apricot Cream (p. 338)

- Buy extra spinach for leftovers (see next menu).
- See Hint #1 (p. 15), crusty bread.
- Buy pesto and cake ready-made.
- Autumn and Winter: Pepperidge Farm® makes good frozen pound cake.
- Summer: For pasta salad, choose a pasta that will trap the dressing and herbs such as orecchiette (little ears) or small seashell.

Made with leftovers from previous menu.

SEASONAL SUGGESTIONS

Autumn

Pasta with Salmon and Sun-Dried Tomato Sauce (p. 292)

Steamed Spinach with Lemon Oil Drizzle (p. 283)

Simple Greens Salad (p. 254) with Italian Vinaigrette (p. 273)

Sautéed Apples (p. 316) on Pound Cake

Winter

Pasta with Caponata (p. 115) and Salmon

Garlic Bread

Simple Greens Salad (p. 254) and Dijon Vinaigrette (p. 273)

Sautéed Apples (p. 316) and Dried Cranberries on Pound Cake

Summer

Pasta Salad (p. 266) with Salmon, Beans, Tomato, and Fresh Basil

Italian Vinaigrette (p. 273)

Garlic Bread

Fruit Cobbler (p. 309)

Country Cheese Soufflé

I can see my grandmother's wrinkly freckled hands stirring the cheese sauce for our Sunday night soufflé. This is an old family favorite, and easy because it's made with bread.

Country Cheese Soufflé (p. 164)

Spinach Salad with Orange Sections and Almonds

Dijon Vinaigrette (p. 273)

Berry Sorbet and Cookies

- Don't skimp on the cheese here. Good quality, aged, sharp cheddar will make this soufflé fabulous.
- No time? Buy the cookies.
- Summer: This macaroni version is a new experience!

SEASONAL SUGGESTIONS

Autumn

Cheddar Soufflé (above) with
Caramelized Onion (p. 231)
Steamed Chard (p. 224) with Lemon
Oil Drizzle (p. 283)
Mixed Greens Salad (p. 254) with
Sliced Apples and Dijon Vinaigrette
(above)
Pumpkin Ice Cream

Winter

Cheese Soufflé with Sun-Dried
Tomato Pesto (p. 284)
Spinach Salad with Tangerines,
Shaved Red Onion, and Dijon
Vinaigrette (above)
Eggnog Ice Cream

Summer

Macaroni and Good Cheese (p. 150)
Steamed Green Beans (p. 224) with
Lemon Oil Drizzle (p. 283)
Simple Greens Salad (p. 254) with
Tomato Vinaigrette (p. 273)
Sliced Melon, Strawberries, and
Cookies

Potato and Italian Sausage Tart

This is traditional European high country pie. Notice how the mood changes with different sausages in different seasons.

Potato and Mild Italian Sausage Tart (p. 240)

Broiled Crusty Bread with Parmesan Cheese

Mixed Greens Salad (p. 254) **with Orange Sections**

Orange Shallot Vinaigrette (p. 274)

Fresh Stawberries with Lemon Cream (p. 338)

- **No time? Use refrigerated dough for tart.**
- **See Hint #1 (p. 15), crusty bread.**
- **See Hint #2 (p. 15), grating Parmesan cheese.**
- **Autumn: Use gingerbread mix.**

Made with leftovers from previous menu.

SEASONAL SUGGESTIONS

Autumn

Potato Tart (above) with Bratwurst Sausage, Caramelized Onion (p. 231), and Jarlsberg Cheese

Salad (above) with Apple and Dijon Vinaigrette (p. 273)

Gingerbread with Apricot Cream (p. 338)

Winter

Potato Tart (above) with Polish Sausage, Fennel Seed, Muenster Cheese, and Spinach

Salad (above) with Tangerine, and Orange Shallot Vinaigrette (p. 274)

Cranberry Apple Crisp (p. 309)

Summer

New Potato Tart (above) with Chicken Sausage, Tarragon, Zucchini, and Monterey Jack Cheese

Salad (above) with Dijon Vinaigrette (p. 273)

Warm Berries in Currant Jelly (p. 311) over Ice Cream

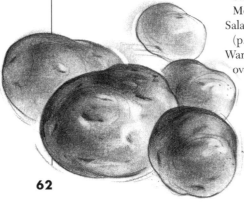

Pasta with Morel Mushrooms, Roasted Garlic, Tomato, and Chard

The bow-tie shape of farfalle pasta looks really pretty with mushrooms and chard. This is a celebration of the season's first morel mushrooms.

Pasta with Sautéed Mushrooms, Roasted Garlic (p. 225), **Tomato, and Chard** (p. 145)

Grated Parmesan Cheese

Simple Greens Salad (p. 254)

Italian Vinaigrette (p. 273)

Crusty Bread

Lemon Bars (p. 330)

- For meat addition to this menu, add prosciutto or paper-thin sliced ham.

- If you can't get wild morels, use dried or leave them out and use more roasted garlic.

- See Hints #2 (p. 15), #3 (p. 15), and #26 (p. 18), about grating Parmesan cheese, selecting pears, and wild mushrooms.

- The Lemon Bar recipe is excellent and worth baking!

- Autumn: Switch to wild chanterelles and shiitakes.

- Winter: Use brownie mix. For Easy Chocolate Frosting, see p. 326.

SEASONAL SUGGESTIONS

Autumn

Pasta with Mushrooms (above)
Mixed Greens Salad (p. 254) with
    Vinaigrette (above)
Bread (above)
Poached Pears in Port (p. 313)

Winter

Pasta (above) with Steamed Winter
    Squash, Roasted Garlic (p. 225),
    Tomato, and Chard (p. 145)
Salad and Bread (above)
Chocolate Brownies

Summer

Pasta (above) with Sautéed Greens
    (escarole or arugula), Tomato, and
    Roasted Garlic (p. 225)
Salad and Bread (above)
Fresh Berries with Lemon Whipped
    Cream Sauce (p. 337)

Summer

Cracked crab, steaming hot corn on the cob, tiny anemone fountains squirting up between your toes, water balloon fights, and bare feet all day. Grimy campers with tear-rendering grins return triumphant from a whole week away from home. Gardens flourish and roadside stands burst with baskets of succulent berries, peas in the pod, sun-warmed tomatoes, deep purple eggplant, and pale yellow wax beans. About the second week of August, dewdrops backlighted by a coral pink sunrise provide glistening definition to the miraculous geometry of spiderwebs. It's time once again for that early morning walk through the brambles to pick the biggest bucket of wild blackberries ever.

Menus

Steamed Shellfish and Corn on the Cob

Clam Fritters and Coleslaw

Caribbean Barbecued Chicken with Beans
and Rice

Cold Caribbean Chicken with Beans and
Rice Salad

Barbecued Flank Steak with Red Chili Sauce

Santa Fe Steak Salad

Farmers Market Pasta

Barbecued Tuna and Two Salads

Fresh Tuna Sandwiches and Gazpacho

Summer Tomato Cheese Tart and Salad

Barbecued Sausage and Bread Kabobs

Crab Cakes with Cajun Tartar Sauce

Salad Samplers

Steamed Shellfish and Corn on the Cob

Clams, mussels, scallops, crab, lobster, or whatever is available. A celebration of simple foods that are absolutely fresh. Provide bibs and hand towels.

Steamed Shellfish (p. 185)

Corn on the Cob with Herb Butter (p. 278)

Crusty Bread

Sliced Cucumbers, Tomatoes, and Fresh Basil

Caesar Dressing (p. 276)

Strawberry Shortcake

- **Cook extra shellfish for leftovers (see next menu).**
- **See Hint #1 (p. 15), crusty bread.**
- **Dampen terry cloth hand towels with lemon water and heat for 1 minute in the microwave.**
- **I use Krusteaz® scone mix for shortcake. Avoid those spongy things in a package.**
- **Winter and Summer: This is a really fun way to cook shellfish!**

SEASONAL SUGGESTIONS

Autumn

Steamed Mussels (p. 185) and Red Potatoes (p. 224)

Sautéed Zucchini with Onions and Tomato (p. 225)

Fresh Peach or Nectarine Shortcake

Winter

Seafood and Pasta Cooked in Parchment (p. 187)

Simple Greens Salad (p. 254) with Dijon Vinaigrette (p. 273)

Crusty Bread

Winter Fruit Compote (p. 315) over Ice Cream

Spring

Clams, Mussels, and Calamari Cooked in Parchment with Pasta (p. 187)

Simple Greens Salad (p. 254) with Dijon Vinaigrette (p. 273)

Crusty Bread

Poached Pears (p. 313) with Frozen Berry Sauce (p. 333)

Clam Fritters and Coleslaw

A very quick and easy dinner.

Clam or other Leftover Shellfish Fritters (p. 166)
with Quick Tomato Salsa (p. 287)

Cole Slaw (p. 255)

Crusty Bread

Cut Fruit Salad

Ice Cream Bars

- There is no way around the fat needed for frying fritters. No-cholesterol oils are more healthful, but fat is fat. Use a deep, heavy pan!
- See Hint #1 (p. 15), crusty bread.
- For a great taste change, try Ginger Sesame Vinaigrette (p. 275) instead of salsa or tartar sauce with seafood fritters.
- Autumn: See Hint #2 (p. 15), grating Parmesan cheese.
- Autumn and Winter: Buy ready-made dessert sauces.
- Spring: See Hint #3 (p. 15), selecting pears.

SEASONAL SUGGESTIONS

Autumn

Fritters with Cajun Tartar Sauce (p. 281)
Broiled Crusty Bread with Parmesan Cheese
Chocolate Sundae

Winter

Puget Sound Cioppino (p. 191), using only One or Two Varieties of Fish
Broiled Crusty Bread with Parmesan Cheese
Hot Butterscotch Sundae

Spring

Seafood Fritters (p. 166) with Salsa (p. 287)
Warm Garlic Bread
Sautéed Pears (p. 316) over Ice Cream

Made with leftovers from previous menu.

67

Caribbean Barbecued Chicken with Beans and Rice

Another menu inspired by the Bahamas.

Barbecued Chicken with Caribbean Dijon Glaze (p. 105)

Quick Fruit Chutney (p. 287)

Jamaican Beans and Rice (p. 249)

Chopped Salad with Orange, Shaved Red Onion, Tomato, Cucumber, Mint, and Basil (p. 260)

Lime Cumin Vinaigrette (p. 274)

Cornbread

Frozen Yogurt with Chopped Candied Ginger

- **Cook extra chicken for leftovers (see next menu).**
- **Select a fairly hot mango chutney as a base for Quick Fruit Chutney.**
- **Use "just add water" cornbread mix. Make extra for next menu dessert.**
- **Other seasons: Bake chicken if it's too cold outside to barbecue.**
- **Autumn: See Hint #3 (p. 15), selecting pears.**
- **Winter: No time? Buy beans and rice pilaf in a box.**

SEASONAL SUGGESTIONS

Autumn
Chicken and Chutney (above)
Black-Eyed Peas and Brown Rice
Cucumber, Yogurt, and Mint Salad (p. 256)
Cornbread
Pumpkin Ice Cream

Winter
Chicken and Chutney (above)
Wild Rice and Bean Pilaf (p. 248)
Mixed Greens Salad (p. 254) with Chopped Spinach, Red Onion, Avocado, and Grapefruit
Cornbread
Coconut Ice Cream

Spring
Baked Chicken with Spicy Caribbean Sauce (p. 297)
Black Beans and Rice with Tomato
Steamed Asparagus (p. 224) with Chopped Peanuts and Lime Cumin Vinaigrette (p. 274)
Cornbread
Ice Cream with Chopped Pineapple and Candied Ginger

Cold Caribbean Chicken with Beans and Rice Salad

Mince any leftover cucumber salad from previous menu, and add it to the fruit chutney to make a crunchy, sweet-hot salsa.

Cold Caribbean Glazed Chicken with Tropical Fruit Salsa (p. 290)

Beans and Rice Salad (p. 265)

Lime Cumin Vinaigrette (p. 274)

Sliced Melon

Cornbread Pudding (p. 319) **with Fresh Berries**

- **Cornbread pudding may be habit forming.**
- **Spring: See Hint #3 (p. 15), selecting pears.**

Made with leftovers from previous menu.

SEASONAL SUGGESTIONS

Autumn

If the weather has turned cold, substitute Caribbean Chicken Casserole (p. 250)

Sliced Tomato Salad with Caesar Dressing (p. 276)

Cornbread Pudding (above) with Melted Pumpkin Ice Cream Sauce

Winter

Warm Leftover Chicken

Wild Rice Pilaf Salad (p. 248) with Chopped Spinach

Cornbread Pudding (above) with Dried Cranberries and Quick Vanilla Sauce (p. 335)

Spring

Rice Salad (p. 265) with Black Beans, Frozen Peas, Leftover Chicken, and Asparagus

Sliced Fresh Pears with Cream Cheese and Chutney

Cornbread Pudding (above) with Pineapple and Candied Ginger

Barbecued Flank Steak with Red Chili Sauce

The red chili sauce adds a different twist to good old flank steak.

Barbecued Flank Steak (p. 88) **with Red Chili Sauce** (p. 298)

Sautéed Bell and Anaheim Peppers (p. 228)

Grilled New Potatoes (p. 226)

Mixed Greens Salad (p. 254)

Lime Cumin Vinaigrette (p. 274)

Strawberries Dipped in Sour Cream, Cinnamon, and Powdered Sugar (p. 312)

- Make shallow cuts both ways across the grain of flank steak before grilling.
- Cook extra steak and peppers for leftovers (see next menu).
- Spring: Toss uncooked frozen French fries with minced garlic and chopped oregano and broil according to manufacturer's directions.

SEASONAL SUGGESTIONS

Autumn

Flank Steak and Peppers (above)

Corn on the Cob

Warm Tortillas with Lime Cilantro Butter (p. 278)

Sliced Tomatoes, Fresh Oregano, Drizzled Lime, and Olive Oil

Fan-Sliced Fresh Peach Halves with Warm Currant Jelly and Blueberries

Winter

Flank Steak and Peppers (above)

Santa Cruz Hominy (p. 247)

Tortillas with Cilantro Butter (p. 278)

Simple Greens Salad (p. 254) with Orange Sections and Lime Cumin Vinaigrette (p. 274)

Vanilla Ice Cream Sprinkled with Cinnamon and Brown Sugar

Spring

Flank Steak and Peppers (above)

Broiled French Fries

Sautéed Broccoli Stems and Carrot Slices with Lemon Oil Drizzle

Mixed Greens Salad (p. 254) and Lime Cumin Vinaigrette (above)

Coffee Ice Cream with Grated Chocolate and Cinnamon

Santa Fe Steak Salad

This is a very light and flavorful salad, using leftover flank steak and peppers.

Santa Fe Salad (p. 267) **with Cold Flank Steak, Peppers, Avocado, Jack Cheese**
Red Chili Dressing (p. 276)
Quick Tomato Salsa (p. 287) **and Sour Cream**
Warm Tortillas with Lime Chili Butter (p. 278)
Sliced Sugared Strawberries and Watermelon Chunks

- **The Santa Fe Salad is a beautifully arranged vehicle for leftovers—be creative.**
- **Autumn: Add leftover red chili sauce to lime cumin vinaigrette for salad dressing.**
- **Winter and Spring: Use brownie mix or buy ready-made. For Easy Chocolate Frosting, see p. 326.**

Made with leftovers from previous menu.

SEASONAL SUGGESTIONS

Autumn

Santa Fe Fajitas (p. 267) with Leftover Corn and Peppers, Salsa (above), and Sour Cream
Refried Black Beans (p. 251)
Simple Greens Salad (p. 254) with Red Chili Vinaigrette (see box at left)
Vanilla Ice Cream with Blueberries and Peaches

Winter

Santa Fe Fajitas, Salsa (above), and Sour Cream
Chopped Tomato, Cucumber, Hominy, Onion, and Broccoli Salad with Lime Cumin Vinaigrette (p. 274)
Chocolate Brownies

Spring

Santa Fe Salad, Salsa (above), and Sour Cream
Chocolate Brownies

Farmers Market Pasta

This colorful pasta recipe was inspired by the wonderful Pike Place Farmers Market in Seattle, my home. Let what's fresh today determine the vegetables you include. A very quick dinner.

Farmers Market Pasta (p. 148) **with Shaved Parmesan Cheese**
Simple Greens Salad (p. 254)
Dijon Vinaigrette (p. 273)
Crusty Bread
Strawberry Ice Cream Cones

- **See Hint #2 (p. 15), grating Parmesan cheese.**
- **Try farfalle (bow-tie) or rigatoni pasta.**
- **For heartier pasta add smoked salmon, cooked prawns, proscuitto, or julienne-cut salami.**
- **See Hint #1 (p. 15), crusty bread.**
- **Autumn: See Hint #3 (p. 15), selecting pears.**

SEASONAL VARIATIONS

Autumn

Farmers' Market Risotto (p. 152)
Salad, Vinaigrette, and Bread (above)
Fresh Pear Halves with Warm
    Currant Jelly

Winter

Winter Vegetable Pasta (p. 148)
Salad, Vinaigrette, and Bread (above)
Warm Maple Syrup Sundaes

Spring

Pasta Primavera (p. 147)
Salad, Vinaigrette, and Bread (above)
Hot Fudge Sundaes

Barbecued Tuna and Two Salads

Substitute any fresh, firm-fleshed fish (marlin, swordfish, halibut, sea bass, etc.).

Lemon Herb Dijon-Glazed (p. 105)
Barbecued Tuna (p. 182)

Caesar Salad (p. 254) **and Dressing** (p. 276)

Sliced Tomatoes with Fresh Basil and Lemon Oil Vinaigrette (p. 274)

Crusty Bread

Chocolate Pan Cake (p. 325)

- **Fresh is the operative word for cooking fish— and for just a very few minutes! Cook extra for leftovers (see next menu).**

- **This old-fashioned cake is very simple. No time? Buy cake ready-made or frozen.**

- **Other Seasons: Bake fish if it's too cold to barbecue outside.**

SEASONAL SUGGESTIONS

Autumn

Fish (above) with Oven-Roasted New Potatoes (p. 237)

Mixed Greens Salad (p. 254) with Sliced Tomato and Caesar Dressing (p. 276)

Apple Ginger Upside Down-Cake (p. 327)

Winter

Barbecued Fish (above) with Sautéed Winter Root Vegetables (p. 225) and Tomato Concasse (See Hints #28 and #29, p. 18)

Mixed Greens Salad (p. 254) with Dijon Vinaigrette (p. 273)

Pear Ginger Upside-Down Cake (p. 327)

Spring

Fish (above) with Steamed Asparagus (p. 224), Crumbled Blue Cheese and Lemon Oil Drizzle (p. 283)

Baked Potatoes

Simple Greens Salad (p. 254) with Tomato Vinaigrette (p. 273)

Chocolate Pan Cake (p. 325)

Fresh Tuna Sandwiches and Gazpacho

The fresh fish sandwich makes this very quick dinner elegant.

Fresh Tuna (or Other Leftover Fish) Sandwiches
(p. 160) **with Homemade Mayonnaise** (p. 279)
on Crusty Bread

Gazpacho (p. 124)

Sliced Melon with Lime

Leftover Cake or Ice Cream and Cookies

- **This is your chance to try Homemade Mayonnaise—it's so quick, so easy, and so good!**
- **Winter and Spring: See Hint #3 (p. 15), selecting pears.**

Made with leftovers from previous menu.

SEASONAL SUGGESTIONS

Autumn
    Sandwiches (above)
    Quick Tomato Vegetable Soup (p. 121)
    Melon
    Leftover Cake

Winter
    Sandwiches (above)
    Quick Tomato Vegetable Soup (p. 121)
    Sliced Pears with Lime
    Leftover Cake

Spring
    Sandwiches (above)
    Potato Soup (p. 132) with Asparagus
    Sliced Pears with Lime
    Leftover Cake

Summer Tomato Cheese Tart and Salad

This is incredibly easy, but it's so beautiful and delicious you will feel like a professional chef!

Summer Tomato and Cheese Tart (p. 163) **with Red and Yellow Tomatoes**

Mixed Greens Salad (p. 254)

Dijon Vinaigrette (p. 273)

Broiled Garlic Bread

Fresh Melon and Berries with Cookies

- The Seasonal Suggestions tarts are variations of the tomato and cheese tart. Use Japanese eggplant for the Autumn tart; it does not need to be salted to leach out bitterness as regular eggplant does.
- See Hint #1 (p. 15), crusty bread.
- Spring: See Hint #3 (p. 15), selecting pears.

SEASONAL SUGGESTIONS

Autumn
>   Tart (above) with Eggplant, Tomato, and Cheese
>   Simple Greens Salad (p. 254) with Dijon Vinaigrette (above)
>   Sliced Nectarines and Blueberries, with Cookies

Winter
>   Tart (above) with Eggplant, Zucchini, Tomato, and Cheese
>   Simple Greens Salad (p. 254) with Dijon Vinaigrette (above)
>   Winter Fruit Compote (p. 315) with Cookies

Spring
>   Tart (above) with Asparagus, Tomato, and Cheese
>   Salad and Vinaigrette (above)
>   Fresh Pears with Frozen Berry Sauce (p. 333)

Barbecued Sausage and Bread Kabobs

This is a take-off on one of Italy's most traditional outdoor rotisserie oven foods.

Barbecued Italian Sausage, Bell Peppers, Onion, and Bread Kabobs (p. 222)

French New Potato Salad (p. 263)

Sliced Tomatoes with Fresh Basil and Lemon Oil Vinaigrette (p. 274)

Fresh Berries with Lemon Cream (p. 338)

- **Make extra kabobs and potato salad for leftovers (see p. 78).**
- **Enjoy completely different taste combinations for each season.**
- **Spring: Follow cooking instructions on package for Spaetzle.**

SEASONAL SUGGESTIONS

Autumn

Kabobs (above) with Peppers, Zucchini, Onion, and Sausage, without Bread

Mustards and Horseradish

Dark Rye Bread with Swiss or Jarlsberg Cheese

German Potato Salad (p. 262)

Gingerbread with Lemon Whipped Cream Sauce (p. 337)

Winter

Grilled Italian Sausage and Caramelized Onions (p. 231) with Polenta (p. 245)

Mixed Greens Salad (p. 254) with Dijon Vinaigrette (p. 273)

Pear Upside-Down Gingerbread Cake (p. 327)

Spring

Grilled Italian Sausage with Buttered Spaetzle

Sweet and Sour Red Cabbage (p. 229) Light Rye Bread

Simple Greens Salad (p. 254) with Dijon Vinaigrette (above)

Pineapple Upside-Down Cake (p. 327)

Crab Cakes with Cajun Tartar Sauce

These crab cakes are very light and a little spicy. If crab is too expensive in your area, see recipe (p. 189) for substitutions.

Crab Cakes (p. 189) **with Cajun Tartar Sauce** (p. 281)
Coleslaw (p. 255) **with Coleslaw Dressing** (p. 277)
String Beans Marinated (p. 257) **in Dijon Vinaigrette** (p. 233)
Garlic Bread
Blackberry Cobbler (p. 309)

- **See Hint #1 (p. 15), crusty bread.**

Made with leftovers from previous menu.

SEASONAL SUGGESTIONS

Autumn
> Smoked Salmon Cakes (p. 189) with Sour Cream Cucumber Sauce (p. 256)
> Mixed Greens Salad (p. 254) with Tomato Vinaigrette (p. 273)
> Ice Cream with Sliced Nectarines

Winter
> Codfish Cakes (p. 189) with Red Chili Tartar Sauce (p. 281)
> Marinated Cucumbers (p. 255)
> Winter Fruit Compote (p. 315) over Ice Cream

Spring
> Shrimp Cakes (p. 189) with Cajun Tartar Sauce (p. 281)
> Bell Pepper and Cabbage Slaw (p. 255) with Coleslaw Dressing (p. 277)
> Strawberry Rhubarb Crisp (p. 309)

Salad Samplers

I almost always order salad samplers for lunch because I can't choose just one. Small portions of each salad work best.

Cold Seafood Salad (p. 268)

Potato Salad (p. 261) **with Homemade Mayonnaise** (p. 279) **and Leftover Sausage**

Chopped Leftover Vegetable Salad with Blue Cheese

Fruit Salad

Broiled Pesto Bread

Cookies

- **These salads are ideas—let refrigerator leftovers and your imagination guide yours!**
- **Buy pesto ready-made.**

Made with leftovers from previous menu.

SEASONAL SUGGESTIONS

Autumn
   Smoked Salmon Seafood Salad
      (above) with Leftover Sour Cream
      Cucumber Sauce (p. 256)
   Leftover Potato Salad with Sausage
   Ice Cream with Sliced Nectarines

Winter
   Quick Tomato Soup (p. 121)
   Seafood Salad (above) with Cod, and
      Red Chili Tartar Sauce (p. 281)
   Leftover Vegetables with Cucumbers
   Cookies

Spring
   Seafood Salad (above) with Shrimp
      and Cajun Tartar Sauce (p. 281)
   Coleslaw (p. 255) with Coleslaw
      Dressing (p. 277)
   Cookies

Just in Case You Give A Party!

More Menus

Italian Fish Dinner

Pork Tenderloin with Cranberry Demi-Glace

A Casual Pasta and Grilled Sausage Dinner

Grilled Flank Steak—A Tex-Mex Barbecue

Autumn Chicken Breasts with Lentils and Wild Mushrooms

A Simple Risotto Supper

Steamed Shellfish Dinner

An Autumn or Winter Mixed-Game Buffet

A Make-Ahead Dinner

Composed Luncheon Salad

Late Afternoon Lunch—Wild Mushroom Soup and Salad

Italian Fish Dinner

Deceptively simple, colorful and light, this dinner is an assortment of tastes. The pears make a gorgeous scarlet finale.

HORS D'OEUVRES

Prosciutto (Resources, p. 340) **Drizzled with Extra Virgin Olive Oil and Cracked Pepper**

Tapenade (Resources, p. 340)

Marinated Chevre Rounds (p. 112) **with Crostini** (p. 119)

DINNER

Dijon-Glazed (p. 105) **Grilled or Oven-Roasted Swordfish*** (p. 182) **with Lemon Herb Demi-Glace** (p. 107)

Sautéed Julienne-Cut Carrots, Beets, and Zucchini (p. 225) **with Lemon Oil Drizzle** (p. 283)

Roasted Potato Wedges (p. 237) **with Olive Oil, Oregano, and Parmesan Cheese**

Simple Greens Salad (p. 254) **with Homemade Croutons** (p. 118) **and Italian Vinaigrette** (p. 273)

DESSERT

Pears Poached in Port with Port Syrup (p. 313) **and Mock Crème Fraîche Swirls** (p. 282)

*Or Chilean sea bass, halibut, sturgeon, ling cod, tuna, mahi mahi, grouper, etc.

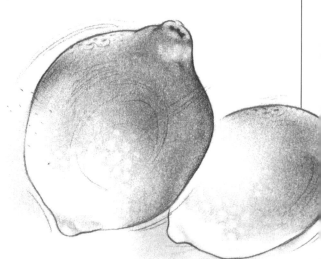

PRESENTATION IDEAS

**If grapes grow anywhere around you, some
grape leaves and part of the vine can make
food presentation pretty dramatic. Put the
marinated chevre rounds directly on a big
grape leaf on a willow cheese tray or glass
plate. Add a tiny bit of the curly vine end also.
Grape vine running down the center of the
table, draping through or around a vase or
included in a flower arrangement on the table
or in the bathroom is fun and interesting. No
grapes? What about large sprigs of rosemary,
or bunches of oregano? Look for long stems
and bunchy leaves. A big head of garlic placed
on the tray or plate next to the chevre rounds
looks great. And if you can't get flowers, how
about a big bowl of beautiful red pears in the
center of the table?**

- **Fish: Buy pieces cut identically, of the same weight and thickness so they will cook at the same rate. I usually buy 7 oz. portion fillets rather than steaks because they are less likely to have bones.**

- **Timing is everything when cooking fish at high heat (p. 14).**

- **Plan the cooking schedule ahead—heat the plates!**

- **See Hint #3 (p. 15), selecting pears.**

- **Autumn: Buy good caramel sauce.**

SEASONAL SUGGESTIONS: Items not repeated
from the primary menu stay the same.

Autumn

> Sautéed Red, Yellow, and Green Bell
> Peppers (p. 228) with Ginger and
> Lemon
> Poached Pears (p. 313) with
> Caramel Sauce

Spring

> Fish (p. 82) with Puttanesca Sauce
> (p. 294)
> Steamed Pencil Asparagus (p. 223) with
> Lemon Oil Drizzle (p. 283)
> Pears with Port Syrup (p. 82),
> garnished with Fresh Raspberries

Summer

> Fish (p. 182) Grilled Outdoors
> Fresh Berry Tart (p. 308)

Pork Tenderloin with Cranberry Demi-Glace

Pork tenderloin is a great item. It's subtle taste is a lot like veal but much less expensive, it is a manageable size to cook, it works with almost any sauce or herb, and it's lean. Carefully wrapped and frozen, it keeps for two or three months.

HORS D'OEUVRES
Melba Rounds or Crostini (p. 119)
with Chopped Scallop Ceviche (p. 111)
and Eggplant Caviar (p. 116)

DINNER
Sage Dijon-Glazed Pork Tenderloin (p. 217)
Dijon Cranberry Demi-Glace (p. 217)
Lentils with Wild Mushrooms and Caramelized Onion (p. 233)
Sautéed Winter Root Vegetables (p. 225)
Tossed with Chiffonade-Cut Spinach (p. 223)
and Lemon Oil Drizzle (p. 283)
Mixed Greens Salad (p. 254)
with Avocado and Grapefruit Sections
Dijon Vinaigrette (p. 273)

DESSERT
Sautéed Apples over Puff Pastry Squares (p. 316) **with Warm Caramel Sauce**

PRESENTATION IDEAS

Sage grows in huge plants that have long stems filled with the beautiful, gray-green leaves. Those and fresh brilliant red apples are a good start for presentation.

- Eggplant Caviar may be made ahead or purchased at specialty food stores.
- Scallops must be fresh!
- Caramelize onions ahead and refrigerate.
- Toss spinach into vegetable sauté for last 2 minutes.
- Add a little brandy to the caramel sauce!
- Spring: See Hint #29 (p. 18), tomato concasse.

SEASONAL SUGGESTIONS: Items not repeated from the primary menu stay the same.

Autumn

Wild Mushroom Demi-Glace (p. 107)

Spring

Tarragon Dijon Glaze (p. 105) and Demi-Glace on Pork Tenderloin

Steamed Asparagus with Tomato Concasse (p. 18)

Salad (p. 84) with Chopped, Roasted Hazelnuts

Rhubarb Crisp (p. 309) with Vanilla Sauce (p. 335)

Summer

Moroccan Dijon Glaze (p. 105) on Pork Tenderloin, Grilled Outside

Demi-Glace (with 1 tsp. Dijon, 1 tsp. marinade, 1 tbsp. apricot preserves, and 1/2 cup white wine) (p. 107)

Jamaican Beans and Rice (p. 249)

Steamed Baby Carrots with Short Stems

Salad with Chutney Vinaigrette (p. 274)

Fresh Berries with Apricot Cream (p. 338)

A Casual Pasta and Grilled Sausage Dinner

I use this menu for week night dinners when preparation time is tight, or for guests who don't know each other well. The elaborate antipasti inspires conversation, and pasta makes a wonderful entertaining entrée. It seems so casual, and guests can participate in the preparation. The final pasta boiling and put-togethers can be a lot of fun. (Antipasti can be as complicated as you have time for, and it and the pasta sauce can be made a day or two ahead.)

HORS D'OEUVRES

Antipasti
Crostini (p. 119)**; Salsa Cruda;
Marinated Chevre Rounds** (p.112)**; Roasted Bell
Pepper Wedges** (p. 227)**; Roasted Garlic** (p. 225)**;
Zucchini and Yellow Summer Squash Wedges
with Pesto Vinaigrette Dip** (p. 273)**; Smoked
Salmon; Marinated** (p. 113) **or Calamata Olives or
Sicilian Olives** (p. 113) (Resources, p. 340) **in Cracked
Pepper and Lemon Zest**

DINNER

Pasta* with Puttenesca Sauce (p. 294) **and
Grilled Italian Sausages**

Freshly Grated Parmesan Cheese

Crusty Italian Bread

Mixed Greens Salad (p. 254) **with
Italian Vinaigrette** (p. 273)

DESSERT

Individual Rustic Plum and Nectarine Tarts (p. 305)

*Use a plain, unflavored pasta, such as linguine, fettuccine, vermicelli, orecchiette, farfalle, penne, etc. Shapes are fun to eat and they capture sauce. Very thin spaghetti or vermicelli will collapse against sausage, and filled pastas will detract from the sauce. Dry pasta is fine; fresh takes less time to cook.

PRESENTATION IDEAS

If you can find long sprigs of rosemary, great. Often floral wholesale houses have them, although they have been sprayed and are not edible. Extra loaves of bread, either round or longer baguettes, whole heads of garlic, large beautiful purple eggplants, and artichokes all look wonderful at Italian dinners. No candles dripping out of chianti bottles, please! If you can get sunflowers, they are spectacular in a tall vase, or cut very short in votive candle containers (sunflowers grow all over Italy).

Buy bell peppers of several colors.

Buy 2 flavors of sausage (fennel and lamb?)

If possible, serve pasta in wide, shallow bowls.

See Hint #1 (p. 15), crusty bread.

See Hint #2 (p. 15), grating Parmesan cheese.

Make tart early, then reheat it while pasta boils. It will be almost warm for dessert—yum!

Winter and Spring: See Hint #3 (p. 15), selecting pears.

SEASONAL SUGGESTIONS: Items not repeated from the primary menu stay the same.

Winter

Tuna Carpaccio (raw, Ahi-grade tuna, sliced paper-thin) with Olive Oil and Cracked Pepper in Antipasti

Quick Tomato Sauce (p. 292) with Sun-Dried Tomatoes and Artichoke Hearts for Pasta

Pears Poached in Port (p. 313) with Italian Almond Macaroons

Spring

Steamed, Chilled Asparagus (p. 224) Marinated in Italian Vinaigrette (p. 273)

Prosciutto or Beef Carpaccio with Olive Oil and Cracked Pepper in Antipasti

Pasta with Smoked Salmon in Creamy Tomato Sauce (p. 293)

Pears Poached in Port (p. 313) with Italian Almond Macaroons

Summer

Pasta and Seafood in Parchment (p. 187)

Individual Berry Tarts (p. 308)

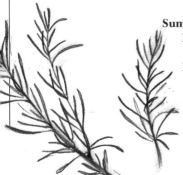

Grilled Flank Steak— A Tex-Mex Barbecue

Simple hors d'oeuvres invite guests to linger outside around the barbecue. The Seasonal Suggestions show just how versatile flank steak can be.

HORS D'OEUVRES

Homemade Tortilla Chips (p. 111) **with Quick Tomato Salsa** (p. 287)

Roasted Mexican Pumpkin Seeds (p. 110)

DINNER

Barbecued Flank Steak (p. 204) **with Red Chili Sauce** (p. 298)

Sautéed Sweet Bell and Anaheim Chili Peppers (p. 228)

Santa Cruz Hominy (p. 247)

Warm Flour Tortillas with Cilantro Butter (p. 278)

Mixed Greens Salad (p. 254) **with Avocado, Jicama, and Sliced Radishes**

Lime Cumin Vinaigrette (p. 274)

DESSERT

Chilled Lemon Soufflé (p. 329) **with Raspberry Sauce** (p. 333)

PRESENTATION IDEAS

I can get hokey with Mexican dinners, so bear with me. Chips served in a Mexican hat; piñata hanging in the powder room; primary colored napkins; dried corn husks as liners; bunches of dried chilies; pepper plants; tiny cacti in 2 - 4" pots as place cards; Mexican jumping beans and dried black or pinto beans scattered on the table . . . stop me before I put on a costume!

MORE PRESENTATION IDEAS

Autumn: **Big beautiful eggplants, garlic heads, pumpkins and other squashes.**

Winter: **Chopsticks, baskets of fortune cookies, Japanese eggplant, ginger flower, enoki mushrooms, rice candies.**

Summer: **Fresh pineapples, wooden serving bowls, tropical flowers, shells, and white sand as a bed for candles.**

If you are unsure about hominy, substitute Fried Polenta (p. 245) with grated Monterey Jack cheese.

Try the soufflé in individual goblets or ramekins.

Autumn: Buy ready-made herb cream cheese.

SEASONAL SUGGESTIONS: Items not repeated from the primary menu stay the same.

Autumn

Herb Cream Cheese, Caponata (p. 115) and Crostini (p. 119)

Steak with Rosemary, Garlic Dijon Glaze (p. 105) and Red Wine Demi-Glace (p. 218)

Sautéed Wild Mushrooms (p. 225)

Oven-Roasted Red Potatoes (p. 237)

Salad with Roasted, Chopped Hazelnuts and Herb Vinaigrette (p. 274)

Apple Pie (p. 302)

Winter

Asian Rice Stick Mix

Shrimp and Scallop Ceviche (p. 117) with Sesame Pita Chips (p. 111)

Steak with Asian Marinade (p. 217)

Fried Rice (from box)

Salad with Tangerines, Green Onions, and Ginger Sesame Vinaigrette (p. 275)

Lemon Soufflé (p. 329) with Candied Ginger and Fortune Cookies

Spring

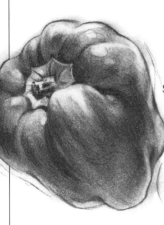

Cumin Pita Chips (p. 111) with Shrimp and Scallop Ceviche (p. 117)

Steak with Spicy Caribbean Sauce (p. 297) and Quick Fruit Chutney (p. 287)

Couscous

Salad with Chutney Vinaigrette (p. 274)

Flourless Dense Chocolate Cake (Resources, p. 340) with Apricot Cream (p. 338)

Autumn Chicken Breasts with Lentils and Wild Mushrooms

If you don't have much time, buy the hors d'oeuvres. The stars of this menu are the chicken, mushrooms, and the julienne-cut vegetables. And you send your guests home basking in the warmth of bread pudding. If you are looking for future favors, this is the menu to set you up.

HORS D'OEUVRES
Dry-Roasted Pistachio Nuts; Three Types of Marinated Brine-Cured Olives (p. 113)**; Sun-Dried Tomato Pesto** (p. 284) **over Brie Cheese**

DINNER
Sage Dijon-Glazed Chicken Breasts (p. 167) **with Sautéed Wild and Button Mushrooms** (p. 225) **over Lentils and Caramelized Onion** (p. 233)

Steamed Julienne-Cut Winter Squash and Root Vegetables (p. 225) **with Chopped Sage and Lemon Oil Drizzle** (p. 283)

Simple Greens Salad (p. 254) **with Sliced Pear, and Warmed Chevre Rounds**

Dijon Vinaigrette (p. 273)

DESSERT
Bread Pudding (p. 319) **with Whiskey Sauce** (p. 336)

PRESENTATION IDEAS
Gourds, several kinds of squashes, and pumpkins of all sizes placed throughout the house; blossoming squash vines as a table runner; bunches of fresh sage; colorful fall leaves under each serving plate (collect the leaves, press them for 24 hours between newspaper).

MORE PRESENTATION IDEAS

Winter: Line a basket tray with dry lentils, and put crackers and spreads on top; put bowls of fresh cranberries around the house; place a basket of huge mushrooms and onions on the table with lentils scattered around.

Spring: Add raw asparagus to flower arrangements or set crocus plants in tiny pots down the center of the table.

Summer: Instead of a flower arrangement on the piano or coffee table, how about a big bowl filled with lemons? or lemons and limes? and big bunches of oregano?

• Remove the top skin from the brie and spread with pesto.

SEASONAL SUGGESTIONS: Items not repeated from the primary menu stay the same.

Winter
> Salad with Grapefruit Sections and Chopped Fresh Cranberry

Spring
> Wild Rice Pilaf (p. 248) (for Lentils)
> Steamed Asparagus
> Salad with Avocado, Crumbled Blue Cheese, and Orange Shallot Vinaigrette (p. 274)
> Bread Pudding with Almonds and Amaretto Sauce (see Whiskey Sauce, p. 336)

Summer
> Barbecued Chicken with Lemon, Garlic, Oregano Dijon Glaze (p. 167)
> Couscous with Chopped Red Onion
> Steamed Green and Yellow Wax Beans with Crumbled Feta Cheese
> Mixed Greens Salad (p. 254) with Sliced Fresh Figs and Pineapple Mint Vinaigrette (p. 275)
> Mixed Berry Tart (p. 308)

A Simple Risotto Supper

*In India it's curry; in Asia it's stir-fry; in Morocco it's couscous.
Risotto is Italy's version of steaming hot, cooked starch with leftovers on top or stirred in; all true supper foods, relaxed, informal,
and ultimately comforting. This is a menu I might use after hiking,
skiing, or trout fishing. Because suppers are light meals, hors
d'oeuvres aren't necessary. If you want to have something to taste
while the risotto is cooking, keep it simple and fresh.*

HORS D'OEUVRES
Salsa Cruda (p. 291) **with Melba Rounds**
Italian Calamata Olives (Resources, p. 340)

DINNER
Smoked Salmon Risotto (p. 151)
with Fresh Asparagus Tips
Freshly Grated Parmesan Cheese
Crusty Bread
Mixed Greens Salad (p. 254)
with Shaved Red Onion
Italian Vinaigrette (p. 273)

DESSERT
Rhubarb Strawberry Crisp (p. 309)
with Grand Marnier Vanilla Sauce (p. 335)

Elaborate "trappings" might overwhelm this casual menu. Votive candles and garlic heads interspersed in sprigs of a ground cover such as salal might set the tone. If you have a big enough shallow serving bowl, put the risotto in the middle of the table, and serve it family style. A small wedge of the Parmesan at the side of the bowl of grated cheese can look wonderful. In Autumn, pumpkins are a natural.

- **Serve Risotto in warm bowls with a bowl of extra cheese.**
- **Use lox-style smoked salmon.**
- **Blanch asparagus first so they will hold their brilliant green.**
- **See Hint #1 (p. 15), crusty bread.**
- **See Hint #2 (p. 15), grating Parmesan cheese.**
- **Strawberries add strong color to the Crisp.**
- **Autumn: See Hint #3 (p. 15), selecting pears.**

SEASONAL SUGGESTIONS: Items not repeated from the primary menu stay the same.

Autumn

Pumpkin Risotto with Prosciutto or Ham

Rustic Pear Tart (p. 305) with Vanilla Sauce (p. 335)

Winter

Risotto with Roasted Garlic (p. 225), Wild Mushrooms, and Pepper Bacon

Cranberry Pudding (p. 321) with Hard Sauce (p. 336)

Summer

Bowl of Peas in the Shell

Risotto with Roasted Garlic, Julienne-Cut Summer Vegetables, and Artichoke Hearts

Warm Berries with Currant Sauce (p. 311) over Pound Cake topped with Lemon Cream (p. 338)

Steamed Shellfish Dinner

This is a peak season menu requiring absolutely fresh, perfect shellfish. It is not a neat and tidy meal to eat, and it's almost impossible without seafood forks. Your guests will appreciate steaming, lemon-scented hand towels before dessert.

HORS D'OEUVRES
Dilly Beans and Carrots (p. 259)

**Water Crackers and Flatbread with
3 or 4 Fine Quality Imported Cheeses**

DINNER
Steamed Shellfish (p. 185) **in Nectar**

Mixed Greens Salad (p. 254) **with
Herb Shallot Vinaigrette** (p. 274)

Crusty Bread

DESSERT
Strawberry Shortcake

- Small, pink-shelled scallops are available fresh, in some locales, for only a very short summer season. With deep purple mussel shells and sand colored clam shells, the three make a stunning combination.
- Dampen towels with lemon water and steam for 1 minute in the microwave.

- **Dilled vegetables are available at most supermarkets. The fresh version in the recipe section are easy, crunchy, and, because they are not cooked, brightly colored.**
- **Make vegetables a day or two ahead, or make crudites with Cucumber Dip (p. 256).**
- **Plan time to prep shellfish.**
- **Remember shell crackers (nutcrackers work) and seafood forks.**
- **Krusteaz® scone mix made with cream makes wonderful shortcake.**
- **Save a whole berry with greens to top each dessert.**

SEASONAL SUGGESTIONS: Items not repeated from the primary menu stay the same.

Autumn
Dilly Carrots (p. 259)
Salad with Red Skinned Apple Slices and Roasted Cashews with Dijon Vinaigrette (p. 273)
Cornbread Pudding (p. 319) with Whiskey Sauce (p. 336)

Winter
Caponata (p. 115)
Salad with Chopped Cranberries and Roasted Pistachios with Dijon Vinaigrette (p. 273)
Gingerbread with Apricot Cream (p. 338)

Spring
Eggplant Caviar (p. 116)
Lemon Tarts (p. 308) with Frozen Berry Sauce (p. 333)

An Autumn or Winter Mixed-Game Buffet

If your butcher does not carry "exotic" poultry or rabbit regularly, it can be ordered through several suppliers throughout the country (ask the butcher for suppliers). The buffet platters will hold quarters of poultry and the saddle of rabbit.

HORS D'OEUVRES
Warm Homemade Parmesan Pita Chips (p. 111)

DINNER
Dijon-Glazed (p. 105) **Grilled Quail, Pheasant, Duck, and Rabbit**

Wild Rice with Toasted Pine Nuts

Sautéed Apples with Caramelized Onion (p. 232)

Pickled Red Cabbage (p. 229)

Chilled, Steamed Green and Yellow Wax Beans Marinated in Herb Vinaigrette (p. 274) **with Crumbled Blue Cheese**

Sliced Tomatoes with Italian Vinaigrette (p. 273) **and Chopped Fresh Basil**

Various Mustards and Chutneys

Rye, Sourdough, and Pumpernickel Bread

DESSERT
Pears Poached in Port with Port Syrup (p. 313) **and Grand Marnier Vanilla Sauce** (p. 335)

- Make chips ahead and reheat to serve warm.
- Grill rabbit and game birds the way you would grill chicken, with Dijon Glaze liberally applied and at high heat. While they cook, brush them several additional times with the glaze to prevent them from drying out.

PRESENTATION IDEAS

If you can get ahold of game bird feathers, they can be used in flower arrangements, lining bread baskets, or tied to raffia and then tied around napkins. Sunflowers, dried corn husks and corn stalks, duck calls, gourds, pumpkins, popcorn (blue and yellow) scattered on the buffet table or used to hold dried stalks in baskets, decoys, raffia sculpture fowl. Define one dominant color, and then repeat it often to provide continuity.

- **Offer as many varieties of mustards and chutneys as you want, at least 3 of each; I recommend including a whole grain mustard, mustard chow chow, and Cranberry Chutney (p. 288)**
- **Pickled red cabbage is also available ready-made.**
- **See Hint #1 (p. 15), crusty bread.**
- **Poach pears ahead— they will keep for 2 or 3 days. See Hint #3 (p. 15), selecting pears.**

SEASONAL SUGGESTIONS: Items not repeated from the primary menu stay the same.

This really is an Autumn or Winter menu that doesn't lend itself to minor modifications. You could grill a combination red meat and sausages, but that's entirely different.

97

A Make-Ahead Dinner

Paella is a show stopper, so serve dinner at the table. Remember shell receptacles and seafood forks. If there is any shellfish left over, remove it from the shell before refrigerating it overnight.

HORS D'OEUVRES

Sicilian or Spanish Olives (Resources, p. 340) **with Olive Oil, Lemon Zest, and Cracked Pepper**

Parmesan Tortilla Chips (p. 111)

Pistachio Nuts Roasted with Spanish Olive Oil, Saffron, and Salt

DINNER

Chicken, Chorizo Sausage, and Shellfish Paella (p. 155) **with Saffron Rice**

Mixed Greens Salad (p. 254) **with Orange Sections and Thinly Shaved Red Onion**

Orange Shallot Vinaigrette (p. 274)

Heated Sliced Crusty Bread with Cumin Butter (p. 278)

DESSERT

Lemon Tarts (p. 308) **with Raspberry Sauce** (p. 333)

PRESENTATION IDEAS

A colorful serape or similar fabric might make a wonderful table runner. Castanets, maracas, very bright paper napkins or candles can pick up or add accent to various corners or rooms in your home. Did you know that saffron comes from crocus plants? Small 4" crocus pots spark up any table or bathroom. And of course, colorful peppers of all varieties are very Spanish and easy to find. Make sure that the serving dish for the paella is wide enough to display the different seafoods, chicken drumettes, and sausage in one layer so that each guest gets at least one or two pieces of everything.

- **Timing is very important with seafood.**
- **Buy only very fresh shellfish.**
- **Buy lemon tarts to save time.**

SEASONAL SUGGESTIONS: Items not repeated from the primary menu stay the same.

Autumn or Winter

Cumin Pita Chips (p. 111) and Chilled Shrimp with Cucumber Yogurt Dip (p. 256)

Moroccan Chicken with Couscous (p. 169)

Mixed Berry Tarts (p. 308) with Grand Marnier Vanilla Sauce (p. 335)

Composed Luncheon Salad

A touch of Mexico, or Asia, or France, or . . .

LUNCH

Santa Fe Salad (p. 267) **with Flank Steak, Avocado, Corn, Chevre, and Red Chili Dressing** (p. 276) **on Mixed Greens with Lime Cumin Vinaigrette** (p. 274)

Quick Tomato Salsa (p. 287) **and Sour Cream**

Warm Tortillas with Cilantro Butter (p. 278)

DESSERT

Dense, Flourless Chocolate Cake (Resources, p. 340) **Dusted with Powdered Sugar and Cinnamon**

A Mexican fabric or serape used as a table runner on a solid-colored table cloth sets a subtle tone. Line the tortilla basket with dried corn husks, use brightly colored crepe paper flowers, and scatter Mexican jumping beans or dried corn on the table.

- **If you are not using leftover flank steak, grill the steak a day ahead.**
- **Buy cake.**

SEASONAL SUGGESTIONS: Items not repeated from the primary menu stay the same.

Autumn

Asian Chicken Salad (p. 271) (smoked chicken breast if available) with Chilled, Steamed Asparagus (p. 224) and Ginger Sesame Vinaigrette (p. 275)

Warm Sesame Pita Chips (p. 111)

Poached Pears (p. 313) with Quick Ginger Sauce (p. 337) and Fortune Cookies

Spring

Seafood Salad (either salmon, tuna, or other firm-fleshed fish) (p. 268)

Crusty Bread

Individual Rustic Apple Tarts (p. 305)

Summer

Marinated Vegetables (green and yellow wax beans, fennel, asparagus, baby carrots, celery, yellow teardrop and cherry tomatoes) and White Bean Salad (p. 257) with Herb Vinaigrette (p. 274) and Crumbled Blue Cheese

Warm Parmesan Pita Crisps (p. 111)

Chilled Lemon Soufflé (p. 329) with Berry Sauce (p. 333)

Late Afternoon Lunch— Wild Mushroom Soup and Salad

This menu reminds me of a Sunday afternoon with friends who came over for a long walk on the beach and a late lunch (or early supper). The soup is piping hot and woodsy, and the cheese invites you to linger at the table.

HORS D'OEUVRES

Blanched and Raw Vegetables (p. 223) **with Italian Vinaigrette** (p. 273) **for Dipping**

LUNCH

Creamy Wild Mushroom Soup (p. 136)

Crusty Bread with Imported Cheeses: Muenster, Aged Provolone, Cambazola Brie, and Chevre

Mixed Greens Salad (p. 254) **with Sliced Pears**

Lemon Oil Vinaigrette (p. 274)

DESSERT

Warm Apple Crisp (p. 309) **with Vanilla Sauce** (p. 335)

- See Hint #26 (p. 18), wild mushrooms.
- Button mushrooms should be firm and plump, indicating that they haven't lost moisture. A few opened under the cap and a little dark will add flavor, but too many will make the soup bitter.

PRESENTATION IDEAS

A simple basket of really big button mushrooms, unwashed with stems, can be stunning. If you are near the woods, salal, those big woody fungi, or dried moss all fit this meal. I often put cheese on pressed leaves (see box, p. 90) **that are set on a flat piece of driftwood. Or I lay a lichen-covered branch on the table and scatter big mushrooms around it.**

• **Don't wash mushrooms! Brush off dirt or pine needles. Separate the stems from the caps of the wild mushrooms. Reserve tops. Put the stems in the processor with the button mushrooms. Process until they are minced.**

SEASONAL SUGGESTIONS: Items not repeated from the primary menu stay the same.

Winter
>Soup with Fresh Crimini and Button Mushrooms and Dried Wild Mushrooms (p. 137)
>Salad (above) with Tangerine Wedges and Orange Shallot Vinaigrette (p. 274)
>Apple Cranberry Crisp (p. 309) with Vanilla Sauce (p. 335)

Spring
>Salad (above) with Sliced Kiwi and Orange Shallot Vinaigrette (p. 274)
>Rhubarb Crisp (p. 309) with Crème Fraîche (p. 282)

Summer
>Fresh Clam Chowder (p. 144)
>Marinated Summer Vegetable Salad (p. 257)
>Warm Berries with Lemon Whipped Cream Sauce (p. 337)

The
Recipes

Dijon Glaze

This glaze seals the pores of fish, meat, or chicken during high heat cooking (roasting, grilling, or frying). The seal prevents loss of natural juices, and the Dijon herb combination adds delicious, basic flavor. I promise that this glaze will change your cooking dramatically. See High Temperature Cooking, p.14.

Yield: 3/4 cup
Preparation time: 5 minutes

> 1/4 cup Dijon mustard (one part)
> 1/2 cup extra virgin olive oil (two parts)
> 1 tbsp. fresh herb, minced, or 1 tsp. dried herb (optional)
> 1 tsp. minced garlic, onion, shallot, chive (optional)

For poultry: Add the herb of your choice and, if you are not going to make a sauce, add minced onion, garlic, or shallots to the glaze. **For pork or game:** Minced onion and sage. **For lamb:** Minced garlic and rosemary. **For beef:** Minced garlic and thyme. **For fish:** Minced shallot or chive, a mild herb such as tarragon, savory, or sorrel, and tsp. of lemon juice.

Caribbean Dijon Glaze: Add 1 tsp. Jerk seasoning (Resources, p. 340), or 1 tsp. Pickapeppa® Sauce, 1/4 tsp. allspice, 1 tsp. lime juice.

Moroccan Dijon Glaze: Add 1 tsp. Moroccan Spice Paste (p. 286) or Garam Masala Curry Paste® (Resources, p. 340).

Pesto Dijon Glaze: Add 1/4 cup prepared basil pesto, without nuts.

In a processor or blender or using a whisk, slowly add the oil to the mustard until the mixture emulsifies to the consistency of the mustard originally. Stir in the herbs. If you put fresh herbs in a processor or blender too soon, they will be chopped so fine that the glaze will turn green.

This spread will keep, tightly covered and refrigerated, for several weeks. Keep adding to it and use it often.

I make Dijon Glaze in a large batches, divide it among several small jars, and flavor each differently, leaving one plain. That way you will have several glazes on hand ready to go.

Low-Fat Dijon Glaze

*See Dijon Glaze (p. 105) for an explanation of what it does to
poultry and meat. It calls for 2 parts olive oil to 1 part mustard.
This low-fat adaptation substitutes stock for most of the oil and
uses cornstarch to thicken the sauce. It works just as well as the
other version.*

Yield: 3/4 cup
Preparation time: 10 minutes

See recipes for
Homemade and
Modified
Canned Stock
(p. 108).

1 tsp. cornstarch
1/2 cup chicken stock
3 tbsp. Dijon mustard
1 tsp. extra virgin olive oil
1 tbsp. fresh herb, minced, or 1 tsp. dried
herb (optional)
1 tsp. minced garlic, onion, shallot, chive
(optional)

1. In a small bowl, mix stock into cornstarch and whisk until the
   cornstarch is smoothly blended with the stock. Microwave
   (covered) at high temperature for 40 seconds, or cook in a
   small saucepan over low heat until it boils slightly and clears
   (about 5 minutes). Cool to room temperature.

2. Whisk oil, mustard, and herbs of choice into the cornstarch
   mixture until it is blended.

3. Brush over poultry, fish, or meat.

Demi-Glace

VARIATIONS: DIJON DEMI-GLACE, FLAVORED DEMI-GLACE

Demi-glace is sauce made by adding liquid to cooking residue, then cooking it until it is reduced by half, hence "demi." It is the quickest and easiest way to make delicious sauce.

Yield: 3/4 cup
Preparation time: 5 minutes

> **1/2 cup meat, chicken, or vegetable stock, or wine**
> **drippings from cooked fish, meat, or poultry**

1. Transfer meat, chicken, or fish from cooking pan to warmed serving dish or plates.

2. Put the cooking pan on medium high heat, add stock, wine, and any extra flavorings, and scrape cooked-on residue from the bottom of the pan into the liquid. Simmer until the liquid is reduced by half, about 3 - 5 minutes. If waiting meat, chicken, or fish loses any liquid, add it to the sauce.

3. To serve: Ladle the sauce over the meat, chicken, or fish, and serve immediately.

DIJON DEMI-GLACE
Add 1 tsp. Dijon Glaze (p. 105).

FLAVORED DEMI-GLACE

> **1 tbsp. chopped fresh herb,** *or*
> **2 tbsp. tart berries, chopped,** *or*
> **2 tbsp. sautéed mushrooms,** *or*
> **2 tbsp. finely chopped shallots,** *or*
> **1 tbsp. pesto or tomato paste**

Homemade Stock

Stock provides flavored, nutritious liquid for soups, gravies, sauces, etc. The flavor of the vegetables, herbs, and bones of homemade stock is unmatchable! The longer stock is boiled and reduced, the more intensely flavored it will be. And smaller containers take up less storage room.

Yield: 1 quart stock
Preparation time: 5 minutes. Cooking time: several hours
(Please read "The Magic Stock Bag," p. 12)

> 1 **full Stock Bag** (p. 12)
> 2 **gallons water**
> 1 **tbsp. kosher salt**
> 10 **peppercorns**
>   **meat, chicken, or fish bones and scraps if that flavor is desired**

1. Combine all ingredients in stock pot. Bring to a rolling boil, turn down to a low simmer and cook, uncovered until liquid reduces to 1 quart.

2. Strain stock through a fine strainer into a bowl and refrigerate, covered, until fat solidifies on the top.

3. Remove and discard fat (or freeze, see box p. 179). Transfer to recycled plastic containers and freeze for up to 6 months.

Modified Canned Stock

The low sodium, reduced-fat stocks are very good.

Yield: 1 quart
Preparation time: 5 minutes

> 2 **16 oz. cans chicken stock**
> 1 **tsp. dried thyme**
> 2-3 **turns fresh ground pepper**
> 1 **tsp. minced garlic**
> 1/2 **cup finely chopped onion (green or yellow)**

Mix all ingredients in a small saucepan (or 6-cup glass container for microwave), cover, and simmer over medium low heat for 5 minutes (or microwave on high for 3 minutes), until garlic and onion are soft and have absorbed their flavors into stock.

Flavored Nuts

A good thing about making your own flavored nuts is creating the flavors you like, with as much or as little salt as you choose.

> 8 oz. nuts (almonds, cashews, pecans, peanuts, or walnuts)
> 2 tsp. peanut oil*
> 1/4 tsp. kosher salt
> 1 tsp. dried herb (thyme, tarragon, sage, or savory)
> spice of choice

GARLIC ALMONDS

> 8 oz. whole almonds, skin on
> 2 tsp. pure olive oil
> 1 tsp. minced garlic

GARLIC PINENUTS

> 4 oz. pinenuts
> 2 tsp. olive oil
> 1/2 tsp. minced garlic

SAFFRON PISTACHIOS

> 8 oz. roasted pistachios, shelled
> 2 tsp. Spanish olive oil
> 4-5 saffron threads
> salt

*For a drier consistency substitute spray olive or corn oil.

Preheat oven to 250°.

1. Put all flavor ingredients into a mixing bowl. Add nuts and toss. Transfer to a roasting pan into which the nuts will fit in one single layer.

2. Roast for 20 minutes or until nuts begin to color. Transfer to a paper towel to drain excess oil.

Store in air-tight container, preferably tin.

> **Want to make a great impression? Take some of these to your hostess or give them as holiday presents.**

Roasted Mexican Pumpkin Seeds

These are really, really good to have on hand (and to hide in a container in the glove compartment of your car).

Yield: 1/2 lb.
Preparation time: 30 minutes

> 1/2 lb. raw Mexican pumpkin seeds
> (green, small)
> spray olive or corn oil
> 1/2 tsp. ground chili powder (not pure cayenne)
> 1/2 tsp. crushed red pepper flakes
> 1/2 tsp. kosher salt

Preheat oven to 250°.

1. Mix chili powder, pepper flakes, and salt.

2. Put the seeds in a bowl, and spray them with oil. Sprinkle the dried spices over them, tossing to distribute evenly.

3. Spread on a baking sheet in one layer and bake until you hear them popping and they are browned slightly, between 5 and 10 minutes. Cool completely and store in an air-tight container.

Another great gift item!

Tortilla or Pita Chips

VARIATIONS: CUMIN CHIPS, PARMESAN CHIPS, SESAME CHIPS

Several companies now make tortilla and pita chips with interest-ing flavors. Homemade chips are easy to make, but pay attention while they cook—they burn quickly. Served warm, they are unbeatable!

Yield: about 6 dozen
Preparation time: 30 minutes. Cooking time: 30 - 40 minutes

TORTILLA CHIPS

             1 package 7 or 8" flour tortillas, or
                1 package 7 or 8" pita or pocket bread
             1 cup olive oil
             1 tsp. kosher salt
         1/2 tsp. crushed red pepper flakes
             1 tsp. dried herb (optional)

Preheat oven to 400°. Line sheet pans with parchment (cooking
   2 batches at a time is faster).

1.   In a large, wide mixing bowl, mix oils, spices and/or herbs.

2.   Stack tortillas or pita and cut into 6 wedges. Pull the wedges
     apart into 2 pieces each.

3.   Put the wedges into the bowl with the oil mix, and toss with
     your hands until the oil has coated the wedges. Put them on
     pans and bake until they are just golden brown. (You may have
     to turn them if bottoms are not crisp and brown.)

CUMIN CHIPS

             1 cup pure olive oil
             1 tsp. dark, Chinese sesame oil
             1 tbsp. cumin
                kosher salt to sprinkle or grind

> In an air-tight container these chips will stay crisp for up to two weeks.

Follow procedure above.

PARMESAN CHIPS

             1 cup olive oil
             1 tbsp. dried oregano, basil, rosemary
                (crushed), or marjoram leaves
    1/2 - 3/4 cup finely grated Parmesan cheese

Same as above, but sprinkle cheese over the chips before they go
   into the oven, and cook them only on one side. When the
   chips are golden brown and crisp on the top, they will be
   cooked on both sides.

SESAME CHIPS

- **1 cup light sesame oil**
- **1 tsp. dark, Chinese sesame oil**
- **1 tsp. full-strength soy sauce**
- **1/2 tsp. crushed red pepper flakes**
- **1 egg white, beaten to stiff peaks**
- **1/2 cup toasted sesame seeds**

1. Fold beaten egg white into oil-spice mixture.

2. Lay the wedges onto the parchment-lined baking sheets and brush the tops with the oil-spice mixture. Bake one side, turn them, brush the other side, and sprinkle sesame seeds over the oil mixture. Bake until golden brown.

Marinated Chevre Rounds

A delicious and pretty way to serve chevre, a soft, fresh goat cheese. Use a brand of chevre that is log-shaped.

Yield: 8 oz. / 6 rounds
Preparation time: 10 minutes, plus 1 1/2 hours for marinating

- **1 8 oz. log of chevre**
- **1/2 cup extra virgin olive oil**
- **1/2 tsp. crushed red pepper flakes**
- **1 tbsp. finely chopped fresh rosemary leaves**
- **1 tbsp. finely chopped lemon zest**

1. Chill the cheese log in the freezer until it is very cold, but not frozen. With a cheese wire or very sharp wet knife, cut the log into 6 rounds, and place them in a shallow, non-reactive bowl just large enough to hold the rounds without touching.

2. Mix remaining ingredients, and pour over the rounds. Cover with plastic wrap and refrigerate for 30 minutes. Uncover, and carefully turn the rounds over. Re-cover and marinate at room temperature for 1 hour.

To serve: Remove the rounds from the marinade with a slotted spoon. Sprinkle zest over top. Serve with the marinade and crackers or Crostini (p. 119).

There are several very good chevres produced domestically. If your market does not stock chevre, ask the grocer to order it.

Marinated Black Olives

VARIATION: SICILIAN OR SPANISH OLIVES WITH LEMON ZEST AND
CRACKED PEPPER

*If pitted calamata olives are unavailable, this works as a substitute
for Mixed-Olive Mayonnaise (p. 114) or as a snack. It does not
work for Tapenade (p. 280).*

Yield: 8 oz.
Preparation time: 10 minutes

> 1 tsp. minced garlic
> 2 tbsp. red wine vinegar
> 1 tbsp. dried Italian seasoning
> 1 tbsp. extra virgin olive oil
> 1/4 cup caper juice
> 1 1/2 tsp. kosher salt
> 1/2 tsp. cracked black pepper
> 1/4 tsp. crushed red pepper flakes
> 1/2 cup water
> 8 oz. pitted medium or large black
> olives, drained

1. Mix marinade ingredients in a glass jar. Add olives.

2. Combine all ingredients in a non-reactive container, cover, and
   marinate at room temperature for at least 1 hour.

SICILIAN OR SPANISH OLIVES WITH LEMON ZEST AND CRACKED PEPPER

> 1/2 pint large green Sicilian or Spanish olives,
> drained
> 2 tbsp. extra virgin olive oil (Italian for Sicilian
> olives, Spanish for Spanish olives)
> 1 tbsp. lemon zest
> 1 tsp. lemon juice
> 1 tsp. freshly cracked pepper

Prepare as above.

- These will last for several weeks stored
  refrigerated in an air-tight container.
- See Hint #30 (p. 18), non-reactive container.

Tapenade

Commercial tapenade is very good, but the flavor is so intense and salty that it has limited appeal as a spread. This recipe dilutes the saltiness, adds a little complexity to the flavor, and extends the amount.

Yield: 1 pint
Preparation time: 5 minutes

> 8 oz. pitted, medium or large black olives, drained
> 1 tsp. finely chopped rosemary
> 1 tsp. finely minced garlic
> 1 tbsp. extra virgin olive oil
> 1/2 pint pitted calamata olives, drained (save the juice)
> 1/4 cup pinenuts (optional)

1. Put all ingredients except pinenuts into a processor and pulse until the olives are finely chopped.

2. Add pinenuts and pulse 3-4 times.

3. Transfer to a non-reactive container or serving dish. Serve with Crostini (p. 119), crackers, or fresh crusty bread.

- Tapenade will last for several weeks stored refrigerated in an air-tight container. I keep it on hand as an instant hors d'oeuvre (see box, p. 116).
- See Hint #30 (p. 18), non-reactive container.

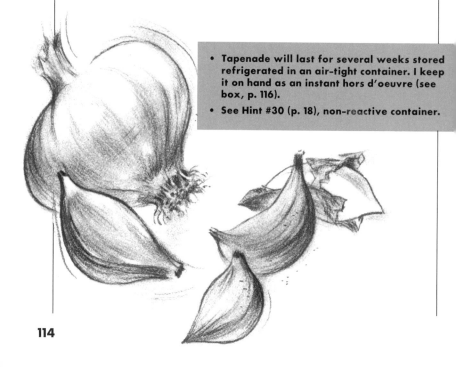

Caponata

*Caponata, the Italian version of French ratatouille, is a thick,
flavorful vegetable relish or stew that is used as a spread for bread.
I keep it in my refrigerator throughout the summer, and use it as
an hors d'oeuvre spread, a sandwich filling, or a relish with cold
chicken or fish.*

Yield: 1 quart
Preparation time: 45 - 50 minutes

STOCK BAG
Remember
your Stock
Bag (p. 12).

1/4	cup extra virgin olive oil
1	large yellow onion, peeled and diced (1 cup)
2	large carrots, peeled and diced
1	large eggplant, stem removed and cut into 3/4" cubes
1	cup raw zucchini, diced
1	tbsp. chopped garlic (about 3 cloves)
1/4	cup finely chopped fresh basil leaves, *or*
1	tbsp. dried basil leaves
1/4	cup finely chopped fresh Italian parsley
1	14 1/2 oz. can premium diced tomatoes in purée
1/2	cup dry red wine
1/4	cup capers
2	tbsp. caper juice
1/4	cup coarsely chopped, pitted calamata or Marinated Black Olives (p. 113)
1/4	cup red wine vinegar
1/2	tsp. crushed red pepper flakes
	kosher salt to taste

1. In a 3-quart saucepan over low heat, cook the onion in oil until
   it is translucent (about 6 - 8 minutes). Add carrot and eggplant, and steam, covered, for 6 - 8 minutes. Add zucchini,
   garlic, and herbs, and simmer uncovered for 10 more minutes,
   tossing to blend flavors.

2. Add tomatoes and wine, and simmer until all the vegetables
   are completely cooked (10 - 15 minutes).

3. Add the other ingredients, mixing thoroughly, and simmer for
   15 - 20 more minutes to blend flavors and thicken the stew.

4. Transfer to a non-reactive bowl, cover loosely with plastic wrap or a damp towel, and let it cool to room temperature.

5. Taste and correct seasoning if necessary. It should be flavorful, slightly tart, and have just a tiny bite from the red pepper.

6. Refrigerate, tightly covered, until ready to serve. It will last a week refrigerated if there is very little air between the sauce and its lid.

> • Store pesto, mayonnaise, salsas, chutneys, etc., with the least amount of air possible between the food and the lid. Mold spores live in that air. Zip-type plastic bags are the best.
>
> • See Hint #30 (p. 18), non-reactive container.

Eggplant Caviar

This is also called Texas Caviar, although this flavoring is more Mediterranean than Texan.

Yield: 1 pint
Preparation time: 45-50 minutes

> 1 **eggplant**
> 1/2 **cup extra virgin olive oil**
> 1 **head garlic, roasted and mashed,** (p. 225)
> 2 **tbsp. minced fresh oregano, or 2 tsp. dried leaves**
> 1/4 **cup minced brine-cured green olives or capers**
> 1/2 **tsp. crushed red pepper flakes**
> 2 **tsp. lemon juice**

1. Peel and slice the eggplant into 1/2" slices. Place on paper towel, sprinkle with kosher salt, and "sweat" for 30 minutes, to leach acid from the eggplant. Rub off juice and salt, and dice.

2. Heat 1/4 cup oil in a skillet over medium heat. Add eggplant and cook until soft and translucent, about 10 minutes.

3. Put eggplant, garlic, oregano, olives (not capers), and crushed pepper into a processor, and pulse several times until all ingredients are blended and minced. **Stop before it purées**. Stir in remaining oil, lemon juice, and capers if you are using them.

To serve: Put in non-reactive serving bowl and serve with crackers, melba toast, or Crostini (p. 119).

Scallop Ceviche

The citric acid in the lime juice "cooks" scallops in about 30 minutes. If they marinate longer than about 1 hour, the flesh begins to break down, and they get mushy. Chopped, this makes a delicious hors d'oeuvre topping for Crostini (p. 119) or melba toast.

Yield: 1 pint
Preparation time: 20 minutes, plus marinating

> 1 cup **Lime Cumin Vinaigrette** (p. 274)
> 2 tbsp. finely chopped shallot
> 2 tbsp. finely chopped cilantro
> 1/2 tsp. crushed red pepper flakes
> 3/4 cup tiny scallops, coarsely chopped (in quarters)
> kosher salt to taste
> 1/4 cup small diced tomato (optional)

1. In a plastic zip-type bag or glass bowl, mix shallot, cilantro, and pepper flakes into the vinaigrette.

2. Add chopped scallops and marinate, refrigerated, for 15 minutes. Taste and correct seasoning with salt if necessary. Add tomato and continue to marinate for another 15 minutes. Serve with a slotted spoon as an hors d'oeuvre, with Crostini (p. 119), or melba rounds to put it on.

Other seafood may be added or substituted. Crab, shrimp, or lobster should be precooked slightly first.

Croutons

This is a great use of stale bread. If it's so stale that it won't slice, refresh it in a 350° oven in a foil-covered pan with 3-4 drops of water.

Yield: 4 cups
Preparation time: 10 minutes. **Cooking time:** 15 minutes

> 4 cups cubed stale French or sourdough bread (1/2" x 1")
> 2 tbsp. extra virgin olive oil
> 1 tsp. minced garlic
> 1/2 tsp. kosher salt
> 1 tbsp. minced fresh rosemary, or 1 tsp. dried leaves, crushed (optional)

Preheat oven to 350°.

1. Place bread cubes in bowl.

2. Mix oil, garlic, salt, and rosemary, then pour it around the sides of the bowl. Toss immediately.

3. Put seasoned bread cubes on a parchment-covered sheet pan and bake until golden brown (about 15 minutes).

4. Remove from oven, cool to room temperature, and store in air-tight tin or bag.

Croutons freeze very well. Thaw frozen croutons in a 250° oven until they are crisp.

Crostini

VARIATIONS: MOZZARELLA BASIL CROSTINI, ROASTED GARLIC CROSTINI

Salsa Cruda (p. 291), Tapenade (p. 114), and Italian Sandwich Spread (p. 158) are particularly tasty accompaniments for Crostini.

Yield: 30 - 40 slices
Preparation and cooking time: 30 minutes

> 3/4 **cup extra virgin olive oil**
> 1 **tsp. minced garlic**
> 1/4 **tsp. crushed red pepper flakes**
> 1 **long baguette loaf French bread**

Preheat oven to broil. Put oven rack low. Line sheet pan with baking parchment.

1. Mix the garlic and pepper flakes with the oil, and let the flavors set while you are slicing the bread.

2. Slice the loaf into 1/3" slices and brush oil mixture on one side. Toast the oiled sides until they are golden. Turn and toast the plain side also.

3. Cool completely before storing in an air-tight container. Crostini freezes very well.

This only works with fresh mozzarella.

MOZZARELLA BASIL CROSTINI
> 1 **slice fresh mozzarella cheese per slice**
> 1 **fresh basil leaf per slice**

Chill the mozzarella and slice it as thin as possible. Warm to room temperature. Place a basil leaf on each crostini, at a diagonal, and then place a slice of mozzarella, centered, on top of the leaf. Serve immediately.

ROASTED GARLIC CROSTINI
> 1 **clove Roasted Garlic** (p. 225) **per slice**
> **eliminate the garlic from the oil mixture for this version**

1. Place a clove of roasted garlic on each crostini, gently mashing and spreading slightly.

2. Serve immediately.

Judy's Mother's Homemade Biscuits

My dear friend Judy was taught this recipe by her mother, who probably learned it from her mother. It produces the lightest, flakiest biscuits ever. They take a little more time than other recipes, but they turn out perfectly and are well worth the effort.

Yield: 1 doz. 3" biscuits
Preparation time: 25 minutes; cooking time 10 minutes

> 2 **cups unsifted all-purpose flour**
> 1 **cup plus 2 tbsp. unsalted butter, at room temperature**
> 4 **tsp. baking powder**
> 1/2 **tsp. cream of tartar**
> 1 **scant tsp. kosher salt**
> 2/3 **cup milk**

Preheat oven to 450°.

1. Process flour, baking powder, cream of tartar, and salt with 1 cup butter.

2. Transfer to a bowl and mix milk in with a fork until the dough holds together.

3. Place dough on waxed paper and pat it into a 12" square, about 1/2" thick. Fold in half. Repeat seven more times. The last square should be about 3/4" - 1" thick.

4. Melt remaining butter and put it in a bowl. Cut biscuits in desired shape°, dip in butter, and place on a parchment-covered baking sheet. (At this point the uncooked biscuits may be covered with plastic wrap and held for up to 2 hours before baking. Brush tops with melted butter just before baking.)

5. Bake for 10 minutes or until tops are golden brown.

°Have fun with the shapes; try hearts, or stars, or crescent moons, or . . .

Quick Tomato Soup

VARIATIONS: CREAMY TOMATO BISQUE, CURRIED TOMATO BISQUE

This soup transforms easily into fish soup or mixed vegetable soup or meat soup by adding those ingredients and using appropriate stock.

Yield: 4 servings
Preparation and cooking time: 15 minutes

For low-fat option, use spray olive oil or simply eliminate oil, and do not garnish with cheese.

2	**tsp. extra virgin olive oil**
1/2	**cup yellow onion, chopped (1 small)**
2	**14 1/2 oz. cans premium diced tomatoes in purée**
1/4	**cup chopped fresh basil, tarragon, or oregano, or 2 tsp. dried herb leaves**
2	**cups vegetable or chicken stock**
1/2	**tsp. crushed red pepper flakes**
	kosher salt to taste
	coarsely grated Parmesan cheese (optional)

1. In a small saucepan, over medium low heat, cook chopped onion until it is translucent (5 minutes).

2. Add tomatoes, stock, herbs, and pepper flakes, and simmer for about 5 minutes.

3. Correct seasoning with salt, if necessary.

To serve: Ladle into preheated bowls. Sprinkle each serving with freshly grated Parmesan or other dry, aged Italian cheese.

CREAMY TOMATO BISQUE
Add 1/2 pint whipping cream.

Purée all ingredients but cream and cheese, and simmer on medium low for about 5 minutes. Add cream and continue to simmer until thickened slightly. Garnish as above.

CURRIED TOMATO BISQUE
Eliminate crushed pepper flakes and cheese and add:

See Hint #2 (p. 15), grating Parmesan cheese.

2 1/4	**tsp. curry powder**
1/2	**pint whipping cream**
2	**tbsp. yogurt**

1. Add 2 tsp. curry powder to original ingredients and simmer on medium low for about 5 minutes. Add cream and continue to simmer until thickened slightly.

2. Mix remaining curry powder with yogurt and swirl on top of each serving.

Basic Vegetable Soup

VARIATION: CHICKEN NOODLE

This is one of my favorite homemade soups because it is quick, easy, and delicious. I use pasta most often, but if I have leftover rice or barley, I use that. Note: Be cautious about overcooking the vegetables; mushy vegetables ruin otherwise wonderful soups.

Yield: 4 servings
Preparation time: 25 minutes

1 1/2	cups chopped yellow onion (about 2 medium)
2	tbsp. olive oil
5	cups Homemade Stock (p. 108) or Modified Canned (chicken or vegetable)
6	cups water (for cooking pasta)
1/2	lb. fresh or frozen pasta or 1 cup dry
1/4	cup chopped fresh herbs, or 1 tbsp. dried herb leaves
1/4	tsp. crushed red pepper flakes
2	cups fresh vegetables, blanched if appropriate, and cut into bite-sized pieces (consider color, texture, and taste)
1	tsp. kosher salt
1	tbsp. minced fresh Italian or regular parsley

> **STOCK BAG**
> Remember your Stock Bag (p. 12).

1. Sauté onion in oil over medium heat until it is translucent (5 - 6 minutes). Bring stock, herbs, pepper flakes, and salt to a boil. Add onions and firm vegetables (carrots, winter squash, or winter roots), turn down heat and simmer for 10 minutes.

2. Meanwhile, cook pasta in boiling water until it is al dente (3 - 5 minutes for fresh pasta; 12 - 15 minutes for dried). Drain and add to the soup, along with the softer vegetables, herbs and crushed pepper flakes or add leftover cooked rice or barley at this point. Simmer for 4 - 5 minutes, until all vegetables are cooked. Taste and correct the seasoning with salt, if necessary.

3. Add the parsley and serve in heated bowls.

CHICKEN NOODLE
Add chicken, eliminate the tomato, and you will have wonderful chicken noodle soup.

> Al dente—
> "to the tooth"
> —or just soft
> enough so
> that it still
> must be
> chewed.

Vegetable Soup

VARIATION: TOMATO VEGETABLE SOUP

This recipe, with its modifications, will produce a clear broth-based soup or a thick tomato-based vegetable soup that highlights vegetables. Both are quick, easy, and delicious. Add pasta, rice, or legumes if you wish. Be loose and creative with this soup. If you have fresh vegetables and a flavorful stock, you can't miss!

Yield: 6 servings
Preparation time and cooking time: about 45 minutes

<table>
<tr><td>2</td><td>tbsp. extra virgin olive oil</td></tr>
<tr><td>1</td><td>large yellow onion, peeled and finely chopped*</td></tr>
<tr><td>3</td><td>tbsp. chopped mixed fresh herbs, or 1 tbsp. dried</td></tr>
<tr><td>2</td><td>quarts vegetable or chicken stock, preferably Homemade</td></tr>
<tr><td>1/2</td><td>tsp. crushed red pepper flakes</td></tr>
<tr><td>4</td><td>cups prepared fresh vegetables (peeled, chopped, etc.) kept separated by type</td></tr>
<tr><td>1</td><td>tbsp. lemon juice</td></tr>
<tr><td></td><td>kosher salt to taste</td></tr>
<tr><td>2</td><td>cups cooked pasta, rice, or legumes (optional)</td></tr>
</table>

STOCK BAG
Remember your Stock Bag (p. 12).

See recipes for Homemade and Modified Canned Stock (p. 108).

°Or 1/4 cup minced shallots, 1 cup sliced leeks, or 3 tsp. minced garlic.

1. Put oil and onion (shallot, leek, or garlic) in a large soup pan over medium low. Cook until soft and translucent, about 5 minutes.

2. Add herbs, stir to mix, and cook a few more minutes.

3. Add stock and crushed pepper, and bring to a boil. Add vegetables according to the amount of time they take to cook (peas or broccoli should be added last). When the vegetables are cooked, add the lemon juice. Taste and correct seasoning if necessary with salt.

4. Turn heat down to simmer, add cooked pasta, rice or legumes, and cook for 3 - 4 more minutes.

TOMATO VEGETABLE SOUP

<table>
<tr><td>1</td><td>14 1/2 oz. can premium diced tomatoes in purée</td></tr>
<tr><td>1</td><td>cup tomato purée</td></tr>
</table>

Hint #19: Tomato purée and tomato sauce are not the same. Tomato sauce is seasoned; tomato purée is 100% tomato.

Add tomatoes and purée after vegetables are cooked.

123

Gazpacho

Traditionally, gazpacho contains raw egg. However, because of the health hazard potential of raw egg, I use egg substitute.

Yield: 6 - 8 servings
Preparation time: 30 minutes

See Hint #28 (p. 18), peeling tomatoes.

1/4	cup red wine vinegar
1/4	cup extra virgin olive oil
1	14 1/2 oz. can premium diced tomatoes in purée, *or*
3	large ripe tomatoes, peeled and coarsely chopped, with their juice, plus 3/4 cup tomato juice
1/2	cup egg substitute (optional)
2	red bell peppers, coarsely chopped, seeds and pith removed
1/4	cup diced red onion
1	large shallot, peeled and coarsely chopped
1	large cucumber, peeled and coarsely chopped
1/4	tsp. crushed red pepper flakes kosher salt to taste
1/4	cup chopped fresh dill
8	tbsp. Crème Fraîche (p. 282) or sour cream

1. In a mixing bowl, whisk together the vinegar, olive oil, reserved fresh tomato juice, canned tomato juice, and eggs.

2. Process the tomatoes and other vegetables in the processor or purée in small batches in a blender, adding the juice gradually. **Do not purée completely, as the soup should have plenty of texture.**

3. Stir in the pepper, salt, and dill. Cover with plastic wrap and chill for at least four hours.

To serve: Stir the soup and correct seasoning if necessary. Ladle into chilled bowls and top with a dollop of Crème Fraîche or sour cream.

Simple Pasta and Vegetable Soup

This is very simple, very quick, and very good. The fresher the broccoli, the better the soup. For a heartier version, add cooked sausage or chicken to the soup.

Al dente—"to the tooth" —or just soft enough so that it still must be chewed.

Yield: 4 servings
Preparation and cooking time: about 25 minutes

See recipes for Home-made and Modified Canned Stock (p. 108).

3	cloves garlic, minced
1/4	cup extra virgin olive oil
2	quarts chicken stock, preferably Homemade
4	oz. dried penne, orecchiette, or raddiatori pasta cooked al dente, rinsed, and drained
2	cups broccoli flowerets (cauliflower works well also)
1/4	tsp. crushed red pepper flakes
1/2	cup finely chopped, fresh Italian parsley
1	cup coarsely grated Parmesan cheese

1. Cook garlic in olive oil over low heat until it is softened and golden.
2. Transfer to a soup pot and add stock. Bring to a low boil and add pasta, broccoli, parsley, and crushed pepper. Cook until the broccoli is just done (3 - 4 minutes).

To serve: Ladle the soup into preheated bowls and top each serving with 1/4 cup Parmesan. Serve with crusty Italian bread.

LEFTOVERS
The leftovers from Oven-Roasted Chicken (p. 167) might just be enough to add to this soup.

STOCK BAG
Remember your Stock Bag (p. 12).

125

Wild Rice, Potato, and Mushroom Soup

Crusty Italian bread is wonderful with this quintessential Autumn soup.

Yield: 4 servings
Preparation time: 20 minutes with already-cooked rice

If you don't have ham stock, add 2 drops of liquid smoke to the stock .

1	**quart meat or chicken stock (I use ham stock), preferably Homemade**
3	**green onions—mince the white parts, slice the green parts diagonally, about 1/2" long**
1	**cup cooked wild rice**
3 - 4	**red potatoes, sliced 1/4"**
2 - 3	**tbsp. fresh chopped herbs (tarragon, marjoram, or basil)**
3/4	**cup sliced fresh button or crimini mushrooms (wild are great in this soup)**
1/2	**tsp. crushed red pepper flakes**
	kosher salt to taste
1/2	**cup shaved Parmesan**

1. Put stock, minced onion, and potato slices in a saucepan, cover, and cook on low heat for 10 minutes or until potatoes are just soft, about 6 - 8 minutes.

2. Add rice, onion greens, herbs, mushrooms, crushed pepper, and liquid smoke if necessary. Simmer for 5 - 6 more minutes and correct seasoning.

To serve: Ladle into warmed bowls and garnish with cheese shavings.

Note: Add 4 oz. julienne-cut ham, smoked chicken, or smoked pork for variety.

- **See Recipes for Homemade and Modified Canned Stock (p. 108).**
- **See Hint #1 (p. 15), crusty bread.**
- **See Hint #2 (p. 15), grating Parmesan cheese**
- **See Hint #26 (p. 18), wild mushrooms.**

Puréed Vegetable Soup

This recipe works for almost any vegetable and results in a smooth, creamy soup that is the color of the vegetable. Think about a garnish for the finished soup: swirled yogurt, chopped parsley or a sprig of fresh herb, heated croutons, etc.

Yield: serves 6
Preparation time: 1 hour (you may eliminate 30 minutes if you use canned, pureed pumpkin!)

See recipes for Home-made and Modified Canned Stock (p. 108).

> **4 cups of raw vegetable* (1 variety), washed, peeled with tops and bottoms removed if necessary, and chopped (if you have a juicer, add enough additional vegetables to make 1 cup juice)**
> **1 large yellow onion, peeled and chopped**
> **2 tbsp. pure olive oil**
> **4 cups chicken or vegetable stock**
> **1 tbsp. lemon juice**
> **1/2 cup heavy cream (for low fat, use evaporated skim milk)**
> **1 tsp. kosher salt**
> **1/4 tsp. crushed red pepper flakes**
> **2 tbsp. minced fresh herb, or 2 tsp. dried herb leaves**

*For pumpkin soup, substitute 2 cups puréed canned pumpkin.

1. In a covered container with 3/4 cup water, steam (about 15 minutes) or microwave (about 10 minutes) raw vegetable until soft. Transfer with the cooking water to a processor or blender. Purée and set aside.

2. Put olive oil and chopped onion in large saucepan over medium heat and cook until the onion is softened and translucent, about 6 minutes. Add it to the purée and process again until the mixture is completely smooth. Return it to the saucepan with the heat on medium low.

3. Add the remaining ingredients, except garnish, and simmer, stirring continuously, until the soup has thickened slightly and all the flavors have blended, about 10 minutes. If you have a juicer, add uncooked vegetable juice at this point and continue to simmer until it is heated. Taste and add salt if necessary.

To serve: Ladle into heated soup bowls and garnish imaginatively!

For variations, see next page.

SOUPS

VARIATIONS
Suggested herb or spice combinations:

Beet Soup: Thyme, 1 tbsp. orange zest, and 1/4 cup fresh
    orange juice

Broccoli Soup: Minced garlic

Carrot Soup: Tarragon or thyme; spices: curry powder°; ginger,
    powdered, or 1 tbsp. grated fresh

Cauliflower Soup: Minced garlic; spice: curry powder°, mace,
    chopped lemon zest

Celery Root Soup: Savory or thyme

Chilled Cucumber Soup: Savory (substitute yogurt for cream
    in soup)

Fennel Soup: 3 tbsp. chopped fennel leaves

Pea or Green Bean Soup: Thyme or savory

Pumpkin Soup: Curry powder°

Spinach Soup: Nutmeg

Winter Root Soup: Tarragon, thyme, savory, or sage

Winter Squash Soup: Thyme or sage; spice: mace, curry
    powder°

°You may substitute an equal amount of Garam Masala Curry
    Paste® (Resources, p. 340) or Moroccan Spice Paste (p. 286).

> **Remember your Stock Bag (p. 12)—this could fil**
> **it! If you have a juice machine, the added cup o**
> **juice produces a spectacular color and intense**
> **flavor to this soup.**

Three Bean and Lentil Soup

This complex carbohydrate filled soup is delicious, vegetarian, and non-fat.

Yield: 8 servings
Preparation and cooking time: 2 hours (but you don't have to stay in the kitchen with the soup as it cooks!). Freeze extra for another time.

See recipes for Home-made and Modified Canned Stock (p. 108).

1	large yellow onion, chopped
2	tsp. cumin seeds
4	cups water
1	cup dried lentils
1/3	cup pearl barley
2	quarts chicken or vegetable stock, preferably Homemade
2	carrots, finely diced
1	turnip, finely diced
1	16 oz. can black beans, rinsed and drained
1	16 oz. can garbanzo beans, rinsed and drained
1	16 oz. can red kidney beans, rinsed and drained
1	14 1/2 oz. can premium diced tomatoes in purée
1	tbsp. powdered cumin
1/2	cup finely chopped fresh basil
1/2	cup finely chopped fresh Italian parsley
1/2	tsp. crushed red pepper flakes
	kosher salt to taste
1	tbsp. minced fresh Italian parsley
1/2	cup non-fat yogurt

1. In a covered soup pot over medium heat, cook the onion and cumin seeds in 1/2 cup stock for 5 minutes.

2. In another pot, cook the lentils in the water. When they have cooked for 25 minutes, add the barley and more water if necessary. Cook 20 minutes more or until the barley is done. Strain and save the water.

3. Add the remaining stock, the carrots, and the turnip to the soup pot, bring to a low boil, and cook, covered, for 10 minutes.

4. While the vegetables are cooking, process half of the black and garbanzo beans into a purée. When the vegetables are cooked, transfer about half of the soup to the processor and process with the bean purée until the whole mixture is puréed. Return the puree to the soup pan, add the remaining beans, the tomatoes, and the other ingredients, except salt, minced parsley and yogurt.

5. Continue to cook the soup on low simmer until the flavors are blended, about 30 minutes. Taste and add salt if necessary.

To serve: Mix minced parsley with yogurt and swirl 1 tbsp. over each serving.

If the barley and lentils are cooked ahead, this soup takes only about 30 minutes to prepare.

STOCK BAG
Remember your Stock Bag (p. 12).

Leftover Meat or Chicken Soup

This recipe makes Scotch Broth (Lamb and Barley), Chicken and Barley, or almost any leftover meat or poultry soup. Basically, it's juice from the meat, plus stock, vegetables, and a starch. Use your imagination and the contents of your refrigerator!

Yield: 6 servings
Preparation time: 1 hour

1 1/2 lbs. leftover meat (all you can cut from the bone, roast, or carcass)
       any leftover cooking juice
   1 quart water
   1 cup chopped yellow onion (save the skin, tops, and bottoms)
   2 tbsp. olive oil
   2 tsp. minced garlic
 1/2 cup dry barley (or 2 cups cooked), or lentils, or rice
   1 quart stock, preferably Homemade
   3 carrots, peeled and chopped
   1 bay leaf
   1 tsp. thyme
   1 tsp. oregano
   1 tsp. marjoram or rosemary
      any other "chopable" vegetables in the refrigerator, celery is great
   1 tsp. kosher salt

STOCK BAG
Remember your Stock Bag (p. 12).

See recipes for Home-made and Modified Canned Stock (p. 108).

1. Cut all the meat off the bones, then cut it again into bite-sized pieces. Set it and cooking juices aside.

2. Put the bones, the onion trimmings, and the bay leaf into the 1 quart water and bring to a hard boil. Boil, uncovered, for 15 minutes. Strain.

3. In a soup pot over medium low heat, cook the onion and garlic in the olive oil for 2 minutes. Add strained stock, the other quart of stock, the carrots, other raw vegetables, and the barley, and boil uncovered for 10 minutes.

4. Add the meat, the herbs, the leftover cooking juice, and continue cooking for 10 minutes.

5. If you want to thicken the soup, add 2 tbsp. cornstarch mixed with 1/2 cup water, and simmer until it thickens. Taste and add salt if necessary.

Potato Soup

VARIATIONS: POTATO PEANUT SOUP, POTATO LEEK SOUP, VICHYSSOISE

Improvise with Potato Soup. Add grated cheddar or Parmesan cheese, or sliced carrots or celery, or a flavorful herb such as tarragon, or cooked smoked sausage or ham, or hard smoked salmon (at the very end). Its rich base flavor is just asking for leftovers.

Yield: 6 servings
Preparation and cooking time: 30 minutes

See recipes for Home-made and Modified Canned Stock (p. 108).

1 large yellow onion, peeled and coarsely chopped (about 1 cup)
2 tbsp. unsalted butter or olive oil
3 large russet potatoes, peeled and diced (about 3 cups)
2 cups chicken or vegetable stock, plus 3 cups potato cooking water
1 cup milk
1 tsp. kosher salt
1/2 tsp. crushed red pepper flakes
1/4 cup finely chopped Italian parsley

One-Pot Quick Method
1. Cook diced potatoes, onion, and 2 cups stock in the microwave. Add 1 tbsp. butter or 1 tbsp. olive oil and 2 cups milk to the cooked potatoes, transfer to a blender and purée.
2. Transfer to a soup pot, and complete Steps 4 and 5 on next page.

Traditional Method
1. Put the diced potatoes and 6 cups water into a 6-quart pan. Add 1/2 tsp. kosher salt and bring to a boil. Cover and cook the potatoes until they are soft. Drain and save the water. (Strain out any potato chunks.)
2. While the potatoes are cooking, cook the onion in butter or oil in the soup pot over low heat until onion is translucent and softened, about 5 minutes.
3. Put the potatoes, onions, stock (in batches if necessary), and milk into a blender (**not a processor**) and purée. If you need more liquid, add reserved potato cooking water. When the potato is puréed, return it to the soup pot.

4. Cook over medium low heat, stirring often. Add reserved potato cooking water (or more milk) until it is the consistency you like. Add pepper flakes and 1/4 cup parsley, turn the heat to simmer, and cook about 3 - 4 minutes to blend the flavors. Add more potato water or milk if soup is too thick.

5. Taste and add salt if necessary.

To serve: Ladle into preheated bowls and garnish with remaining parsley or toasted peanuts.

POTATO PEANUT SOUP
Add 1/2 cup creamy peanut butter in step 4 and garnish with toasted, chopped, dry-roasted peanuts.

POTATO LEEK SOUP
Substitute sliced leeks for onion.

VICHYSSOISE
Transfer soup to a non-reactive metal, glass, or plastic container, cover with plastic wrap laid directly on the soup, and refrigerate until well chilled. Serve in glass bowls, if possible, and garnish with a slice of lemon and chopped chives or parsley.

- *Never* purée potatoes in a processor. The power of the blade breaks down the starch too far, and the result is *irreversible glue.*
- Caution: the starch in potatoes will cause the soup to stick to the pan if it isn't stirred as it cooks.
- See Hint #30 (p. 18), non-reactive container.

STOCK BAG
Remember your Stock Bag (p. 12).

Cauliflower Bisque With Curried Croutons

VARIATIONS: CURRIED ASPARAGUS, GINGER CARROT, GREEN PEA, ARTICHOKE

This vegetable bisque adapts to lots of different vegetables. Curried Asparagus Bisque, Ginger Carrot Bisque, Green Pea Bisque, Artichoke Bisque, etc. In this version the curry flavor is in the croutons.

Yield: 4 servings
Preparation time: 30 minutes. Cooking time: 30 minutes

Soup

- 1 **lb. fresh cauliflower, cooked until soft**
- 2 **pints chicken or vegetable stock, preferably Homemade**
- 1/2 **cup chopped scallion**
- 1 **tsp. cumin**
- 1/2 **pint heavy cream***
- 1/4 **cup Crème Fraîche** (p. 282)

*For lower fat: substitute evaporated skim milk, plus a paste made of 2 tbsp. water mixed into 1 tbsp. cornstarch.

Croutons

- 4 **oz. baguette, sliced 1/2" thick, then cut into cubes**
- 2 **tbsp. extra virgin olive oil**
- 1/2 **tsp. kosher salt**
- 1 **tsp. curry powder**

1. Mix the oil, salt, and curry powder for the croutons. Toss the bread cubes in the oil mixture and bake for 20 minutes, at 275°.

2. Purée the cauliflower with the stock until it is perfectly smooth. Add the onion and spices.

3. In a saucepan, bring the purée to a simmer and add the cream (or evaporated milk and cornstarch paste). Bring to a simmer on medium low heat, and cook until the soup thickens (about 6 - 8 minutes).

4. Taste and correct seasoning with salt, if necessary.

To serve: Ladle soup into preheated bowls, swirl 1 tbsp. Crème Fraîche into each serving, and top with warm croutons.

See recipes for Homemade and Modified Canned Stock (p. 108).

CURRIED ASPARAGUS BISQUE
Substitute asparagus for cauliflower, curry powder for cumin, and
yogurt for Crème Fraîche.

GINGER CARROT BISQUE
Substitute carrot for cauliflower and 1 tbsp. grated ginger
for cumin.

GREEN PEA BISQUE
Substitute frozen or fresh peas for cauliflower and thyme
for cumin.

ARTICHOKE BISQUE
Substitute cooked artichoke hearts and/or bottoms for cauliflower,
and thyme for cumin.

- **If you have a juicing machine, see Step 3 of Puréed Vegetable Soup (p. 127).**
- **Do you know the difference between scallions and green onions? Scallions are the white part of green onions.**

STOCK BAG
Remember your Stock Bag (p. 12).

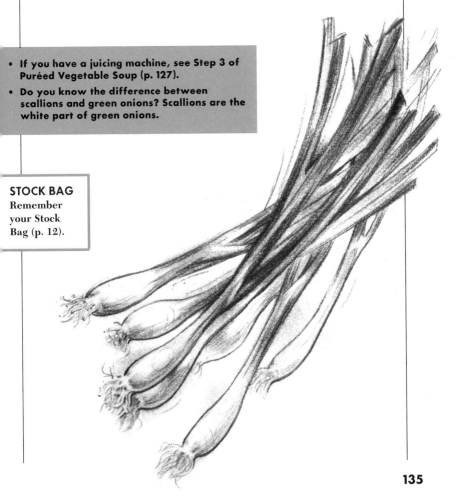

Wild Mushroom Soup

If fresh wild mushrooms are not available, dried can be substituted. To locate dried wild mushrooms, see Resources, p. 340.

Yield: 4 servings
Preparation time: 45 minutes

See recipes
for Home-
made and
Modified
Canned Stock
(p. 108).

2	tbsp. extra virgin olive oil
1/4	cup minced shallots
1	lb. button mushrooms
1	lb. mixed fresh wild mushrooms (chanterelles, shiitaki, hedgehog, oysters, portabello, crimini, porcini—whatever is available)*, separate 3 oz. to slice for the soup
1	quart chicken stock, preferably Homemade
3	tbsp. chopped fresh or 1 tbsp. dried tarragon, save unchopped tips for garnish
1/2	pint heavy whipping cream (or milk and roux) (see *, p. 134)
1/2	tsp. crushed red peppers
1/4	cup dry sherry
	kosher salt to taste

*If fresh wild mushrooms are not available, substitute 2 oz. of dried wild mushrooms, re-hydrated, and double the amount of buttons. Separate 3 oz. to slice for the soup.

Some wild mushrooms, such as criminis and some shiitaki, actually are cultivated. Crimini look like dark button mushrooms; they cost a little more than buttons and have much more flavor. Other wild mushrooms are expensive, so selection is crucial. They should not be soggy (no point in paying for water when they will be in liquid) or slimy, and except with porcini and lobster mushrooms, the stems should be minimal in proportion to the caps.

1. **Don't wash mushrooms! Brush off dirt or pine needles.** Separate the stems from the caps of the wild mushrooms. Reserve tops. Put the stems in the processor with the button mushrooms. Process until they are minced.

2. Put the oil, shallots, stock, and the processed mushrooms into a frying pan. Bring the liquid to a boil, cover the pan and reduce heat to low. Simmer for 5 - 6 minutes or until the mushrooms have shrunk to half their size. Transfer to a strainer (not a colander) over a soup pan, and strain out the stock. Press the mushrooms to get all the liquid you can, and discard pulp.

3. Slice or tear tops of remaining uncooked mushrooms into bite-sized pieces and add with cream and tarragon to liquid. Cook on a low boil until the soup has thickened slightly. Add remaining sherry and cook for 2 - 3 more minutes. Correct seasoning with salt, if necessary.

To serve: Ladle into warmed bowls and garnish each serving with the tip of a tarragon leaf or a swirl of Crème Fraîche (p. 282).

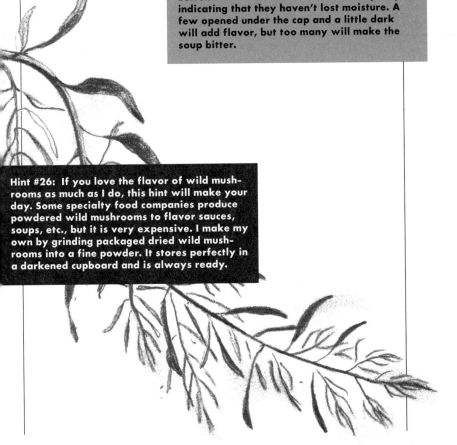

Button mushrooms should be firm and plump, indicating that they haven't lost moisture. A few opened under the cap and a little dark will add flavor, but too many will make the soup bitter.

Hint #26: If you love the flavor of wild mushrooms as much as I do, this hint will make your day. Some specialty food companies produce powdered wild mushrooms to flavor sauces, soups, etc., but it is very expensive. I make my own by grinding packaged dried wild mushrooms into a fine powder. It stores perfectly in a darkened cupboard and is always ready.

Black Bean Chili

Fermented black beans (packaged in small plastic bags), are available in Asian markets. Their musky flavor cannot be duplicated, but they are salt-cured, so soaking is essential. The Chinese black bean sauce found in most grocery stores is made with these beans. However, it often contains lots of garlic, so decrease the garlic by 1 tsp.

Yield: 6 servings
Preparation and cooking time: 1 hour (not counting the soaking time for fermented beans)

See recipes for Home-made and Modified Canned Stock (p. 108).

2 tbsp. prepared black bean sauce, or 1/2 oz. fermented black beans (Resources, p. 340), soaked in water for 3 hours, then rinsed
1 tbsp. corn oil
1 large yellow onion, peeled and diced (about 1 1/2 cups)
4 large cloves garlic, minced, or 3 tsp. dehydrated minced garlic
1 tbsp. cumin seed, crushed (put it between 2 sheets of waxed paper and smash)
2 large Anaheim chili peppers, seeded and chopped, or 8 oz. canned mild green chilies, chopped
1 1/2 pints chicken stock, preferably Homemade
1 cup chopped fresh cilantro (about 2 bunches)
2 tbsp. unsweetened cocoa powder
2 tsp. ground cumin
3 tbsp. chili powder
2 15 oz. cans black beans, rinsed and drained (purée half the beans)
2 14 1/2 oz. cans premium diced tomatoes in purée
1/2 tsp. crushed red pepper flakes
zest and juice from 1 lime
kosher salt to taste
sour cream, plain yogurt or Cilantro Crème Fraîche (p. 282) for garnish
1 cup Quick Tomato Salsa (p. 287)

1. If you are using fermented beans, prepare them ahead. Rinse them several times, then soak them in water for 3 hours (or overnight). Rinse again. Purée with 1 cup stock.

2. In a large saucepan on medium heat, cook onion in oil until translucent (about 6 - 8 minutes). Add garlic, cumin seed, and chopped pepper, and cook 5 minutes more. Reduce heat to low.

3. Add remaining stock, 1/2 cup cilantro, cocoa powder, cumin, chili powder, beans, tomatoes, and black bean sauce or puréed fermented bean mixture. Simmer about 5 minutes. Add lime zest. Simmer for 15 minutes more, then add lime juice and correct seasoning. The longer it simmers the thicker it will become. Add the remaining 1/2 cup cilantro about 3 minutes before serving.

To serve: Ladle into warmed bowls and garnish with Salsa and sour cream, yogurt, or cilantro Crème Fraîche (p. 282).

Vegetable Chowder

VARIATIONS: CHICKEN CHOWDER, VEGETABLE COBBLER

I prep all the vegetables first (sometimes the day before), then make the chowder. The peelings will almost fill the Stock Bag!

Yield: 6 servings
Preparation time: 40 minutes. Cooking time: about 35 minutes

STOCK BAG
Remember your Stock Bag (p. 12).

See recipes for Homemade and Modified Canned Stock (p. 108).

2 tbsp. pure olive oil
1 large yellow onion, peeled and coarsely chopped (about 1 cup)
1/4 cup chopped fresh herb, or 2 tbsp. dried herb (a premixed, or your own blend of thyme, sage, and tarragon)
1 carrot, peeled and thinly sliced
1 large baking potato, peeled and diced (or equivalent red or yellow potatoes with skin on)
2 stalks celery, sliced
3 cups chicken or vegetable stock, preferably Homemade
1 tbsp. lemon juice
1 bay leaf, cracked in 2 or 3 places
1 14 1/2 oz. can premium diced tomatoes in purée
3 cups various other vegetables, peeled and chopped or diced (about 1 lb.)
1/2 tsp. crushed red pepper flakes
1/2 pint heavy cream, or 1/2 cup half-and-half or evaporated skim milk mixed with 2 tbsp. corn starch
1 tsp. kosher salt

1. Prep all vegetables but keep them separate so they can be added separately.

2. Put oil in a large saucepan. Sauté onion on medium high until it is browned, about 8 minutes. Turn heat down to medium. Add herbs, vegetables, 1 cup stock, lemon juice, and bay leaf. Cover and cook until the vegetables are just soft, about 10 - 15 minutes.

3. When the vegetables are cooked, add remaining stock, salt, tomato, herbs, and pepper flakes. Bring to a boil, turn the heat down to simmer and cook for 6 - 8 minutes. Remove bay leaf.

4. Add cream, or put cornstarch into a small bowl, add half-and-half or evaporated skim milk, and stir into a paste. Stir into chowder, and simmer until chowder thickens slightly. Add salt.

To serve: Ladle into warmed bowls and serve.

CHICKEN CHOWDER
To Vegetable Chowder recipe add:

>   **chicken stock, preferably**
>   **Homemade**
> **8 - 10 oz. cooked chicken**
> **1 cup chicken Demi-Glace** (p. 107)

> **LEFTOVERS**
> **This recipe is based on leftover Oven-Roasted Chicken (p. 167) and vegetables. I do not recommend making it from scratch.**

Eliminate canned tomato. Follow Steps 1 and 2 above, adding chicken and Demi-Glace along with the herbs. Proceed with Steps 3 and 4.

VEGETABLE COBBLER

> **3 tbsp. cornstarch mixed with cream to form a paste**
> **2 cups biscuit mix, mixed**
> **2/3 cup milk**

The sauce needs to be a little thicker for cobbler than it does for chowder, so you will add more cornstarch mix.

Preheat oven to 400°.

1. Follow step 1 and 2 of the Vegetable Chowder recipe.

2. While the vegetables are cooking, make the cobbler dough by mixing biscuit mix with the milk until it is just blended. Set aside.

3. Add cornstarch paste to the chowder and simmer until the mixture thickens. Transfer to an oven-proof baking dish.

4. Drop biscuit dough by spoonfuls onto the top of the vegetable mixture. With a wet rubber spatula, spread dough together into a single crust as well as you can. Bake for 15 minutes or until crust is golden brown.

To serve: Ladle into warmed shallow soup or pasta bowls, taking care to serve the crust brown-side up.

Add the vegetables in stages according to the amount of time they need to cook, i.e., peas and summer squash only need warming, but carrots and potatoes take awhile.

Spicy Corn Chowder

This recipe wakes up the flavor of traditional corn chowder.

Yield: 5 servings
Preparation and cooking time: 20 minutes

See recipes for Home-made and Modified Canned Stock (p. 108).

- 2 **cups fresh or frozen corn kernels**
  zest and juice of 1 lime
- 2 **tbsp. corn oil**
- 1 **large yellow onion, peeled and minced**
- 1 **quart chicken stock, preferably Homemade**
- 2 **cups peeled, diced russet potato**
- 1 **tsp. ground red chili powder**
- 1/2 **tsp. crushed red pepper flakes**
- 1 **tsp. ground cumin**
- 1 **Anaheim pepper, stem and pith removed, seeded and chopped**
- 1 **red bell pepper, stem and pith removed, seeded and chopped**
- 1 **cup heavy cream**
- 1/2 **cup chopped fresh cilantro, plus 5 sprig tops for garnish**
- 1/2 **tsp. kosher salt**
- 1/2 **cup Quick Tomato Salsa** (p. 287) **for garnish**

1. In a mixing bowl, squeeze lime juice over corn and mix in zest with a spoon. Set aside.

2. In a large saucepan over medium heat, cook oil and onion until the onion is translucent and softened. Add stock, potato, chili powder, red pepper flakes, and cumin and bring to a boil. Turn heat down to medium low, cover, and cook until potatoes are just soft. Add Anaheim and red bell pepper and cook another 5 - 6 minutes, uncovered until potatoes are very soft.

3. Add corn and cream, and continue to cook, uncovered, until soup thickens. Add cilantro and simmer a few more minutes. Taste and correct seasoning with salt if necessary.

To serve: Ladle into warmed bowls, garnish with a cilantro sprig and a dollop of Salsa on each serving, and serve immediately.

Puget Sound Chowder

VARIATIONS: FRESH CLAM CHOWDER, MANHATTAN STYLE CHOWDER

Puget Sound, an inland waterway adjacent to Seattle, offers an abundance of seafood year round. This recipe was created one day when I simply could not choose between fish and shellfish for dinner. The only seafood limit here is availability.

Yield: 4 servings
Preparation time: 35 minutes. Cooking time: 10 - 15 minutes

STOCK BAG
Remember
your Stock
Bag (p. 12).

2	**tbsp. olive oil, vegetable oil, or enough spray to coat pan**
1	**medium yellow onion, peeled and diced (about 1 cup)**
2	**carrots, peeled and sliced into half-rounds, about 1/4" thick**
1/4	**tsp. crushed red pepper flakes**
1	**pint Homemade Fish Stock** (p. 108) **or clam juice**
3	**tbsp. fresh tarragon or basil, chopped**
2	**stalks celery, thinly sliced**
1	**large russet potato, peeled and cubed (about 1+ cup)**
16	**fresh mussels, about 1 lb.** (see box, p. 144)
1/2	**cup dry white wine**
1	**lb. medium prawns, shelled**
4	**oz. fresh scallops**
1 1/2	**cups heavy cream**
4	**oz. Ling or true cod, cut into 2" pieces**
3	**oz. hard-smoked salmon**
1	**tbsp. lemon juice**
	kosher salt to taste
2	**tbsp. fresh Italian parsley, chopped, for garnish**

1. In a medium-sized saucepan, sauté onion in oil over medium heat, until translucent, 3 - 5 minutes. Add carrot, red pepper flakes, and fish stock, cover and cook until carrots begin to soften, about 10 minutes. Add herbs, celery, and potato, turn heat to low, and simmer for 10 more minutes so the flavors will blend.

2. Meanwhile, poach mussels in wine for 5 - 6 minutes. Strain nectar into stock. Pick the mussels from their shells and set aside.

3. Add prawns, scallops, and cream to chowder and simmer until chowder thickens slightly, 3 - 5 minutes.

4. Add fresh fish, smoked salmon, and lemon juice, and cook 2 - 3 minutes more. Taste and correct seasoning if necessary.

To serve: Ladle into warmed bowls, garnish with Italian parsley, and serve.

FRESH CLAM CHOWDER

Substitute 3 lbs. washed fresh clams for all other fish or seafood.

1. Follow Step 1, eliminating the carrots.

2. In a steamer or in a colander set in a larger pot, steam clams in wine. Strain nectar into stock, shell clams, and set aside.

3. Add cream to the stock and simmer on medium low heat until the chowder thickens slightly. Add clams and simmer for 5 more minutes. Taste and correct seasoning with salt if necessary.

MANHATTAN STYLE CHOWDER

Eliminate the cream.

Add 1 14 1/2 oz. can premium diced tomatoes in purée.

Follow above instructions substituting tomato for cream. It will not be thick.

Fish is very delicate and should be cooked as little as possible. It will continue to cook if the chowder is left on heat, so this is not a soup that should simmer on the back of the stove for hours. If it is not going to be served immediately, remove from heat and keep it covered. Reheat on high, just until it is hot, and serve immediately.

Farmed mussels grow attached to netting. As they are harvested, part of the fiber sticks to the mussel, and it should be removed before cooking. Hold the mussel, narrow end down, and pull the fiber down, away from the shell.

Pasta with Sautéed Vegetables

This quick, easy, and straightforward pasta recipe has been dinner hundreds of times in my house. Timing is important: fresh pasta cooks in 3 - 5 minutes, but dried pasta takes up to 12 - 15 minutes. I usually cook dried pasta first, drain it, toss it with 1 1/2 tbsp. olive oil and cover it while the vegetables cook.

Yield: 4 servings
Preparation and cooking time: 15 - 20 minutes

STOCK BAG
Remember your Stock Bag (p. 12).

See Cooking Fresh Vegetables (p. 223).

See Hint #2 (p. 15), grating Parmesan cheese.

- 1 lb. fresh pasta, or 1/2 lb. dried
- 2 tbsp. extra virgin olive oil
- 2 cloves peeled garlic, thinly sliced
- 3 cups raw, prepped vegetables (see below)
- 1/4 cup chopped fresh basil or other fresh herb, or 1 tbsp. dried
- 1 large or 2 medium ripe tomatoes, peeled, seeded, and chopped, or 1 14 1/2 oz. can premium diced tomatoes in purée
- 1/4 tsp. crushed red pepper flakes
  kosher salt to taste
- 1/2 cup grated Parmesan cheese

Suggested Vegetable Options
- 1/4 cup diced yellow onion or chopped green onion (onion flavor enhances most sautéed vegetables)
- 1 bell pepper, stem, seeds, and pith removed, sliced into thin strips
- 1 zucchini or summer squash, chopped or cut into thin, 2" long wedges
- 1 cup sliced mushrooms (about 3 oz.)
- 1 cup winter squash, julienne-cut
- 1 Japanese eggplant, diced
- 1 bunch fresh spinach, leaves only, chiffonade-cut (p. 223)
- 2 or 3 chard leaves, chiffonade-cut, with stems, thinly sliced

1. Bring 1 gallon of water to a boil in a large pot. Add dried pasta, and cook to al dente—to the tooth— (just soft enough so that it still must be chewed). Drain in a colander. For fresh pasta, turn the heat down to low, cover the pot and hold water on warm until the vegetables are almost done before you cook the pasta.

2. Put oil and garlic into a large skillet. Turn the heat to medium and cook the garlic just until it begins to color, not beyond or it will burn and be bitter. Add the vegetables in the order that they will cook, starting with those that will take the longest. Move them constantly with a spatula so they will not overcook in one spot. For fresh pasta, reboil the water at this point, and cook the pasta during final minutes of cooking the vegetables. Drain.

3. Add the herbs to the vegetables and mix to distribute. When the vegetables are almost cooked (still a bit too crunchy), add canned tomato and crushed pepper flakes, turn the heat down to low, and simmer for 3-4 minutes to blend the flavors. Taste and add kosher salt if necessary.

To serve: Transfer the cooked, drained pasta to the plates (with tongs) or to a pasta platter. Ladle the vegetables over the pasta and garnish each serving with 2 tbsp. Parmesan cheese.

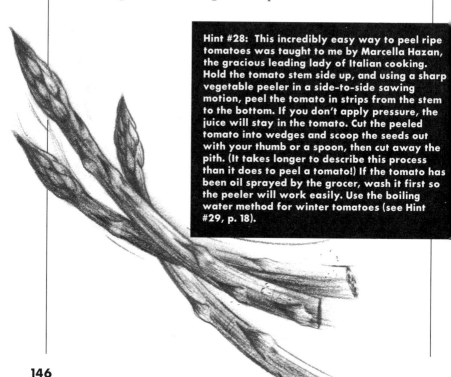

Hint #28: This incredibly easy way to peel ripe tomatoes was taught to me by Marcella Hazan, the gracious leading lady of Italian cooking. Hold the tomato stem side up, and using a sharp vegetable peeler in a side-to-side sawing motion, peel the tomato in strips from the stem to the bottom. If you don't apply pressure, the juice will stay in the tomato. Cut the peeled tomato into wedges and scoop the seeds out with your thumb or a spoon, then cut away the pith. (It takes longer to describe this process than it does to peel a tomato!) If the tomato has been oil sprayed by the grocer, wash it first so the peeler will work easily. Use the boiling water method for winter tomatoes (see Hint #29, p. 18).

Pasta Primavera

VARIATIONS: FARMERS MARKET PASTA, WINTER VEGETABLE PASTA

*Traditional Pasta Primavera is made with a garlic cream sauce,
but I don't like creamed vegetables, so this is my recipe. Use
whatever fresh vegetables are available, considering color and
texture in the mixture.*

Yield: 6 servings
Preparation and cooking time: 35 minutes

TOCK BAG
emember
our Stock
ag (p. 12).

6	quarts water, for cooking the pasta
1 1/2	cups fresh carrots, peeled, match stick cut (about 3 carrots)
6	oz. fresh cauliflowerets (about 1 cup)
4	oz. fresh broccoli flowerets, or fresh green beans cut in 2" pieces and blanched, *or* 1/2 lb. fresh pencil asparagus cut into 3" pieces
1	tbsp. lemon zest
2 1/2	lbs. fresh pasta or 3 cups dried
1/2	cup extra virgin olive oil
1	tsp. minced garlic
1/2	tsp. crushed red pepper flakes
1/2	lb. fresh mushrooms, sliced (about 2 cups)
3 to 4	Roma tomatoes, coarsely chopped
1	cup tiny green peas, fresh, or frozen, thawed
1/4	cup chopped fresh basil, tarragon, or Italian parsley
1 1/4	cup coarsely grated Parmesan cheese

1. Blanch vegetables that need it.

2. Bring the pasta water to a boil in a large, covered saucepan, turn the heat down to warm and hold.

3. Steam the vegetables (except the mushrooms, tomatoes, and peas) with the zest. As soon as they are cooked just enough to be pierced easily with a sharp knife, rinse them with cold water, drain, and set aside.

- If you are not experienced at cooking vegetables "just beyond the vine," see Cooking Vegetables (p. 223).
- See Hint #2 (p. 15), grating Parmesan cheese.

147

4. Reheat the pasta water to a hard boil, add a pinch of salt and the pasta, and cook until the pasta is al dente—to the tooth—(just soft enough so that it still must be chewed). Fresh pasta will take 3 to 5 minutes; dry will take up to 15 minutes. Drain the cooked pasta in a colander.

5. While the pasta is cooking, cook the garlic and pepper flakes for 1 - 2 minutes in half the oil, in a large skillet over medium low heat. Turn the heat up to medium high, add the mushrooms, tomatoes, and peas, and sauté for 3 more minutes, continually moving them in the pan with a wooden spoon. Add the blanched vegetables and chopped herb, toss to mix, and cook until vegetables are heated. If they are cooked before the pasta, remove them from the heat until the pasta is drained and ready.

6. Transfer the pasta into a large, heated serving bowl or platter, and toss it with the remaining oil. Add the vegetables and 1/2 cup grated Parmesan, and toss to mix.

To serve: Put pasta in heated pasta bowls, garnish each serving with grated Parmesan, and serve immediately.

FARMERS MARKET PASTA
Substitute whatever vegetables are fresh and locally grown.

WINTER VEGETABLE PASTA
Substitute winter vegetables such as roots, winter squash, or Brussels sprouts.

Hint #16: Pasta can be precooked and held, refrigerated, for 2 or 3 days. Cook, rinse (in cool water to stop the cooking), and drain the pasta. Toss it with a little olive oil and put it into a zip-type plastic bag. Press the air out of the bag before sealing it. To reheat: Boil water in a saucepan, put the cold pasta in a strainer and plunge the strainer into the water for 2 minutes. Remove the strainer, let the pasta drain, and serve immediately.

Spicy Vermicelli Noodles

This very popular dish is delicious by itself, or with cooked, chilled seafood, sliced duck, or grilled or smoked chicken sliced and layered on top.

Yield: 2 servings
Preparation time: 20 minutes

> **1/2** **lb. vermicelli noodles**
> **1** **cup Ginger Sesame Vinaigrette** (p. 275)
> **2** **tbsp. soy sauce**
> **2** **tsp. pure sesame oil**
> **2** **green onions, diagonally cut into pieces about 1/2" long**
> **2** **tbsp. toasted sesame seeds**

1. Cook pasta to al dente—to the tooth— (just soft enough so that it still must be chewed), drain, and set aside.

2. While the pasta is cooking, make the vinaigrette, adding soy sauce and sesame oil.

3. Pour the sauce over the pasta while it is still warm, and toss to mix. Marinate for 10 minutes.

4. Toss green onions with pasta and sprinkle with sesame seeds.

Tongs are a good utensil for serving cooked noodles.

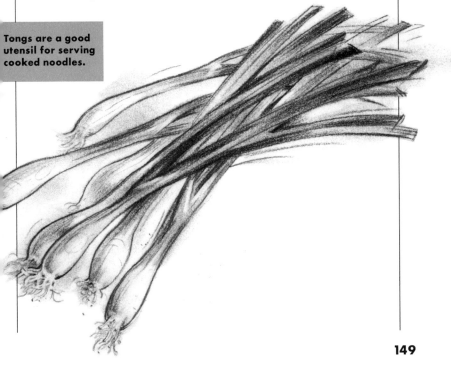

Macaroni and Good Cheese

As a child, I loved macaroni and cheese. Later on I made it with sliced hot dogs for my own children. I still love the idea, but, I prefer good cheeses and more interesting pasta. Try it and see what you think.

Yield: 4 - 6 servings
Preparation and cooking time: 50 minutes

See recipes for Home-made and Modified Canned Stock (p. 108).

2   cups dry raddiatori, or orecchiette pasta
2   tbsp. unsalted butter or margarine
2   tbsp. all purpose flour
2   cups warmed chicken stock, preferably Homemade
3/4   cup coarsely grated provolone cheese
1/2   cup coarsely grated Parmesan cheese, plus 1/4 cup for breadcrumb mixture
1/2   cup plus 1 tbsp. finely chopped Italian parsley
3/4   cup ricotta cheese
1/2   cup bread crumbs mixed with 1/4 cup of the Parmesan cheese and 1 tbsp. chopped Italian parsley

Preheat oven to 350°.

1. Cook pasta in boiling water until it is al dente—to the tooth—(just soft enough so that it still must be chewed). Rinse, drain, and set aside.

2. In a large saucepan, melt butter or margarine over low heat. When it bubbles, add flour and stir into a paste. Cook for 3 - 4 minutes, but don't let it burn. Add stock slowly, stirring constantly to form a smooth sauce.

3. Add provolone and Parmesan cheese, stirring to blend. Add parsley.

4. Transfer the cooked pasta to an oiled casserole dish, and, using a teaspoon, dot the pasta with the ricotta cheese. Pour cheese sauce over the pasta, sprinkle the bread crumb mixture over the top, and bake for 30 minutes, until bubbly golden brown.

- The highest sales volume pasta product in this country is the macaroni and cheese dinner that comes in a box. Does that interest or scare you?
- See Hint #2 (p. 15), grating Parmesan cheese.

Risotto

VARIATIONS: RISOTTO PRIMAVERA, FARMERS MARKET RISOTTO

Risotto, an Italian staple, has become very popular in the U.S. It should have a creamy, almost soupy consistency and be served in a pasta bowl. The rice most commonly used is Italian arborio, a short grain, high starch content rice (long grain rice will not work). Thomas Jefferson is credited for bringing Risotto to America.

Yield: 4 servings
Preparation time: 40 minutes

<table>
<tr><td>2</td><td>tbsp. extra virgin olive oil</td></tr>
<tr><td>8</td><td>small fistfulls of arborio rice unwashed</td></tr>
<tr><td>5+</td><td>cups of simmering chicken, beef, or vegetable stock, preferably Homemade</td></tr>
<tr><td>1/4</td><td>cup wine</td></tr>
<tr><td>2</td><td>tbsp. heavy cream, optional*</td></tr>
<tr><td>1/2</td><td>cup freshly grated Parmagiano Reggiano or other fine, dry, aged Italian cheese</td></tr>
<tr><td>1/4</td><td>cup chopped fresh herb or 2 tsp. dried herb, optional</td></tr>
<tr><td>1</td><td>cup vegetables, meat, poultry, fish or other flavorings you wish to add, cut into bite size pieces and partially pre-cooked if necessary, as it will cook for 2-3 minutes with the risotto</td></tr>
</table>

STOCK BAG
Remember your Stock Bag (p. 12).

*For lower-fat risotto, substitute evaporated skim milk for the cream.

1. Heat the oil in a fry pan on medium high, and add the rice. Cook it until it turns slightly golden.

2. Turn heat down to low, add enough simmering stock just cover the rice, and simmer uncovered until the liquid is absorbed. Stir the rice several times during this liquid absorption.

3. Repeat three or four more times, until there is enough liquid left for one more addition.

4. At the last addition, add whatever other ingredients that you wish mixed into the risotto (vegetables, seafood, fresh herbs, etc.) Simmer a few more minutes, add half the grated cheese, the wine, cream, and a little more stock. Mix it into the risotto gently, cover, and remove from heat for 5 minutes.

• See recipes for Homemade and Modified Canned Stock (p. 108).

For Winter Squash or Pumpkin Risotto:
Add 1/4 cup chopped yellow onion
2 cups canned pumpkin **or**
1# winter squash cut into matchstick pieces
Steam the onion and add it to the canned pumpkin, or steam it
with the winter squash, until the squash begins to soften, but
is still crunchy, about 2 minutes.

For molded or timbale or scooped consistency, eliminate the very
last addition of stock.

To serve: Spoon into warmed pasta bowls or onto a warmed
platter, and garnish with remaining grated cheese.

RISOTTO PRIMAVERA
vegetable stock, preferably Homemade
1 cup julienne-cut carrots, blanched (p. 223)
1 cup frozen peas, thawed
1 cup sliced fresh mushrooms
1 cup julienne-cut yellow summer squash*

*Use outside cut only so each piece shows yellow; put the inside
into the stock bag.

Proceed as above. While risotto is cooking, sauté the mushrooms.
Add all the vegetables with the last addition of stock.

FARMERS MARKET RISOTTO
Add 2 cups sliced or julienne-cut sautéed fresh, seasonal vegetables (see Sautéed Vegetables, p. 225) to the rice with the
last addition of stock.

Proceed as above. While risotto is cooking, sauté the mushrooms.
Add all the vegetables with the last addition of stock.

- **Continued stirring throughout the additions of stock releases and distributes the starch, giving risotto its creamy texture.**
- **The fat from the cream and cheese gives the broth a velvety, smooth consistency that is a hallmark of risotto. Using a non-stick pan, low-fat cheese, and eliminating the cream will reduce the fat content but also modify the consistency of the risotto.**
- **See Hint #2 (p. 15), grating Parmesan cheese.**

Roasted Pepper and Tomato Risotto

This is basic risotto, modified with cooked vegetables in a sauce. The sauce will determine the flavor of the risotto, so taste it as it cooks to get the flavor balance you want.

Yield: 4 servings
Preparation: 40 minutes

STOCK BAG
Remember your Stock Bag (p. 12).

See recipes for Homemade and Modified Canned Stock (p. 108).

1/4	cup extra virgin olive oil
1/2	cup chopped yellow onion (about 1 medium)
3	tsp. minced garlic
2	red bell peppers, roasted (p. 227), peeled, seeded, and puréed
1/4	tsp. crushed red pepper flakes
1/2	cup tomato purée, or 2 tbsp. tomato paste
1	14 1/2 oz. can premium diced tomatoes in purée
2	tbsp. lemon juice
8	small fistfulls arborio rice *unwashed* (about 2 cups)
5+	cups of *simmering* chicken stock
1/4	cup Italian parsley, finely chopped
1/4	cup fresh oregano, marjoram, thyme, rosemary, basil, or other Italian herb, finely chopped with 1 stem per portion reserved for garnish
1/2	cup Chianti or other red table wine
2	tbsp. heavy cream
1/2	cup grated Parmesan cheese

1. In a pan different from the risotto pan, sauté the onion and garlic over medium heat in half the olive oil until softened and translucent, 3 - 5 minutes. Add the puréed pepper, pepper flakes, crushed tomato and purée, and heat to a simmer. Turn off the heat and stir in the lemon juice.

2. Heat the remaining olive oil in a large skillet over medium heat, and cook the rice until it turns golden on the edges.

3. Add enough simmering stock to cover the rice and simmer until the moisture is cooked away. Repeat the process until all but 3/4 cup of the stock is used. Add the tomato mixture, the herbs, and the wine to the rice, and continue to simmer until the sauce is just thick.

5. Add remaining stock, cream, and 1/4 cup cheese. Stir it in, cover the pan, and remove it from the heat for 8 minutes.

To serve: Ladle the risotto into warm bowls and sprinkle with remaining cheese. Garnish each serving with a sprig of fresh herb.

See previous recipe (p. 151) for explanation of Risotto.

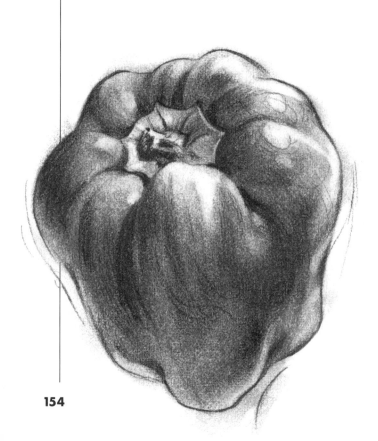

Paella

This is not traditional Spanish paella, but it's based on that concept and reminds me of some of the tastes I enjoyed in Spain, so I call it Paella. The sauce is made with the cooking juices of the ingredients, so the rice is flavorful and moist. Use whatever meat, poultry, and fish is available.

Yield: 6 - 8 servings
Preparation time: 40 minutes. Cooking time: 1 1/2 hour

STOCK BAG
Remember your Stock Bag (p. 12).

See recipes for Home-made and Modified Canned Stock (p. 108).

1/2	lb. small clams, washed
1/2	lb. mussels, washed and bearded
18	medium prawns (18 - 24 to a pound)
1 1/2	cups white wine
2	tbsp. olive oil (preferably Spanish)
1	cup chopped yellow onion
3	tsp. minced garlic
24	chicken drumettes
1/2	lb. chorizo or other spicy sausage in casing, cut into 16 pieces (a smoked Polish sausage works fine)
1	small green bell pepper, seeded and coarsely chopped
1	yellow bell pepper, seeded and coarsely chopped
1 1/2	cups dry red wine
1 1/2	cups long grain white rice
3	cups chicken stock, preferably Homemade
4-5	saffron threads
1 1/2	cups frozen or fresh peas
2	14 1/2 oz. cans premium diced tomatoes in purée
1	tsp. kosher salt
1/4	cup fresh lemon juice
1/4	cup fresh oregano, chopped, or 1 tbsp. dried leaves
1/2	tsp. crushed red pepper
1/2	cup whole or halved large green Spanish olives, pitted

Farmed mussels grow attached to netting. As they are harvested, part of the fiber sticks to the mussel, and it should be removed before cooking. Hold the mussel, narrow end down, and pull the fiber down, away from the shell.

Warning: These instructions look more complicated than they actually are.

1. Leave the clams and mussels in their shells, and peel the shrimp, leaving the tails on. Poach the clams, mussels, and shrimp separately in 1/2 cup white wine plus the peelings, tops, and bottoms of the onion, and the stems of the herbs (add wine as needed). Strain nectar, add the garlic and set aside. Set seafood aside.

2. In a large skillet over medium heat, cook onion in oil until softened, 3 - 4 minutes. Add chicken and cook until browned and almost done, about 15 minutes. Add bell pepper and cook until it just begins to soften. Remove everything with a slotted spoon and reserve. Add 1/2 cup wine to the pan, scraping any residue, and simmer for 5 minutes.

3. Meanwhile, cook the rice in the chicken stock with the saffron. When it is done, mix the thawed but uncooked peas into the hot rice.

4. Put tomato, strained nectar, herbs, lemon juice, pepper flakes, remaining wine, and olives into a large saucepan, and add sausage, chicken mixture, and sauce. Simmer for 10 minutes. Add peppers and set aside.

5. Transfer the rice to a large, oven-proof casserole or a paella pan. Add the chicken, sausage and peppers, mixing them carefully into the rice with a fork. Add half the sauce to the rice, mixing it in gently. Arrange the cooked seafood (reheated if necessary) over the top of the Paella. Spoon the remaining sauce over it. Olé!

Make-Ahead Dinner Party: Immediately after the seafood is cooked, put it in a plastic zip-type bag and refrigerate it. Put things from Step 4 into another zip-type bag and refrigerate. Combine the cooked rice (without peas) and part of the sauce in a large pan, cover with foil and set aside (or refrigerate if it's a day ahead) until about an hour before the guests arrive. Cover the remaining sauce and refrigerate or set aside.

An hour before dinner, reheat the sausage/chicken mixture. Reheat the rice, covered, in a 350° oven for 20 minutes. Reheat and hold the remaining sauce. Just before serving, heat the peas, transfer the rice to the warmed serving dish or paella pan, and add the peas, sausage, chicken, etc. Continue with Step 5 (reheat the seafood by steaming it, covered, over very high heat for 2 - 3 minutes).

Grilled Italian Sandwich

This is one of the heartiest and most flavorful sandwiches around.

Yield: 4 sandwiches
Preparation and cooking time: 40 minutes

8	slices crusty Italian bread
1/2	cup **Mixed Olive Mayonnaise** (p. 280)
1	**tbsp. Dijon mustard**
1/2	cup **Italian Sandwich Spread** (see next page)
24	very thin slices summer sausage or salami
8	oz. fresh mozzarella cheese, cubed, or 4 oz. processed mozzarella, sliced
1	**Roasted Bell Pepper** (p. 227)**, in 16 slices**
4	oz. provolone or feta cheese, thinly sliced or crumbled
1/4 - 1/2	cup extra virgin olive oil

1. Spread mayonnaise inside tops and bottoms of the bread and spread mustard on the inside tops only. Cover bottoms with sandwich spread.

2. Layer the salami, mozzarella, the pepper slices, and provolone in that order over the spread.

3. Put the sandwiches together, brush the outside tops and bottoms with olive oil, and grill until the crusts are golden brown and the cheeses have melted. Transfer the sandwiches to a cutting board, let them set up for 2 minutes, cut, and serve.

Chicken Sandwich: Substitute 8 oz. cooked chicken, torn into bite-sized pieces or sliced for salami.

Vegetable Sandwich: Substitute 12 fresh spinach leaves, washed and patted dry with paper towel, for salami.

Cold Sandwich: Use 4 small panini loaves in place of bread. Put the sandwiches together, wrap in waxed paper and let the flavors set for 15 minutes before serving. Serve at room temperature.

For the ungrilled version, cut baguette-style bread loaf horizontally into long sandwiches. Consider the height of the bread in relation to your mouth size—nothing like a sandwich you cannot wedge between your gaping jaws!

Italian Sandwich Spread

This recipe yields enough for four Grilled Italian Sandwiches.

Yield: 1 cup, enough for 4 sandwiches
Preparation time: 15 minutes

> 3 oz. frozen or canned artichoke hearts
>   (not marinated in oil), drained and
>   coarsely chopped (about 1/2 cup)
> 2 tsp. minced garlic
> 1/4 cup chopped fresh basil
> 1 tbsp. dried oregano or marjoram leaves
> 1/4 cup diced tomato (1 medium)
> 2 tbsp. extra virgin olive oil
> 1 oz. pitted calamata olives (Resources, p. 340), **or**
>   **Marinated Black Olives** (p. 113), **coarsely
>   chopped**
> 2 tbsp. capers, drained

Mix all ingredients in a non-reactive bowl. Use as a spread
for Grilled Italian Sandwich (see previous page) or as a
topping for Crostini (p. 119).

- **See Hint #19 (p. 17), tomato sauce.**
- **See Hint #30 (p. 18), non-reactive
  container.**

Grilled Ham, Caramelized Onion, Apple, and Cheese Sandwiches

I discovered this sandwich first on a restaurant menu, and could hardly wait to taste it. When it came, it was oddly bland; they left out the apple! I made a special market stop on the way home to make them for dinner, and I'm hungry now just writing about it.

Yield: 4 sandwiches
Preparation and cooking time: 35 minutes

8 **slices (1/2" thick) crusty bread, preferably sourdough**
Dijon Glaze (p. 105)
mayonnaise, preferably Homemade (p. 279)
3/4 **cup Caramelized Onion** (p. 231)**, room temperature**
4 **thin slices of ham at room temperature**
1 **crisp, tart apple, cored, and sliced about 1/4" thick**
4 **slices Jarlsberg or Swiss cheese**
olive oil

1. Brush one side of each slice of bread with a thin coating of Dijon Glaze. Spread mayonnaise on 1 slice per sandwich.

2. Layer 1/4 of the onion and ham, a layer of apple slices, a slice of cheese on mayonnaise slice, and top with remaining slice of bread.

3. Brush the top and bottom of each sandwich with oil and grill in a pan or sandwich grill (don't press the top of the grill) until the bread is crisp and golden brown and the cheese has melted.

If you have Caramelized Onion in the freezer, this can be thrown together in a few minutes. If you don't, caramelize 2 or 3 this time so they will be waiting the next time.

Fresh Fish Sandwiches

VARIATION: BROILED SANDWICHES

Fresh fish sandwiches make it hard to open a can of tuna ever again.

Yield: 4 sandwiches
Preparation and cooking time: less than 10 minutes

> 4 slices of crusty sourdough bread, or
> 2 English muffins, sliced into 4 halves
> Mayonnaise (if not homemade, add a
> little caper juice and a few crushed red
> pepper flakes to the amount you would
> use on a sandwich) (Homemade Mayonnaise, p. 279)
> 1 tsp. lemon juice
> 1 tbsp. capers
> Dijon mustard
> 8 oz. poached or cooked fish, at room
> temperature
> 1/2 cup grated Parmesan or Mozzarella
> cheese (optional)

BROILED
1. Toast both sides of bread or the cut sides of English muffin.
2. Mix lemon juice and capers into mayonnaise and spread it on the bread. Add a small amount of Dijon mustard.
3. Break fish apart with a fork so that it is flaky. Put it on the spread. Put cheese or a dollop of flavored mayonnaise over the top and broil until bubbly and golden brown.

FRESH
Use 2 slices of bread per sandwich. Add lettuce and sliced, room temperature tomato, and omit the cheese.

Try this with Mixed Olive Mayonnaise (p. 280).

Hint #23: Cooked fish for cold sandwiches or salads should be brought to room temperature before using. The cold fat is quite firm, and it creates a tough consistency. At room temperature, it is soft and delicate.

Quick Pasties or Turnovers

*Pasties, predecessors of the sandwich, originated in Europe
(Italians and Irish both claim the invention) where herders needed
hearty food that would last two or three days. Turnovers provided
meat and vegetables in one portable package. British and Irish
pubs have taken the concept to a fine art.*

Yield: 6 pasties
Preparation time: 20 minutes. Baking time: 25 minutes

Filling

1/2	lb. ground sausage (pork, chicken, or turkey), or 2 cups leftover cooked chicken, sausage, fish, or meat
1	cup diced yellow onion
1	cup diced potato (about 1 potato—frozen French fries work)
1	cup diced or sliced carrot (packaged frozen ones work)
2	tsp. dried herbs, or 3 tsp. chopped fresh herbs
1/4	cup Dijon mustard
1	tsp. dried thyme or sage leaves
1/2	tsp. crushed red pepper flakes kosher salt to taste
3	uncooked, refrigerated or frozen pie crusts egg wash (1 beaten egg white with 1 tbsp. water added)
1/4	cup grated Parmesan cheese (optional)

Preheat oven to 375°.

1. Put 1/2 cup water in a skillet over medium heat. Add the onion,
    potato, and carrots and cook, covered, until the carrots are just
    soft enough to pierce with a fork, 6 - 8 minutes. Pour off water.
    Add sausage if you are using it. Stirring several times, cook the
    sausage uncovered for 5 minutes. Pour off excess fat and
    transfer the mixture to a mixing bowl.

2. Mix in herbs, mustard, and pepper flakes, taste and correct
    seasoning if necessary. If you are using cooked meat, add it,
    the herbs, mustard, and pepper flakes to the cooked vegetables
    in a mixing bowl, and mix together with a fork. Refrigerate
    to cool.

3. While the filling cools, roll the pie dough to about 1/4" thickness and cut it into six 6" rounds. Brush the edges of the circles with egg wash to ensure a seal.

4. Place the cool filling mixture in the center of each round, fold the dough over, and crimp the open edges, forming a turnover.

5. When all the pasties are made, brush the tops with egg wash and sprinkle cheese over the tops. Put them on a baking sheet and bake for 25 minutes, or until they are golden brown.

Serve with Coleslaw (p. 255), mustard, and horseradish.

- **With frozen potatoes, carrots, and refrigerated pie crust, this is a very quick, easy dinner.**
- **This is a standby when I am cooking dinner i a rented condo because all the ingredients are so available, even in tiny grocery stores And the dinner feels so homespun and cozy.**

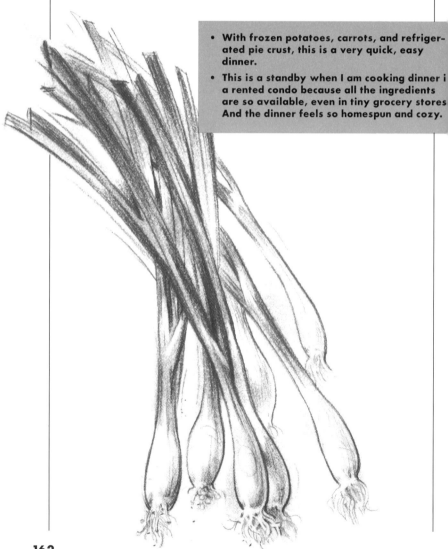

Tomato Tart

VARIATION: TOMATO CHEESE TART

This simple, beautiful tart is the kind of food we "discover" in tiny European cafes. It really only works with vine-ripened, plump fresh tomatoes.

Yield: 4 - 6 servings
Preparation time: 15 minutes. Cooking time: 30 minutes plus 30 minutes cooling time

>   1   uncooked pie crust, frozen (thawed) or
>   refrigerated, or dough mix
> 1/4   cup Sun-Dried Tomato Pesto (p. 284)
>   or store-bought, at room temperature
>   3   medium sized, vine-ripened tomatoes
>   (1 yellow if possible), sliced 1/3" thick and
>   drained on paper towel
>   1   tbsp. lemon juice
>   1   bunch fresh basil, leaves washed, picked
>   from stem and dried between paper towels
> 1/4   cup coarsely grated Parmesan cheese

Preheat the oven to 400°.

1. Place the dough into a pie plate, and push edges down so the sides are about 1/2" high. Re-crimp the edge if necessary. Cover the bottom with a circle of parchment, prick the bottom all over, through the parchment, and put pie weights or rice over the paper.

2. Bake the crust for 10 minutes (partial bake) and remove from the oven. Turn the heat down to 350°.

3. Gently spread the tomato pesto onto the bottom of the pie crust.

4. Alternate tomato slices and basil leaves, in a single layer over the pesto. If you use a yellow tomato, intersperse it with the red. Sprinkle the lemon juice and cheese over the top and bake for 20 minutes more, or until the crust edge is brown and the tomatoes are set.

5. Remove from the oven and cool on a wire rack to room temperature.

TOMATO CHEESE TART
Add 4 oz. sliced fresh mozzarella cheese (not processed). Prepare as above except in Step 5, alternate slices of mozzarella with tomatoes and basil. There will about 2 - 3 tomato and basil slices per slice of mozzarella. Bake as directed.

Country Cheese Soufflé

Another salute to my very creative grandmother.

Yield: 4 - 6 servings
Preparation time: 15 minutes. Cooking time: 30 - 35 minutes

4 tbsp. unsalted butter or margarine
2 tbsp. all-purpose flour
2 cups skim milk at room temperature or warmer (microwave)
8 oz. extra sharp cheddar cheese, grated
1/2 tsp. dry mustard
1 tsp. Worcestershire sauce
1/2 tsp. crushed red pepper flakes
2 eggs, beaten
6 slices white or sourdough bread, cubed

Preheat the oven to 375°.

1. Butter the bottom and sides of an oven-proof casserole dish, and add the bread cubes.

2. Heat butter in a saucepan over low heat, until it bubbles. Add flour and stir into a paste. Cook, stirring often, for about 3 minutes, until the flour is cooked and it begins to brown at the edges (careful, it burns easily—if it burns, start over. You'll never get the burn taste out). Add the milk, stirring constantly until it becomes a smooth, creamy sauce.

3. Add 6 oz. of the cheese, stirring to blend. Add the Worcestershire sauce and pepper, and more milk if it is too thick.

4. Pour a little of the cheese sauce into the beaten eggs and stir to blend. Then pour the mixture back into the cheese sauce and blend. Pour over bread cubes.

5. Sprinkle the remaining cheese over the top and bake for 30 - 35 minutes, until the top is golden brown.

Note: Italian sausage or ham taste terrific in this soufflé. Sprinkle over bread before you add the cheese sauce.

Chili Corn Fritters

VARIATIONS: SEAFOOD FRITTERS

Fritters are deep-fried food . . . requiring a lot of fat. My theory is, if I am going to eat fat, "shoot the moon" and choose something as crisp and delicious as fritters. The stiff egg whites and cornstarch make these very crisp and light. I won't even guess about the calories!

Yield: 4 - 6 servings
Preparation time: 30 minutes. Cooking time: 20 minutes

- 2 **eggs, separated**
- 1 **can or bottle beer**
- 1 **cup biscuit mix, or 1 cup all-purpose flour plus 1 tbsp. baking powder and 1/4 tsp. kosher salt**
- 1 **cup cornstarch**
- 1 **10 oz. package frozen corn kernels, thawed**
- 1/2 **cup finely chopped onion (1 small)**
- 1/4 **cup seeded, stem removed, and finely chopped Anaheim chili pepper (about 1 pepper)**
- 2 **tbsp. minced fresh cilantro, or 2 tsp. dried leaves**
- 1 **tsp. ground cumin**
- 1/2 **tsp. ground red chili pepper (not pure cayenne)**
- 1 **tbsp. lime juice**
  cooking oil (according to deep fat fryer directions, or enough for 3" depth in fry pan)

1. Combine egg yolks and 1 cup of the beer. Set aside. Mix dry ingredients and set aside.

2. Mix corn, onion, pepper, cilantro, cumin, ground pepper, and lime. Add liquid and mix thoroughly. Stir in dry ingredients, adding more beer if the batter is too thick to stir. Cover with plastic wrap, and refrigerate for 1 hour.

3. Heat oil and prepare paper towel over parchment (grocery bags work) on a sheet pan. While the oil is heating, beat the egg whites to stiff peaks. Fold gently into the fritter batter.

4. Drop batter, by tablespoonful, into oil and fry until golden brown. Turn with a mesh scoop or slotted spoon. Drain thoroughly.

Serve immediately with your favorite sauce, Quick Tomato Salsa (p. 287), or Ginger Sesame Vinaigrette (p. 275).

Fritters will hold in a 350° oven as long as it takes for the batch to be cooked. Don't try to make them ahead and hold them though, because they begin to soften on the inside after about 20 minutes.

SEAFOOD FRITTERS

Follow ingredients for Corn Fritters but substitute: 1 1/2 cups clam juice for beer; green onion for yellow; 1 cup finely chopped, drained (add any drained liquid to clam juice), firm-textured seafood for corn; 1/2 tsp. crushed red pepper flakes for ground red pepper. Eliminate Anaheim pepper and cumin. Add 1 tsp. Worcestershire and 2 limes, cut into wedges. Squeeze 1 tbsp. lime juice into batter. Serve remaining wedges with the fritters.

Prepare batter and cook as on previous page. These are wonderful served with Ginger Sesame Vinaigrette (p. 275) or Cajun Tartar Sauce (p. 281).

Grilled or Oven-Roasted Chicken with Dijon Glaze

VARIATIONS: WHOLE ROASTED, WITH DEMI-GLACE

This glaze seals the pores of the skin or flesh, trapping the moisture in the chicken while it is cooked at very high temperature. The glaze also provides a delicate base flavor. The result is moist, delicious chicken in a few minutes. This works equally well for grilled or barbecued chicken. See High Temperature Cooking, p. 14.

Yield: 4 servings
Preparation time: cut-up chicken, 5 minutes; whole chicken, 10 minutes. Cooking time: cut-up chicken, 20 minutes; whole chicken 35 - 40 minutes. Demi-Glace: 5 minutes.

> **2 chickens, cut in halves, quarters or pieces**
> **1/4 cup herb-flavored Dijon Glaze** (p. 105)

Preheat oven to 450°.

1. Wash the chicken and pat it dry with paper towel.

2. Brush Dijon Glaze over all the surface area, top and bottom.

3. Place pieces in single layer, 1/2" apart, in heavy, oven-proof pan.

4. Cook for 15 - 18 minutes or until juices run clear when the chicken is pricked with a knife.

OVEN-ROASTED WHOLE CHICKEN
Stuffing
> **1 or 2 carrots, cut into 2" chunks**
> **1 tbsp. dried, or 1 whole stem fresh herb**
> **4 garlic cloves**

Roasting
> **2 tbsp. chopped fresh, or 2 tsp. dried mixed herbs added to the Dijon Glaze**

Demi-Glace
> **1 tbsp. chopped fresh, or 1 tsp. dried mixed herbs**
> **1 cup dry white wine**
> **1 additional tsp. Dijon Glaze**

Preheat oven to 450°.

1. Put the carrot, herb stems, and garlic into the cavity of the chicken and tie it closed with trussing skewers and string.

2. Brush entire surface with Dijon Glaze.

3. Place the chicken on a rack in a roasting pan and roast for 30 - 35 minutes, until skin is dark golden brown, a leg jiggles easily, and the juice runs clear when the skin is pierced with a knife.

DEMI-GLACE

1. Remove chicken from roasting pan and transfer to a heated platter. Skim fat off the residue juice, and put the pan on medium high heat. Add wine and Dijon Glaze to the cooking juice, and scrape up any cooking residue as the sauce heats.

2. Whisking continually, simmer the sauce until it thickens (3 - 5 minutes) and reduces by half.

To serve: Remove and discard stuffing. Carve the chicken and ladle Demi-Glace over each serving.

LEFTOVERS

If there is any chicken left, make Leftover Chicken Soup (p. 131) or Simple Pasta and Vegetable Soup (p. 125), or Chicken Chowder (p. 141), or Quick Pasties or Turnovers (p. 161), or Chicken Quesadillas (p. 175), or Asian Chicken Salad (p. 271).

Moroccan Chicken With Couscous

VARIATION: MOROCCAN CHICKEN SOUP

Yield: serves 8 with enough for leftovers
Preparation and cooking time: 45 minutes

STOCK BAG
Remember
your Stock
Bag (p. 12).

- **8 boneless chicken breasts**
- **18 chicken thighs**
- **1/4 cup Dijon Glaze** (p. 105) **flavored with 1 tbsp. Garam Masala Curry Paste®** (Resources, p. 340)**, or 1 tbsp. Moroccan Marinade** (p. 286)
- **3 cups cooked couscous (follow instructions on package)**
- **2 14 1/2 oz. cans premium diced tomatoes in purée**
- **1 large yellow onion, sliced, and Caramelized** (p. 231)
- **3 oz. sliced black olives**
- **3 tbsp. Garam Masala Curry Paste®, or Moroccan Marinade**
- **1 cup chicken stock, preferably Homemade**
- **1 green pepper, seeded, pith removed, and coarsely chopped**
- **1/4 cup finely chopped fresh parsley**
- **3/4 cup bread crumbs mixed with 1/4 cup coarsely grated dry sharp cheese**

Preheat oven to 450°.

1. Brush chicken pieces with Dijon Glaze and put them into a heavy oven-proof skillet. Bake for 20 minutes or until the juice runs clear when a piece is pricked with a fork.

2. While chicken is cooking, prepare couscous. When the chicken is done, turn the oven down to 350°.

3. To make sauce: put tomatoes, Garam Masala Curry Paste®, onions, stock, and olives in a saucepan and bring to a simmer over medium low heat. Cook 5 to 8 minutes. Remove from heat and add chopped pepper and parsley.

- **See recipes for Homemade and Modified Canned Stock (p. 108).**

4. Put couscous in an oven-proof casserole dish. Pour half the sauce over it, and using a large fork, mix the sauce gently into the couscous. Place the chicken over the couscous, pour the remaining sauce over the chicken, and sprinkle bread crumb mixture over top. If there is not enough sauce to cover the chicken, add some chicken stock to the sauce, taking care not to thin it too much. (The recipe may be made ahead, up to this point, covered and refrigerated [or frozen°] until 1 hour before serving. To reheat: bring to 50° or slightly warmer than chilled, before baking.)

5. Bake (at 350°) until the chicken is heated through and the top is golden brown, 10 - 12 minutes.

°Thaw completely and bring to room temperature before baking.

MOROCCAN CHICKEN SOUP

>   leftover Moroccan Chicken with Couscous
>   (2 pieces chicken plus 2 cups other stuff)
> 3   cups chicken stock
> 1   14 1/2 oz. can premium diced tomatoes
>   in purée

1. Cut the chicken off the bone. Put it and the leftover casserole contents into a soup pot. Add the stock and tomatoes.

2. Bring to a low simmer and cook until flavors are blended, about 5 minutes.

Serve with fresh crusty bread, warm pita bread, or steaming hot cornbread (from a mix).

LEFTOVERS
This recipe is based on leftovers from Moroccan Chicken with Couscous (p. 169). I do not recommend making it from scratch.

Hungarian Chicken

The only thing Hungarian about this old-time recipe is the Hungarian paprika, which is mellow and lacks the bitterness of other paprikas.

Yield: 6 - 8 servings
Preparation and cooking time: 45 - 50 minutes

STOCK BAG
Remember your Stock Bag (p. 12).

16	chicken thighs, or 6 breasts and 8 thighs, washed and patted dry
2	tbsp. olive oil
1	large yellow onion, peeled and chopped (about 1 cup)
4	oz. mushrooms, sliced about 1/4" thick (2 cups)
2	cups chicken stock
1	quart sour cream
2	tbsp. Hungarian paprika (Resources, p. 340)
1/2	tsp. crushed red pepper flakes
1/2	tsp. kosher salt
3	cups cooked rice or fettuccine

You will need a heavy oven-proof casserole dish.

Preheat oven to 350°.

1. Heat oil in heavy skillet on medium high heat. Cook chicken until it is crisp and brown on both sides, about 15 minutes. Remove from the pan and set aside. Turn the heat down to medium low, add the onion, and cook it until it is softened and translucent, about 5 minutes. Add the sliced mushrooms and cook for 5 more minutes, stirring constantly. Add remaining 5 ingredients, retaining 2 tsp. paprika, and mix thoroughly.

2. Transfer cooked chicken to the casserole dish and pour sauce over chicken. Sprinkle the top with remaining paprika and bake, uncovered for 25 minutes.

3. Serve over steamed rice or wide egg fettuccine.

- See recipes for Homemade and Modified Canned Stock (p. 108).
- Low fat sour cream contains gelatin, which breaks down if it is heated, so it will not work here.

Chicken and Dumplings

VARIATION: CHICKEN COBBLER, CHICKEN POT PIE

The fillings for Chicken and Dumplings, Chicken Cobbler, and Chicken Pot Pie are identical, but the end results are very different and wonderful in their own ways. Pot Pies use up that last bit of stuffing, Chicken Cobbler is the quickest and easiest, and they both are suited perfectly for individually made portions. But there somehow is a magic to dumplings; it's hard to imagine a more comforting food.

Yield: 6 servings
Preparation time: 40 minutes with leftover chicken; 1 hour, without. Cooking time: 20 - 30 minutes

LEFTOVERS
This recipe is based on leftovers from Oven-Roasted Chicken with Dijon Glaze (p. 105). While it can be made from scratch, that is much more complicated.

STOCK BAG
Remember your Stock Bag (p. 12).

See recipes for Home-made and Modified Canned Stock (p. 108).

3 cups cooked chicken torn into pieces about an inch wide and 2 - 3" long
1 cup Demi-Glace (p. 107), or residue from cooking the chicken with stock added
1 yellow onion, peeled and diced (about 1 cup)
1 bay leaf, cracked
2 carrots, peeled and diced or sliced about 1/4" thick
1 large baking potato, diced (about 1 cup)
2 stalks celery, sliced about 1/4" thick, about 1 1/2 cups
1/4 cup chopped fresh Italian or regular parsley
3 tbsp. chopped fresh herb (sage, tarragon, thyme, or savory, or a combination), or 3 tsp. dried herb leaves (reserve 1/3 for dumplings)
8 - 10 fresh mushrooms, sliced about 1/4" thick (you may use a combination of button and wild mushrooms or re-hydrated wild mushrooms, using that mushroom water as part of the stock)
3 tbsp. chicken fat, butter, or margarine
2 tbsp. all-purpose flour
3 cups chicken stock, preferably Homemade, heated (microwave)
1/2 pint heavy cream
kosher salt to taste
1/2 tsp. cracked pepper
1 small box frozen peas, thawed (optional)
2 cups biscuit mix
2/3 cup milk
remaining 1/3 of herbs

You will need a large heat-proof casserole that may be heated on top of the stove.

1. Prepare the chicken and set aside.°

2. Heat Demi-Glace in the casserole over medium heat. Add bay leaf, onion, potato, and carrot, cover and simmer until carrot is just beginning to soften, about 8 minutes. Add celery and continue to cook until celery is just soft, 3 - 4 minutes.

3. Add parsley, 2/3 of the herb, mushrooms, and prepared chicken, stir to mix, add 2 cups of stock, and bring to a simmer.

4. While it is heating, in another pan, melt the fat over low heat until it bubbles. Add the flour and cook for about 3 minutes, or until it turns a little darker than golden brown (not burned and smoking, just brown). Add 1 cup stock slowly, whisking constantly, until it forms a thick, creamy sauce. Slowly add it, stirring constantly, to the larger pot. Add the cream and the pepper, and continue to simmer on low for 5 more minutes. Taste and correct seasoning with salt, if necessary. Add peas and stir to mix.

5. While it is simmering, mix the dumpling dough in a small mixing bowl, adding the remaining chopped herb to the dry mix before adding the milk.

6. Bring the heat under the chicken mix up to a very low but constant boil. Drop the dumpling dough by large spoonfuls onto the chicken stew mixture. Cook, uncovered, for 10 minutes. Cover and cook another 10 minutes. Do not remove the lid for the last 10 minutes (peeking makes sticky, heavy dumplings!).

°**To cook raw chicken:** 1) After washing and drying on paper towel, dredge in a light coating of flour; 2) over medium high heat, brown both sides in olive oil, then add 1/4 cup water or white wine to the pan; 3) turn heat to low, cover pan, and poach for 20 minutes. Remove from the pan, keeping the juice and any residue from the bottom of the pan to use as demi-glace in Step 2. Proceed with the recipe.

CHICKEN COBBLER

2 cups biscuit mix (follow box recipe)
1/2 cup milk
tarragon or thyme

1. Prepare the filling according to preceding recipe.

2. While it is cooking, preheat oven to 400°. Mix the cobbler dough, adding the remaining chopped herb to the dry mix before adding the milk.

3. Transfer the chicken mixture to an oven-proof casserole dish. Drop the cobbler dough by tablespoon onto the chicken mixture and bake, uncovered, until the cobbler crust is golden brown on the top.

CHICKEN POT PIE

2 cups leftover stuffing (or made from mix)
1 tbsp. dried sage leaves
1 uncooked pie crust
egg wash (1 whole egg beaten with 1 tbsp. water)

Preheat oven to 375°.

1. Prepare the filling according to preceding recipe.

2. On a slightly floured surface, roll the crust into a shape 1" larger all around than the pie pan.

3. Put the stuffing on the bottom of the pan; don't press it at all. Pour the chicken filling over the stuffing. Place the crust over the top, and crimp the edges. Prick the crust several times with a sharp knife or fork (to release steam), brush with egg wash, and bake for 25 - 30 minutes, until the crust is cooked and golden brown.

- **Pot pies and cobblers are perfectly suited for individual cooking containers. I make them in small terra cotta casserole dishes (some have handles) that are glazed on the inside, or for pot pies, in small or large terra cotta flower pot saucers, also glazed on the inside. If you are in the mood, cut leaf shapes out of the dough scraps and decorate the Pot Pie crust (use egg wash to hold them on).**

- **Cobblers have a flakey biscuit top cooked over a deep-dish pie filling—sweet or savory. Pot pies have crusts.**

Chicken Quesadilla

A very fresh-tasting version of quesadilla.

Yield: 8 quesadillas
Preparation and cooking time: 25 minutes

1	lb. cooked chicken
1	tsp. ground chili powder (not pure cayenne)
1	tsp. ground cumin
	juice of 1/2 lime
1/2	cup corn oil
1	cup diced yellow or green onion
2	Anaheim peppers, stems and pith removed, and diced, or 8 oz. canned chopped mild green chilies
1	red or green bell pepper, stem and pith removed, and diced
1/2	cup chopped fresh cilantro
8	8" flour tortillas
1	cup grated Monterey Jack cheese
	sour cream
	Quick Tomato Salsa (p. 287)
	8 half slices of lime

Preheat oven to 250°.

1. Shred the chicken. Sprinkle chili powder, cumin, and lime juice over it, mix, and set aside.

2. In a large, non-stick fry pan, heat 2 tbsp. corn oil over medium heat. Add yellow onion and peppers and sauté until onion is translucent and peppers have softened a little (add green onion after pepper is softened). Transfer the mixture to a large bowl.

3. Add cilantro and chicken and toss to distribute evenly.

4. Heat remaining corn oil in the same fry pan. While it is heating, divide chicken mixture among the 8 tortillas, in the center. Sprinkle 2 tbsp. grated cheese on each tortilla.

5. When the oil is hot (not smoking, that's too hot), fold the tortillas in half over the chicken and cook 2 at a time. Press down gently on the tops to seal. Turn when they are golden brown, about 3 minutes. Cook until the second half is golden and the cheese has melted.

6. As they finish cooking, place the quesadillas on a platter and hold them in the oven until all of them are done.

Serve with Salsa, sour cream, and half slices of lime, or with Salsa, Black Bean Sauce (p. 300), and half slices of lime.

LEFTOVERS
This recipe is based on leftovers from Oven-Roasted or Grilled (or barbecued) Chicken (p. 167). (I would be lying if I said I had never made it from leftover take-out chicken!)

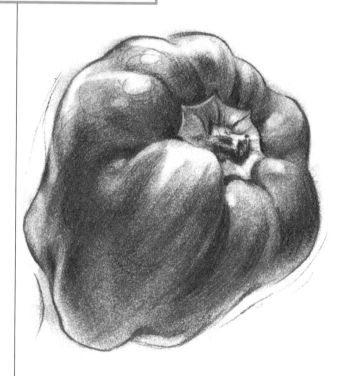

Chicken and Ancho Chili Empanadas or Tacos

This makes a terrific taco filling, or if you add 1 raw egg and 1/2 cup bread crumbs, it becomes great "meatballs" to serve with Jamaican Beans and Rice (p. 249).

Yield: 4 servings
Preparation and cooking time: Empanadas, 50 - 60 minutes; Tacos, 35 minutes

Filling

1	**tsp. ground dried ancho or poblano chili** (Resources, p. 340)
1	**tsp. ground cumin**
1/2	**lb. chicken sausage*, with skin removed**
1/4	**cup chopped fresh oregano or fresh marjoram, or 2 tbsp. dried oregano**
1	**tbsp. minced garlic**
1/4	**cup fresh cilantro, finely chopped**
2	**Anaheim chili peppers, stems and seeds removed, finely chopped**
1/2	**cup coarsely chopped black olives**
3	**oz. grated Monterey Jack cheese**
1/2	**tsp. crushed red pepper flakes**
1	**pint Quick Tomato Salsa** (p. 287)
1	**cup sour cream**

*If you can't get chicken sausage, substitute fresh ground chicken or turkey.

1. Remove the stem and seed from the dried chili. Grind to powder in a spice grinder or blender.

2. Put ground chili and cumin in a small fry pan over high heat. Moving the pan and shifting the spices continuously, cook the spices until they begin to brown, 3 minutes. Remove from heat and set aside.

3. Put sausage in a mixing bowl. Add remaining ingredients and blend thoroughly. The mixture may be made ahead up to this point, covered tightly and refrigerated for 1 day, or frozen for 1 week.

Hint #12: The heat in chili peppers releases as it cooks, so food containing chilies tends to get hotter over time.

Empanadas

enough pie dough for 4, 9" pie crusts (refrigerated or frozen dough works well)
egg wash (1 egg white whisked with 1 tbsp. water)

Preheat oven to 375°. Line a baking sheet (for hors d'oeuvre size, use 2) with parchment paper.

1. Roll out dough to 1/4" thickness. Cut out circles about 7" in diameter for entrée size or 3 1/2" in diameter for hors d'oeuvre size. Place the circles on a lightly floured working surface, and brush the inside edges lightly with egg wash. Place 1/4 cup filling in the center of each circle (1 tbsp. for hors d'oeuvre size), spread slightly, and fold the dough over into the shape of a turnover. Crimp the edges and place the pastries on the baking sheet. When all the pastries are on the sheets, brush the surfaces with egg wash.

2. Bake in the middle of the oven for 15 - 20 minutes, or until crusts are cooked and golden brown.

To serve: Transfer the empanadas to a serving dish and serve Salsa and sour cream on the side.

Tacos

2 tbsp. corn oil
8 taco shells
1/4 head iceberg lettuce, shredded

1. Follow Empanada Steps 1 and 2 to make filling.

2. Heat oil in a fry pan, add the sausage mixture and cook, stirring often, until it is brown. Remove from the pan with a slotted spoon and drain on paper towels.

3. While the sausage is draining, mix the shredded lettuce with the cilantro, and set the taco shells upright so they can be filled easily.

4. Fill the taco shells with the sausage mixture, the olives and grated cheese. Top each taco with Salsa and sour cream, and serve immediately

Chicken Hash

The origin of hash is whatever is leftover stirred together and then fried, so don't be timid about what you add.

Yield: serves 4-6
Preparation and cooking time: 50 minutes

LEFTOVERS
Use leftover steamed potatoes, or raw, or a combination.

3	cups diced (1/4") Idaho russet potatoes, washed, patted dry (I leave the skin on) (about 2 large potatoes)
1	pint chicken stock
2	tbsp. chicken fat, or 1 tbsp. pure olive oil plus 2 tbsp. butter or margarine
3/4	cup diced yellow onion (1 medium)
8	oz. cooked chicken, preferably dark meat
1	green bell pepper, seeded, pith removed and chopped
1	tsp. ground cumin
1/2	tsp. chili powder
1/2	tsp. kosher salt
1/2	tsp. crushed red pepper flakes
1	Anaheim chili, seeded, pith removed and diced, or 8 oz. chopped, mild green chilies
1/4	cup fresh cilantro, leaves only, chopped
2	tbsp. flour (if you are not using any raw potato)
1/4	cup vegetable oil for frying hash
1	lime cut into 6 wedges, for garnish **Quick Tomato Salsa** (p. 287)

A non-stick or seasoned cast-iron fry pan is best for hash.

1. Cook the potatoes in the chicken stock until they can be pricked easily with a fork. Drain and save the juice.

2. While the potatoes are cooking, heat the fat or oil in a large fry pan, and sauté the onion on medium high heat until it is just beginning to brown around the edges (about 5 - 6 minutes). Add the green pepper, the chicken, the spices, and the chilies, and mix until combined. Remove from heat.

When I make chicken stock, I save a little of the fat that hardens on the top of the chilled stock and freeze it for hash. It's very flavorful if not particularly healthful.

3. Add the drained potatoes (and leftovers if you have them) and continue mixing until the ingredients begin to bind (stick together). Correct seasoning with salt.

4. Mix the chopped cilantro in gently with a fork.

5. Transfer the hash to another container, and scrape the residue from the fry pan. Heat oil and chicken fat in pan on medium high. Return hash to pan, spreading it evenly and patting it down gently with a spatula. Fry it until bottom browns, about 8 minutes.

6. Lift the hash with spatula to ensure it will separate easily from the pan. Put a plate upside down over the skillet and invert it so the hash is on the plate. Slide hash back into skillet and brown other side. Or broil the top, but be careful not to dry out the hash.

To serve: Garnish with a wedge of lime and serve immediately (bottom side up if you broiled it), with Salsa on the side.

Chicken Satay

Satay looks pretty presented on a plate or platter lined with curly Napa or bok choy cabbage.

Yield: 8 servings
Preparation time: 40 minutes. **Marinating time:** 2 hours
Cooking time: 15 minutes

This recipe works just as well for meat or shrimp.

- 4 chicken breasts, boned and skinned
- 4 chicken thighs, boned and skinned
- 12" wooden skewers for grilling, soaked in water for one hour (soaking is essential if you want to avoid burned skewers that fall through the grilling grate!)

Spicy Peanut Sauce

- 2 tbsp. minced garlic
- 2 tbsp. fresh ginger, grated
- 2 tbsp. *unseasoned* rice vinegar
- 2 green onions, minced
- 1/4 cup fresh cilantro, minced
- 1/2 cup dry sherry
- 1/4 cup hoisin sauce
- 1/4 cup soy sauce
- 2 tbsp. pure sesame oil
- 2 tbsp. creamy peanut butter
- 2 tbsp. honey
- 1 tsp. crushed red pepper flakes

1. Slice the chicken in long strips, between 1/4 - 1/2" thick. Thread onto the skewers and place in a foil-lined sheet pan, in 1 layer.

2. Mix sauce ingredients thoroughly and pour over the chicken. Cover tightly with plastic wrap and marinate for several hours.

Grilling: Remove the satays from the marinade, and divide marinade in half. Heat half to a low simmer in a small saucepan, and use the other half to baste the chicken while it grills. Barbecue the chicken over low coals, basting constantly to prevent it from drying out. Pour the heated marinade over the chicken and serve.

If you wish to reuse the remaining marinade, boil it for 3 minutes, cool to room temperature in the refrigerator and freeze it. Never reuse chicken marinade without boiling it first.

Baked or Grilled Fish with Dijon Glaze

Most fish is overcooked; its natural moisture is leached out by prolonged heat, so its delicate texture becomes stringy or a little tough. **The less time fish is exposed to moisture-sapping heat, in the oven or on a grill, the moister it will be.** *The hotter the heat, the less time it is exposed. Dijon Glaze seals the pores of the flesh so fish can withstand 500° heat (see p. 14).*

Yield: 4 servings
Preparation time: 10 minutes, including Dijon Glaze (p. 105) and heating the oven or grill. Cooking time: 5 - 10 minutes, depending upon the thickness of the fish

> **4 7 oz. fish fillets or steaks**
> **1/4 cup Lemon Herb Dijon Glaze** (p. 105)
> **1/2 cup dry white wine**
>   **fresh herb for garnish**

You will need a heavy, oven-proof pan, preferably non-stick coated or seasoned cast iron. A pan is not necessary for grilling.

Preheat oven or grill to 500° (or 450° if that temperature is just too scary at first).

1. Heat the pan on high heat, until it is very hot.

2. While it is heating, brush glaze over all surfaces of the fish, particularly all flesh.

3. **To Bake:** When the pan is hot **(using potholders)** put the fish in and brown on one side. Turn the fish after 2 minutes and put the pan into the oven. Bake for another few minutes. **Remember: 5 minutes to the inch of thickness.**
   To Grill: Put fish on grill and cook, turning only once (for 5 minutes per inch).

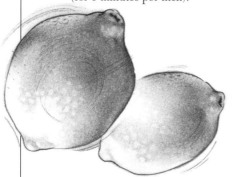

If the fish pieces are less than 1" thick, I recommend cooking it on both sides on top of the stove; the amount of time it will be in the oven isn't worth it.

4. Take the fish out of the oven or off the grill, and immediately transfer it to a warmed serving dish or warmed individual plates.

Note: Before you make the sauce or Demi-Glace (p. 107) make a slight separation in the flesh to stop the cooking.

5. Add wine to the pan and cook at medium high, whisking constantly until the sauce is reduced by half. For grilling, cook wine and 1 tbsp. Dijon glaze in a small pan. Pour over the fish, garnish with fresh herb, and serve immediately.

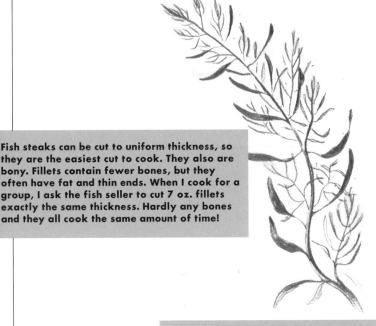

Fish steaks can be cut to uniform thickness, so they are the easiest cut to cook. They also are bony. Fillets contain fewer bones, but they often have fat and thin ends. When I cook for a group, I ask the fish seller to cut 7 oz. fillets exactly the same thickness. Hardly any bones and they all cook the same amount of time!

Timing is everything in cooking fish. If the fish is cooked and the vegetables are not, the fish will be overcooked when the vegetables are done. If the plates are cold when the fish comes out of the oven, the fish will lose its heat instantly. If the fish has to wait at the table while the dog is let out, the phone is answered, and the kids come in from outside, well, you'll just have to figure that one out yourself (or see recipe for Fresh Fish Sandwich, p. 160). Cook everything else first and let it wait for the fish.

Sautéed Seafood

Sautéing is high heat cooking, and because whatever is being cooked needs to be kept in almost constant motion to prevent sticking or burning, it is not a good process for delicately textured fish. Sautéing works best with shrimp, lobster, scallops, halibut cheeks, swordfish, calamari, and chunked or sliced firm-fleshed fish. I recommend using a non-stick or properly seasoned medium-sized sauté pan.

Yield: 4 servings
Preparation time: 15 minutes. Cooking time: 5 minutes

> 2 **tbsp. pure olive oil**
> 1 **tsp. unsalted butter**
> 1 **tsp. minced fresh garlic**
> 1/4 **tsp. crushed red pepper flakes**
> 1 1/2 **lb. seafood, in slightly larger than bite-sized**
> **pieces or smaller, depending upon the dish**
> 1 **tbsp. chopped fresh herb (optional)**
> **(tarragon, thyme, basil, marjoram, oregano,**
> **chives, sorrel)**
> **juice of 1/2 lemon**

Once it is in the pan, the seafood will take about 5 minutes to cook. Be careful not to overcook seafood.

1. Heat butter and oil in sauté pan on medium high. When the butter sizzles (don't let it get to the point of smoking), add the garlic and crushed pepper, moving the pan continuously. Immediately add the seafood and sauté, moving continuously, until the seafood is almost cooked.

2. Sprinkle the chopped herb over the seafood and drizzle the lemon juice immediately.

For Sautéed Shrimp or Scallops: Add 1 tsp. grated fresh ginger at Step 2, eliminating the fresh herb. Substitute 1 tbsp. fresh lime juice for lemon juice.

> **Get everything else ready to serve before you sauté the seafood, so it can be served immediately.**

Steamed Shellfish

The nectar created by steaming clams or mussels is absolutely delicious. Bread dunking is a given. If there is leftover nectar, freeze it. With a little cream and a pinch of curry powder, it is instant soup for a chilly day.

Yield: 4 servings
Preparation and cooking time: 30 minutes

> 2 lbs. mussels, or 3 lbs. clams (1/2 lb. mussels or 3/4 lb. steamer clams per serving), prawns, singing scallops, or crab
> 1 lemon
> 1 cup white wine
> 2 shallots, minced
> 1/2 tsp. crushed red pepper flakes
> 1 tsp. Worcestershire sauce
> 1 tbsp. extra virgin olive oil
> 2 tbsp. chopped Italian parsley, plus 2 tbsp. for garnish

1. Wash shellfish and de-beard mussels.

2. Cut the lemon in half and strain the juice into the steamer pan (if you don't have an official steamer pan, use a colander or vegetable steamer in a stock pot, or just put them directly into a pot; it's not that big a deal).

3. Add remaining ingredients, except shellfish and parsley garnish.

4. Put the shellfish into the steamer, and steam over medium high heat for 10 - 12 minutes.

5. Transfer the shellfish to a serving bowl, and ladle the nectar into a serving container. Sprinkle the remaining parsley over the nectar.

To serve: Provide warmed shallow soup or pasta dishes and small shellfish forks for each person. Remember to provide shell-tossing dishes too. And don't forget the bread!

See box on p. 94, for lemon-scented hand towels.

Farmed mussels grow attached to netting. As they are harvested, part of the fiber sticks to the mussel, and it should be removed before cooking. Hold the mussel, narrow end down, and pull the fiber down, away from the shell.

Fish In Parchment

This is easy and fun to make, and it adds dramatic flare to dinner. It takes longer to preheat the oven than it does to cook the fish!

Yield: 1 serving. Multiply quantities by the number of eaters! Preparation time: 10 minutes for 2 servings, add 5 minutes per serving. Cooking time: 8 minutes per serving

> **All of the fish should be the same thickness so that it will cook evenly. Generally, at high temperature, fish takes 5 minutes per inch of thickness to cook. (See boxes on p. 14).**

6 oz. firm-fleshed fish (halibut, rock fish, seabass, salmon, black cod—avoid tuna, sturgeon, swordfish or other less fatty fish)

1 tsp. Dijon Glaze (p. 105)**, or 2 tbsp. other marinade such as: Moroccan Marinade** (p. 286)**, or Seafood Marinade** (p. 275)**, etc.**

1/6 bell pepper of 3 colors, seeds and pith removed, julienne-cut (see recipe for Sautéed Bell Peppers [p. 228] for suggested technique for removing pith and cutting peppers; it really makes a difference!)

1 tsp. lemon juice

1/6 red onion, thinly sliced and separated into rings

1 12" square of baking parchment (Resources, p. 340)

Preheat oven to 450°.

1. Brush fish with glaze or other seasoning and place it in center of parchment.

2. Sprinkle lemon juice over the peppers and place them and onion slices around the fish.

3. Wrap the edges of the paper over the fish, rolling edges tightly to prevent steam from escaping.

4. Place the parchment package in an oven-proof pan and bake for 5-8 minutes, until fish is cooked rare.

5. Remove from the oven, and prick the parchment package with a sharp knife to release steam.

To serve: Transfer the package onto a preheated plate and let diners open their own. Serve with salsa or chutney of your choice.

> **If your grocer does not carry baking parchment, ask that he or she order it. In a pinch, go to a bakery or restaurant and buy several of their big sheets.**

Pasta and Seafood in Parchment

This is really a fun way to eat pasta and seafood. Don't be afraid to feel a little smug when people open the pouches! Raffia, the natural fibre tying material, looks terrific; it comes in several colors.

Yield: 4 servings
Preparation time: 40 minutes. **Cooking time:** less than 10 minutes

8	pieces cooking parchment, cut into 16" squares
4	pieces of kitchen string or raffia, soaked in water.
1	lb. fresh pasta (spaghetti or linguine), or 8 oz. dried
2	tsp. minced garlic
1/4	cup extra virgin olive oil
1/4	cup chopped fresh Italian parsley
1/2	tsp. crushed red pepper flakes
1	lb. fresh mussels in shell
1	lb. manila or other small steamer clams in shell, washed
4	oz. calamari, cleaned, cut into rings, with tentacles separate
8	oz. firm white fish cut into cubes
1/4	cup chopped fresh thyme or basil leaves, or 4 tsp. dried leaves
1/2	cup fresh tomato, peeled, seeded, and chopped
1	cup dry white wine
2	lemons, sliced with seeds removed

Preheat oven to 450°.

1. Place 4 pieces of parchment flat in a roasting pan, then overlap the other four to form star shapes.

2. Cook pasta in boiling, salted water until not quite al dente (it will cook a little more in the oven). Drain, rinse, and hold.

3. While pasta is cooking, heat olive oil, garlic, crushed pepper flakes, and 2 tbsp. parsley in a large sauté pan over medium heat, and cook until garlic is softened. Add all the seafood, half the fresh herb, the wine, and the tomato.

4. Sauté, stirring continually until seafood is heated, 2-3 minutes.

5. Divide the prepared pasta among the 4 parchment "stars", and ladle the seafood mixture on top of the pasta. Put a lemon slice on each serving, sprinkle remaining herbs over the tops, and pull up the corners of the parchment into packages. Tie each one securely with string or raffia.

6. Bake until parchment is browned on the edges, about 4 - 5 minutes.

To serve: Without untying them, transfer the pouches to heated shallow bowls, pour any juice from the pan into the bowls around the pouches, and serve immediately with crusty Italian bread. Pass the scissors.

If your grocer does not carry baking parchment ask that he or she order it. In a pinch, go to a bakery or restaurant and buy several of their big sheets.

Crab Cakes

VARIATIONS: CODFISH CAKES, SMOKED SALMON CAKES, SHRIMP CAKES

This produces light, flaky, seafood-tasting cakes, as opposed to the more traditional, breadier ones. So mix everything with a fork and use just enough bread crumbs to bind them through the first turn in the pan.

Yield: serves 4
Preparation and cooking time: 1 hour, including chilling time

2 1/2	cups picked, fresh crab meat
1/4	cup lime juice (if cilantro and chilies) or lemon juice (if not)—about 1 large or 2 small
1/2	cup finely chopped green onion
1/2	cup finely chopped fresh cilantro or Italian parsley
1/4	cup finely chopped mild green chili (omit if you are using parsley)
1/2	cup Homemade Mayonnaise (p. 279) (if not homemade, add 1 tsp. wine vinegar; please don't use a sweet or bottled low-fat mayonnaise)
1/2	tsp. crushed red pepper flakes
1	tbsp. Dijon mustard
1	cup bread crumbs
1/4	cup pure olive oil plus 2 tbsp. unsalted butter

1. Put the crab meat into a mixing bowl and drizzle strained lime or lemon juice over it. Add onion, cilantro or parsley, and chopped chili, and mix lightly with a fork.

2. Mix mayonnaise, pepper flakes, and mustard together, then add to crab and mix with fork. Add 1/2 cup bread crumbs, mix, and see if it can hold in a bundle. If not, add more, 1 tbsp. at a time, until it holds. Form into 8 cakes, approximately 3" in diameter and 3/4" thick. Cover with plastic wrap and refrigerate for 30 minutes (chilling is essential or they will fall apart).

3. Heat butter and oil in a heavy skillet over medium high heat. Dredge cakes in remaining bread crumbs and fry until crisp and golden brown on the bottom (3 - 5 minutes). Turn carefully and brown on the other side. Serve immediately.

CODFISH CAKES

Substitute 1 cup soaked and cooked salt cod plus 1 1/2 cups cooked true or Ling cod, and lemon and parsley; substitute green bell pepper for mild chili pepper.

SMOKED SALMON CAKES

Substitute hard smoked salmon for crab; eliminate the cilantro and green chili.

SHRIMP CAKES

Substitute chopped cooked shrimp for crab.

Serve with Quick Tomato Salsa (p. 287), Tartar Sauce (p. 281) or lime wasabi mayonnaise (1 cup good mayonnaise, juice of 1 lime, 1 tbsp. wasabi horseradish).

Puget Sound Cioppino Fish Stew

Like traditional Italian cioppino, this version is a thick, rich tomato-based stew, but it features seafood found in my neighborhood. If Cioppino is made ahead, cool it as quickly as possible to prevent the fish from overcooking as it cools down. Transfer the stew from the cooking pot to a large bowl covered loosely with plastic wrap. Set the bowl on a bed of ice in a larger bowl and refrigerate. To reheat, transfer it back to the cooking pot and heat it over high heat until it simmers, then turn the heat down to medium high to finish heating it through. Serve immediately in heated bowls.

Yield: 6 servings
Preparation and cooking time: 45 minutes

Croutons
4	slices crusty French or Italian bread
1	clove garlic, cut in half
3	tbsp. extra virgin olive oil
1/4	cup coarsely grated Parmesan cheese

Shellfish Nectar
(the shellfish is cooked in this nectar)
1/2	cup white wine
1/3	of the outermost layer of the onion or leek greens
1	stalk of fennel (the bulb will be used in the stew), if not available, substitute 1 tsp. fennel seed, crushed (a rolling pin works) stems from the Italian parsley
1	large clove garlic, slightly crushed with the flat side of knife blade

Stew
1/2	lb. mussels, washed and de-bearded (see box, p. 192)
1/2	lb. clams (manila, butter, or little neck), washed
6	oz. medium shrimp (24 to a pound), peeled with tails left on
2	cups Homemade Fish Stock (p. 108) or clam juice
	juice of 1/2 lemon
2	oz. olive oil
1/2	cup chopped yellow onion or thinly sliced leek

1 bay leaf, cracked
1/2 tsp. fennel seed, crushed
2 tsp. minced garlic
3/4 cup thinly sliced fresh fennel bulb
(if available)
1 14 1/2 oz. can premium diced tomatoes
in purée
1/2 cup red wine (preferably Chianti)
1/2 tsp. crushed red pepper flakes
2 tbsp. chopped fresh basil (or oregano or
marjoram), or 2 tsp. dried leaves
1/2 cup fresh Italian parsley, finely chopped
4 oz. firm white fish, in bite-sized chunks
4 oz. calamari, cleaned, skinned, and sliced
into rings
kosher salt to taste

STOCK BAG
Remember
your Stock
Bag (p. 12).

To make croutons: Brush bread with oil and broil until golden brown. Turn, brush with oil, and broil until golden brown. Remove from the oven, and rub one side with garlic. Sprinkle with cheese and set aside.

Farmed mussels grow attached to netting. As they are harvested, part of the fiber sticks to the mussel, and it should be removed before cooking. Hold the mussel, narrow end down, and pull the fiber down, away from the shell.

To make shellfish nectar:

1. Put ingredients into a shallow saucepan over medium high heat. Add mussels and clams, cover and boil for 5 minutes, until they open. Remove with a slotted spoon and set aside. Put shrimp into the same water, cover and boil until the shrimp turn pink, about 5 minutes. Remove with a slotted spoon and set aside. Squeeze lemon juice over the cooked shellfish, and cover it loosely with plastic wrap.

2. Strain the nectar into a small mixing bowl, and discard residue.

To make stew:

1. Put oil, onion, and fennel seed in a large saucepan over medium heat. Cook until the onion is translucent and softened, 3 - 5 minutes. Add garlic and bay leaf, and cook for 5 more minutes, taking care not to burn the garlic.

2. Add nectar and remaining ingredients, except seafood, turn heat to medium low, and simmer for 10 minutes.

3. Add all seafood, and simmer for 3 more minutes.

4. While the stew is simmering the last time, broil the croutons long enough to melt the cheese.

To serve: Ladle the Cioppino into heated, shallow soup or pasta bowls, taking care to divide the seafood among the bowls evenly. Make room in the center of the bowls and place a crouton in the center of each Cioppino. Sprinkle the remaining parsley over the stew, and serve immediately.

Remember to provide shell waste bowls on the table. For special treatment, dampen terry cloth hand towels with lemon juice and water, and heat them for 3 minutes in the microwave. Pass them to diners as each place is cleared.

Cajun Shrimp Stew

The flavor of the shrimp really comes through in this stew. You can substitute crawfish, other shellfish, cooked chicken, and chicken stock for the shrimp.

Yield: 6 + servings
Preparation and cooking time: 1 hour, including cooking time for rice and shrimp

3	cups water for cooking shrimp
1	lb. raw medium prawns, peeled (18 - 24 to the pound) juice of 1 lemon
2	tbsp. pure olive oil
1/2	cup yellow onion, peeled and chopped
1	tsp. minced garlic
1	red bell pepper, seeded, pith removed, and coarsely chopped
1	green bell pepper, seeded, pith removed, and coarsely chopped
1	stalk celery, peeled and thinly sliced
1	tbsp. fresh thyme or 1 tsp. dried thyme leaves
1	tbsp. filé seasoning (Resources, p. 340)
28	oz. (1 large can) crushed tomatoes in purée
1	cup red table wine
1/2	tsp. crushed red pepper flakes
1	cup shrimp cooking liquid
1 1/2	cups fish stock or bottled clam juice
1	tbsp. paprika
1	tbsp. Worcestershire sauce
1/2	tsp. kosher salt
2	tbs. cornstarch mixed with 1/4 cup water
3/4	cup Italian parsley, stemmed and chopped hold out 1/4 cup for garnish

Filé is ground sassafras.

Cook rice first, and while it is cooking, cook shrimp.

To cook shrimp: Bring water to a boil; add shrimp and boil for 6 - 8 minutes until color changes to pink; rinse in cold water (to stop cooking), and drain.

To make stew:
1. Squeeze juice of 1/2 lemon over cooked shrimp and set aside.
2. Put oil in 6-quart saucepan and cook onion on medium heat until it is softened and translucent, 6 - 8 minutes. Add garlic, chopped peppers, celery, thyme, and filé seasoning and cook for 5 more minutes.
3. Add tomato, wine, pepper flakes, shrimp cooking liquid, fish stock, paprika, Worcestershire sauce, and salt. Simmer for 10 minutes and taste to determine the level of "heat" from the peppers. Add more if necessary. If you want to thicken it, add cornstarch mixture and simmer for 3 - 4 minutes. Add 1/2 cup parsley. **The stew can be made to this point and held for several hours. Add the cooked shrimp just before you are ready to serve.**
4. Add shrimp. When it is heated through, squeeze remaining lemon juice over it and serve.

To serve: Ladle immediately into shallow bowls, garnishing each serving with chopped parsley.

Gumbo

In my kitchen, Gumbo and Cajun Shrimp Stew (p. 194) are very similar, except that Gumbo includes rice, chicken, sausage, and filé seasoning, and it is made with a brown sauce, which makes it gravy-colored. That may not even resemble authentic Gumbo, but it tastes good, isn't so hot that it blows your head off, and it's my kitchen.

Yield: 4 - 6 servings
Preparation time: 50 minutes

1	quart water
1/2	lb. raw medium prawns (18 - 24 to the pound), peeled
1	cup clam juice
	juice of 1/2 lemon
4	oz. Andouille sausage or pepper bacon, cut into bite-sized pieces
2	tbsp. olive oil (or bacon fat)
1/2	medium yellow onion, peeled and chopped
2	tsp. minced garlic
2	tsp. filé seasoning (Resources, p. 340)
1	red bell pepper, seeded and coarsely chopped
1	green bell pepper, seeded and coarsely chopped
1	bunch Italian parsley, stemmed and chopped
2	tbsp. chopped fresh thyme, or 2 tsp. dried thyme leaves
2	tbsp. butter or margarine
2	tbsp. all purpose flour
4	cups chicken stock
2	cups cooked long grain white rice (1 cup uncooked)
8	oz. cooked chicken, torn into 2 - 3" strips
1	cup red wine
1	tbsp. paprika
1	tsp. crushed red pepper flakes
2	tsp. dried sage leaves
1	tsp. ground cumin
1	tbsp. Worcestershire sauce
1	cup tomato purée
1	tsp. kosher salt
4	oz. fresh okra, chopped, or 1 pk. frozen, chopped

Filé is ground sassafras.

1. Bring the water to a boil in a large saucepan over high heat. Add the prawns, cover, and boil for 6 - 8 minutes. Transfer the cooked prawns with a slotted spoon to a bowl and squeeze the lemon juice over them. Set aside.

2. In a skillet over medium high heat, cook the sausage or bacon until it is done, but not crisp. Remove with a slotted spoon and drain on paper towels.

3. Add the onion and garlic to the skillet and cook it at medium heat until softened, 3 - 4 minutes. Add bell pepper, parsley, and thyme and cook until the peppers begin to soften, about 5 more minutes. Transfer that mixture to a plate and set aside.

4. Melt the butter or margarine in the original saucepan over low heat. When it bubbles, add the flour and cook until it begins to brown, 6 - 8 minutes. It should be dark golden brown, but not burned. When it reaches that stage, whisk in 1 cup of the stock, whisking constantly until it is a thick sauce. Add the remaining stock, whisking as it thickens. Add all other ingredients and simmer, uncovered on low heat, for 15 minutes. It should be slightly thicker than regular soup.

To serve: Ladle into warmed soup bowls and serve with crusty French bread or cornbread.

Moroccan Curried Rice with Shrimp

This is a casserole recipe. If the sauce is served separate from the rice, and condiments are added, it becomes a more traditional, but Moroccan-flavored curry. Couscous substitutes well for rice.

Yield: 6 + servings
Preparation time: 40 minutes

1	tsp. lemon zest
	juice of 1 lemon, save the squeezed lemon
1 1/2	lbs. medium shrimp (18 - 24 to a pound), peeled
2	cups water

Sauce

2	tbsp. pure olive oil
1	medium yellow onion, sliced 1/4" thick and **Caramelized** (p. 231)
1/2	tsp. allspice
1	green pepper, seeds and pith removed, sliced into thin strips
3	cups fish stock or bottled clam juice*
1	14 1/2 oz. can premium diced tomatoes in purée
2	tbsp. **Garam Masala Curry Paste**® (Resources, p. 340) **or Moroccan Marinade** (p. 286)
4	cups cooked rice
1/3	cup finely chopped unsalted dry-roasted peanuts or cashews

*You may substitute 1 cup of the shrimp cooking water and 1 cup unsweetened coconut milk.

STOCK BAG
Remember your Stock Bag (p. 12).

Preheat oven to 350°.

1. Cook the shrimp in the water with the squeezed-out lemon. Rinse and drain. **Save the cooking liquid.**

2. While it cooks, make the sauce by combining onions, allspice, and bell pepper in a saucepan with the oil, and cooking over medium low heat for 5 minutes. Add stock, tomato, and curry paste, and simmer for 5 more minutes.

3. Add the cooked shrimp to the sauce.

4. Put the cooked rice into a casserole dish, and mix 2 cups of the sauce with the rice. Pour the remaining sauce over the top. Bake for 8 minutes, to heat through and set flavors.

To serve: Garnish each serving with chopped nuts and serve pickled lime or chutney (ready-made) on the side.

Shrimp Curry

This is more Asian than East Indian. It tastes wonderful, and condiments are unnecessary.

Yield: 4 - 6 servings
Preparation time: 30 - 35 minutes

>   2 cups uncooked Asian or basmati rice
>   2 lbs. medium shrimp (18 - 24 to the pound),
>   peeled, and set aside
>   1/4 cup pure olive oil
>   2 tbsp. minced garlic
>   1/2 cup sliced water chestnuts, rinsed and
>   drained on paper towel
>   2 cans unsweetened coconut milk
>   (Resources, p. 340)
>   1 cup Asian fish sauce (Resources, p. 340) **or**
>   clam juice
>   1/2 tsp. crushed red pepper flakes
>   1/4 cup minced green onion, plus 2 green onions
>   cut in thin slices on a diagonal
>   juice from 2 limes
> 1 1/2 tsp. Garam Masala Curry Paste® (Resources,
>   p. 340) **or Moroccan Marinade** (p. 286)
>   2 tbsp. cornstarch mixed with 3 tbsp. water
>   1/4 cup chopped fresh cilantro

1. Put rice in a saucepan and add cold water to cover by 3/4". Bring to a boil, uncovered. Turn the heat down to low, cover, and simmer for 20 minutes. Remove from heat and let it stand, covered, for at least 10 - 15 minutes.

2. While rice is cooking, heat olive oil in a large skillet over medium high heat, until it is hot but not smoking. Add shrimp, and sauté for 3 minutes, moving the pan continuously to avoid sticking or burning. With a slotted spoon, remove cooked shrimp and set aside.

3. Turn heat down to medium low and add garlic, chestnuts, coconut milk, fish sauce, pepper flakes, minced onion, lime juice, and curry mix. Simmer for 6 - 8 minutes.

4. Add cornstarch paste and simmer for 5 more minutes, until mixture thickens. Put shrimp back into the sauce along with cilantro and half the sliced green onion. Simmer for 3 more minutes. Transfer to a heated serving bowl and garnish with remaining sliced green onion. Serve with cooked rice.

If you can't find unsweetened coconut milk, substitute chicken stock.

Good Old-Fashioned Pot Roast

This recipe had to be invented in the 50's by Mrs. Cleaver; she probably used frozen peas and carrots. Don't despair over the canned soup and packaged soup mix; just try it, then scoff if you will. The time-bake oven gadget was invented for this pot roast; it goes into the oven frozen before breakfast, and comes out 6 p.m., meat-falling-off-the-bone wonderful.

Yield: 6 servings
Preparation time: 10 minutes, including preparing the vegetables.
Cooking time: 5 hours (but you don't have to be there until the last hour)

1	beef chuck or bottom round roast (round bone preferable) approximately 2 1/2 lbs.
1	can cream of mushroom soup, undiluted
1	envelope dried onion soup mix
1	medium yellow onion, trimmed, peeled, and sliced (about 1/3" thick)
3 - 4	sprigs fresh herb (tarragon, thyme, savory), or 3 tsp. dried
3	russet potatoes, washed, peeled and cut into 2" chunks (about 2 cups)
4 - 6	carrots, peeled and sliced on diagonal into 2" chunks

For frozen meat:

1. Unwrap the meat and put it into a roasting pan. Spread the undiluted mushroom soup over the meat and sprinkle the onion soup mix over the mushroom soup. Place the onion slices over the dried soup. Cover with foil, making sure the edges are sealed.

2. Place pan in oven and set the time bake for 4 hours at 275°, so that it will be finished cooking 1 hour before you want to serve it.

3. One hour before serving, unwrap the foil and place the prepared vegetables and herbs around the meat. Seal the foil and continue cooking for an hour.

For thawed meat: Follow the same procedure, but reduce the
initial cooking time to 2 hours.

VARIATIONS
Use tiny new potatoes or cannellini beans, rinsed and drained.
Use those packaged, peeled small carrots and/or winter root
vegetables.
Add 1 fennel bulb, cut in half, then sliced (about 1/3" thick).
Add 1 cup red table wine.
Add 1/2 lb. small button mushrooms with stems removed, or
1/2 lb. fresh wild mushrooms.

Add the potatoes, beans, carrots, fennel, winter roots, or wine at
the final hour; add mushrooms 30 minutes before serving.

LEFTOVERS
**Use leftovers for Pot Roast
Ragu (next page), or
Leftover Meat Soup (p. 131),
or Quick Pasties or Turn-
overs (p. 161), or Shepherd's
Pie (p. 213).**

Pot Roast Ragu

VARIATION: PORK RAGU

This recipe is designed for leftover Good Old-Fashioned Pot Roast (p. 201); it would be too contrived to make it from scratch.

Yield: 4 - 6 servings
Preparation and cooking time: 15 minutes

> **1/2 - 1 lb. leftover Pot Roast** (p. 201) **with vegetables**
> **leftover gravy plus chicken or meat Stock**
> (p. 108) **to equal 2 cups**
> **1 14 1/2 oz. can premium diced tomatoes**
> **in purée**
> **1/2 cup Sun-Dried Tomato Pesto, optional but**
> **fabulous** (store bought, or see p. 284)
> **2 tsp. dried thyme or oregano**
> **1/2 cup red table wine**
> **cornstarch paste if necessary (1 tbsp.**
> **cornstarch mixed with 2 tbsp. water)**

<table><tr><td>STOCK BAG
Remember
your Stock
Bag (p. 12).</td></tr></table>

1. Shred the leftover pot roast and mash the vegetables with a fork.

2. Put the gravy, the meat, and vegetables into a large saucepan and bring it all to a simmer over low heat. Simmer for 10 minutes, to let the flavors blend. If it is thinner than very thick soup, add the cornstarch paste and continue to simmer for 5 more minutes until the starch is cooked. (If that makes it too thick, add a little water.)

This is delicious served over pasta, gnocchi (potato pasta dumplings), polenta, or mashed potatoes.

PORK RAGU
Substitute leftover pork (roast or chops) (p. 201) for pot roast.

- Thin leftover ragu just a little with stock, and it becomes a wonderful, rich soup.
- If the leftover pot roast is in its original cooking pan, pour a little stock or wine into it, and heat it. That will make it easier to get the gravy and scrape out the cooking residue.

Barbecued Pot Roast

VARIATION: BARBECUED FLANK STEAK

*To tenderize and flavor the meat, it must marinate for at least
12 hours, so if you need it tonight and it's not 5 a.m., maybe you
should think about flank steak or burgers.*

Yield: 4 - 6 servings
**Preparation time: 5 - 10 minutes for marinade; 24 hours to
marinate. Cooking time: 40 minutes**

> **1 3 - 4 lb. chuck or bottom round steak (about
> 2 1/2 - 3" thick)**

Marinade
> **1 cup red table wine**
> **1/2 cup Dijon Glaze** (p. 105)
> **1 tbsp. Worcestershire sauce**
> **1 tsp. dried thyme**
> **1 tbsp. fresh rosemary, minced, or 1 tsp.
> dried rosemary, crushed**
> **1/2 tsp. crushed red pepper flakes**
> **whole sprigs of fresh rosemary or parsley,
> for garnish**
> **1 tsp. meat tenderizer**

Barbecue Sauce
Dijon Glaze: Add 2 tbsp. marinade, to additional 1/2 cup of
Dijon Glaze.

Sauce: Add 2 tbsp. extra virgin olive oil to remaining marinade.

1. Blend the ingredients for the marinade.

2. With a sharp paring knife, cut vertical slits all over the surface
   of the roast, penetrating it completely. Put the pot roast in a
   large plastic bag (zip types usually are not large enough to
   close over that size meat, but those cook-the-turkey-in-a-bag
   in the paper section of the market work), and pour the
   marinade over the meat. Close the end of the bag, and place
   it in a pan that is just big enough to hold it, so the marinade
   will be touching the meat.

3. Marinate in the refrigerator for at least 12 and preferably
   24 hours.

4. Remove the meat from the refrigerator and bring to room
   temperature. Heat the barbecue or grill to steak-cooking
   temperature. Remove the meat from the marinating bag and
   pour the marinade into a small saucepan. Set the pan aside.

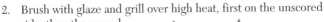

5. Blend the Dijon Glaze, and brush it over the entire surface of the meat. Put the meat on the grill, high enough over the coals so that it can cook through without charring the top and bottom. Because it is so thick, this meat will take longer to cook than most steaks.

6. Whisk the olive oil into the marinade and simmer over low heat for 8 minutes. When the meat has seared, brush baste it with the sauce, first on one side, then on the other.

7. While the meat is cooking, warm a serving platter and make sure your carving knife is very sharp. Reheat the sauce just before the meat is done. When the meat is cooked, transfer it from the grill to a warmed platter and let it rest for about 5 minutes. Slice thin (1/4") with a sharp carving knife.

To serve: Pour warm sauce over the sliced meat, garnish with several sprigs of rosemary or parsley, and serve immediately.

BARBECUED FLANK STEAK
Preparation and cooking time: 30 minutes

> **3 lbs. flank steak (2 large steaks)**
> **1/2 cup Dijon Glaze**

1. Score the steak on one side by making shallow cuts diagonally across the grain first from one direction, then the next.

2. Brush with glaze and grill over high heat, first on the unscored side, then the scored.

Osso Bucco With White Beans and Winter Root Vegetables

Classic country Italian comfort food, Osso Bucco (veal shank), is not well known in America. Because veal is controversial and difficult to obtain, I have substituted beef shank, and it's great. This is the quintessential big pot dinner that will provide leftovers for 1 or 2 nights. It's unpretentious, and bread-soaking scrumptious.

Yield: 8 + servings
Preparation time: 20 minutes. This is a day-at-home dish. It takes about 4 hours to cook to the really tender, fall-off-the-bone stage.

1/2	cup all-purpose flour
2	tsp. dried oregano, basil, or marjoram
4	lb. beef shank, cut 2" thick
	olive oil
1	package onion soup mix
2	cups beef stock or water
2	yellow onions, peeled and cut in half
2	cloves garlic, minced (or 2 tsp. dehydrated, minced garlic)
2	cups Pinot Noir or red table wine
2	14 1/2 oz. cans premium diced tomatoes in purée
1/4	cup chopped fresh marjoram or oregano or 2 tbsp. fresh thyme
3	lb. winter root vegetables (carrot, parsnip, turnip, rutabaga, celeriac), peeled and cut into 2" chunks
2	15 oz. cans large white beans (great northern, cannellini), drained and rinsed
1/2	cup chopped fresh Italian parsley, divided into 2 portions
1/4	cup grated lemon zest

Preheat oven to 350°. You need a big roasting pan or oven-proof casserole.

1. Mix dried herb with flour and dredge the meat pieces in the mixture. Heat oil in fry pan on medium and brown bones (in stages). As meat pieces are browned, transfer them to a heavy oven-proof roasting pan.

2. When all the meat is in the pan, slice the onion halves into 1/4" slices. Add soup mix, stock or water, garlic, wine, tomato, and fresh herbs. Cover pan.

3. Bake for 3 hours or until meat is slightly tender. Skim off any fat on top of the juice. Add the vegetables, cover again, and cook for 45 more minutes.

4. Remove the cover, add the lemon zest, the white beans, and half of the chopped parsley. Continue to cook until the juice thickens slightly and the meat is very tender, 30 - 40 minutes.

To serve: Put pieces of cooked meat and portions of vegetables and beans in heated shallow soup plates. Ladle sauce over the meat and sprinkle each portion with parsley. Serve at once with lots of fresh, crusty French or Italian bread.

Note: This is also delicious without the white beans, and served with mashed potatoes or pasta tossed with chopped parsley and olive oil.

Hint #18: Beano®, a product available in most drug stores and many grocery stores, breaks down undigestible proteins before they reach the large intestine (where bacteria break them down, causing gas). A tasteless liquid, Beano® is added after legumes are cooked, just before they are eaten.

Meat Loaf

VARIATIONS: TUSCAN MEATBALLS, HAM LOAF, GROUND CHICKEN LOAF

Meat loaf sandwich from the 2nd Avenue Athens Cafe: thick slices of homemade sourdough bread with a little mayonnaise and mustard, and a thick juicy slab of warm meat loaf. And a frosty cold beer. Unforgettable! During my childhood, as dependably as candy canes, dinner on the third day after Christmas was ham loaf with mustard sauce, mashed potatoes, peas, and pear salad.

Yield: 6 - 8 servings
Preparation time: 25 - 30 minutes. Cooking time: 1 hour for loaves; 35 minutes for meatballs

          2 lbs. lean ground beef
          1 large yellow onion, diced
      3/4 cup bread crumbs
          2 tbsp. dried Italian or mixed herbs
          2 eggs, beaten slightly
          1 tbsp. Worcestershire sauce
      1/2 tsp. crushed red pepper flakes
      1/4 cup finely chopped Italian parsley
      1/4 cup milk or stock
      1/4 cup tomato paste, mixed with
          2 tbsp. Dijon mustard
          1 tsp. kosher salt

Preheat oven to 350°.

MEAT LOAF
1. In a large mixing bowl, with your hands, blend all ingredients except tomato paste and Dijon mustard.
2. Press into a loaf pan and spread tomato paste mixture over the top. Bake for 1 hour. Drain off excess fat.

TUSCAN MEATBALLS
Add 1 can (14 1/2 oz.) premium diced tomatoes in purée, 2 tsp. minced garlic, and 2 tbsp. dried oregano leaves. Eliminate milk or stock and tomato paste/mustard mixture.

1. Mix all ingredients as in Step 1 above.
2. Form mixture into meatballs (about the size of golf balls). In a large skillet on medium high heat, brown meatballs on all sides. Transfer to a roasting pan and bake for 30 minutes. Drain on parchment paper before serving.

HAM LOAF

Substitute 1 lb. ground ham plus 1 lb. ground chicken for beef, and add 1 tbsp. dried mixed herbs plus 1 tsp. dried sage leaves. Eliminate tomato paste. Mix 2 tbsp. Dijon with 2 tbsp. whole grain mustard. Spread over top and bake for 1 hour.

GROUND CHICKEN LOAF

- 2 lbs. ground chicken
- 1 cup finely chopped green onion
- 1 tsp. kosher salt
- 2 tbsp. crushed sage leaves
- 2 tsp. ground cumin
- 2 Anaheim peppers, stems and pith removed, finely chopped, or 12 oz. canned chopped green chilies
- 2 eggs, slightly beaten with 1/4 cup milk
- 1/2 tsp. crushed red pepper flakes
- 1/2 cup finely chopped cilantro
- 1/2 cup chopped and softened tomatillos (microwave) or canned
- 1/4 cup bottled tomato or green chili salsa

1. Mix all ingredients except salsa, as in Steps 1 and 2 above.
2. Spread salsa over the top and bake for 1 hour.

Roasted or Grilled Lamb

These are expensive cuts of meat, so I recommend asking the butcher to select yours personally.

Yield: 4 - 6 servings
Preparation time: 10 minutes

> **rack of lamb (3 ribs per person) or**
> **1 lamb tenderloin per 2 servings, or**
> **lamb chops (2 – 3 loins per serving; 1 large**
> **shoulder chop per serving)**
> **1/2 cup Garlic Rosemary Dijon Glaze** (p. 105)
> **1/4 cup bread crumbs (for roast or rack only)**

Preheat oven to 500° or grill to hot.

1. Brush entire surface of meat with Dijon Glaze. For roast or rack, mix bread crumbs with glaze first.

2. Bake or grill until desired degree of doneness, 8 - 10 minutes for tenderloin, 5 minutes per side for chops (grilled), up to 18 minutes for a 6-rib rack. Remember, meat cooks for 3 minutes after it is off the heat.

For leg of lamb: I cook Dijon-glazed leg of lamb at 425°, until it shows as rare *beef* on the meat thermometer, because I like *rare* lamb.

LEFTOVERS
Roasted and grilled lamb leftover ideas:
Shepherd's Pie (p. 213), Lamb Curry
(p. 213), Lamb Soup (p. 131), Lamb and
Chevre Salad (p. 269), or Lamb Sandwich
(2 pieces of good bread, Homemade
Mayonnaise [p. 279], salt and pepper, my
father's all-time favorite sandwich).

Lamb Shanks with Orange, Rosemary, and Barley

The beauty of lamb shanks is two fabulous meals: lamb shanks with barley the first night and lamb barley soup the second. The orange in this recipe lightens the meat's flavor density, and accents the garlic and rosemary. Hint: If you haven't bought lamb shanks before, make sure they are split by the butcher so they will fit easily into a casserole dish.

Yield: 6 servings
Preparation time: 35 minutes, including barley.
Cooking time: 3 1/2 hours

6	cups water
1	cup barley
1	cup all-purpose flour
6 - 8	lamb shanks
3	tbsp. pure olive oil
1	head garlic, separated and peeled
2	oranges, unpeeled and cut into 12 wedges
3 or 4	sprigs of fresh rosemary, or 3 tbsp. dried and crushed
1/2	tsp. crushed red pepper flakes
2	cups red table wine

Preheat oven to 275°. You will need a large, oven-proof casserole dish.

1. Boil the barley in water for 10 minutes. Drain and set aside.

2. While it is cooking, dredge the lamb shanks in flour. Heat the oil in a heavy skillet and brown dredged lamb shanks over medium high heat. Remove from the heat, and transfer to a roasting pan.

3. Crush garlic cloves with the flat blade of a large knife, and distribute them among the lamb shanks. Squeeze the orange wedges over the lamb, and toss them in among the shanks. Take the leaves off the rosemary stems, and sprinkle them over the lamb. (Put the herb stems and garlic skins in the stock bag.)

4. Add the partially cooked barley, the crushed pepper, and 1 cup red wine to the lamb shanks.

5.   Cover the pan with a close fitting lid or foil, and bake for
     2 1/2 hours. The lamb should be cooked but still firmly on the
     bones. Uncover, pour the second cup of wine into the pan, and
     continue cooking for another 20 - 25 minutes.

To serve: Take the pan out of the oven and let it cool for
           15 minutes before serving, as the meat can be very hot.
           Transfer to a serving dish or to individual plates and serve.

LEFTOVERS
See Leftover Meat Soup (p. 131) for
a delicious way to use everything
you have left over in one pot.

STOCK BAG
Remember your Stock Bag (p. 12).

Shepherd's Pie

VARIATION: DEEP DISH MEAT PIE

*This is a recipe designed to use up leftover meat and gravy. It is
expensive and time consuming to make from scratch, and it doesn't
have that flavor-penetrated leftover taste. As the name implies, the
traditional meat is lamb, but it is just as good made with leftover
pot roast or pork roast. (Who says pigs can't be herded?) Add
whatever vegetables you wish.*

Yield: 4 - 6 servings
Preparation time: 25 minutes with boxed potatoes.
Cooking time: 20 minutes

LEFTOVERS
Besides
Roasted Lamb
(p. 210), two
other recipes
that will give
you meat for
this pie are
Pot Roast
(p. 202) and
Pork Tender-
loin (p. 84).

8	oz. leftover lamb or other roasted meat, cut into bite-sized chunks (about 2 cups)
2	cups gravy (see next page)
1	medium yellow onion, peeled and diced (about 1 cup)
3	tsp. minced garlic (about 3 cloves)
1	turnip, peeled and diced (about 1 cup)
2	stalks celery, sliced into bite-sized pieces
1	carrot, peeled, sliced
1	tsp. dried herb, or 2 tbsp. chopped fresh herb (thyme, rosemary, tarragon, savory)
1	bay leaf, cracked
1/2	cup water
	kosher salt and cracked pepper to taste
3	cups whipped mashed potatoes from scratch, or enough boxed potatoes, butter, and water to make 3 cups
2	tbsp. grated Parmesan cheese
1 - 1 1/2	tsp. paprika

Preheat oven to 375°.

1. Mix meat with gravy (if you don't have any, make it in a small
   saucepan) and set aside to let flavors blend.

2. If you are using leftover cooked vegetables, cut them into bite-
   sized pieces and put them in the meat mixture. Put all the raw
   vegetables and herbs in a large saucepan with 1/2 cup water,
   on medium high, cover pan, and steam until vegetables are
   just softened enough to be pierced with a fork (al strong
   dente!). The microwave works very well for this step. As they
   cook, you may remove some before others.

3. Drain any remaining water from vegetables. Add the meat and gravy mixture to the vegetables, mix and simmer, uncovered on low heat, for 5 minutes to blend the flavors. Taste and add salt and pepper if necessary. The finished filling should be like stew; if it's too thin, let it simmer 5 minutes longer.

4. While it is simmering, make the whipped potatoes. Add the grated cheese, taste, and correct the seasoning if necessary.

5. Transfer the filling to an oven-proof casserole dish. With a large spoon or rubber spatula, cover the filling to the edge with the potatoes. Make pretty dips and swoops and sprinkle with paprika.

6. Bake until the potatoes begin to brown and the filling bubbles up around them. If you wish to have browned tips on the potatoes, put the pie under the broiler for 3 - 4 minutes.

To serve: This is definitely a "serve at the table item" because it is so pretty. Scoop the pie into shallow soup or pasta bowls.

DEEP DISH MEAT PIE

Add 1 medium-sized potato, peeled and diced. Substitute
1 uncooked pie crust for mashed potatoes.
2 tbsp. egg wash (1 egg white beaten with 1 tbsp. water).

You will need a 9" pie dish or a 3" deep casserole dish.

1. Follow Steps 1- 3 on preceding page.

2. Ladle the meat mixture into the baking dish. Roll out the pie dough into a circle 1" larger in diameter than the dish. Put it over the pie filling and crimp the edges. With a sharp knife, pierce the crust in several places to allow steam to release. Brush egg wash over the crust.

3. Bake for 30 minutes, or until the crust is cooked and golden brown.

If you don't have leftover gravy, use homemade or canned meat stock thickened with cornstarch paste (2 tbsp. water mixed into 1 tbsp. corn starch), 1 tsp. dried or 1 tbsp. fresh chopped herb, 1/4 cup red wine, salt and pepper.

Lamb Curry

*I have always made lamb curry with leftover Lamb (p. 210),
rather than from raw meat. In South Africa, curry often is served
over barley, and with cold beer rather than wine; it is a wonderful
partnership.*

Yield: 4 - 6 servings
Preparation time: 60 minutes

      2 **cups long grain white rice**
   1 1/2 **lb. leftover lamb roast, cut into bit-sized**
          pieces and set aside
          leftover demi-glace or gravy and the residue
          from the roasting pan
      2 **tbsp. butter or margarine**
      2 **tbsp. all-purpose flour**
      3 **cups meat or chicken stock (I usually prepare**
          a day in advance for this and make stock
          with the lamb bone)
      1 **tsp. minced garlic**
      1 **medium yellow onion, chopped (1/2 cup)**
      1 **cup dry red table wine**
      2 **tbsp. Garam Masala Curry Paste**® (Resources,
          p. 340) **or Moroccan Marinade** (p. 286)
      1 **tart apple, cored and diced**
          kosher salt to taste

Condiments

          mango chutney (ready-made)
          finely chopped green onion mixed with
              minced radish
          toasted, shredded or shaved unsweetened
              coconut
          finely chopped roasted peanuts
          minced Anaheim chili pepper
          minced red bell pepper or finely chopped,
              peeled, and seeded tomato
          chopped banana drizzled with lemon juice

**How many condiments are enough? Tradition
calls for 1 per eater.**

1. Put rice in a saucepan and add cold water to cover by 3/4". Bring water to a boil, uncovered, for 3 minutes, turn the heat down to simmer, cover the rice, and cook for 20 minutes. Remove from heat and let it stand, still covered, for at least 10 - 15 minutes.

2. While the rice is cooking, add 1/2 cup water, garlic, and onion to the lamb roasting pan, and bring it to a boil. Scrape the cooking residue away from the bottom, simmer the sauce for 5 minutes, and transfer to a large saucepan. Turn the heat to low and simmer for 5 minutes. Add the demi-glace.

3. In a small pan over medium low heat, melt the butter or margarine and add the flour. Stir the flour as it cooks. When it bubbles and begins to brown, add 1 cup stock; stir into a smooth paste, then transfer to the other sauce. Add remaining stock, wine, cut lamb, curry spice, and apple and simmer for 10 minutes until the curry is thickened slightly. Correct seasoning with salt or more spice mix if necessary.

To serve: Put a portion of rice on a heated plate, and ladle curry over the rice. Serve condiments in small separate containers on the table.

Pork Tenderloin with Demi-Glace

VARIATION: GRILLED DIJON GLAZE PORK CHOPS, CRANBERRY DEMI-GLACE, ASIAN-FLAVORED MARINADE

Pork tenderloin always cooks more quickly than I expect it to, so I have learned (the hard way) to serve it with things I can cook and hold for a few minutes.

Yield: 4 servings
Preparation and cooking time: 30 minutes

> **2 pork tenderloins (3 for leftover recipe)**
> **1/4 cup Dijon Glaze** (p. 105) **with added herbs and chopped shallots or a spicy marinade**
> **1/2 cup dry white or lighter red wine**

1. Brush 2 tbsp. Dijon Glaze over meat on all sides or put marinade over meat and cover while flavors absorb.

2. Heat grill to high or preheat oven to 450°, and heat a heavy non-stick skillet in it or on top of the stove. When the oven or grill is up to temperature, put the meat onto the grill or into the hot pan and cook, turning once just after the meat has seared on one side. Total cooking time, 12 - 15 minutes.

3. While the meat is cooking, mix the wine and the remaining Dijon and herbs in a small bowl.

4. When the meat is done, transfer it to a cutting board and hold it for 2 - 3 minutes so juices will re-absorb. Put the cooking pan on the stove on medium high heat, add the wine mixture, stirring it with any cooking residue in the pan. Cook the sauce until it has reduced and thickened slightly.

To serve: Place sliced meat on heated plates. Pour demi-glace over meat and serve immediately.

DIJON GLAZE PORK CHOPS
Brush chops with Dijon Glaze and grill over very high heat.

CRANBERRY DEMI-GLACE
Add 1 tbsp. finely chopped shallot to the glaze and 2 tbsp. cranberry chutney or chunky cranberry sauce to the wine.

ASIAN-FLAVORED MARINADE
Add 1 tbsp. *unseasoned* rice vinegar, 1/4 cup sake, 1 tbsp. Dijon Glaze, and 2 - 3 tbsp. water to leftover marinade. Reduce by half.

Stuffed Pork Chops

The key to this is lean, thick pork chops.

Yield: 4 servings
Preparation time: 30 minutes. Cooking time, including sauce: up to 30 minutes, depending upon the thickness of the chops

>   2 tsp. granulated sugar
>   1 medium yellow onion, peeled and cut in half, then sliced (1/4")
>   4 large, 1 1/2 - 2" thick pork chops, or 8 thinner ones
>   2 tbsp. Dijon Glaze (p. 105) with 1/2 tsp. dried sage added

Stuffing

> 1/4 cup pine nuts
>   1 tsp. dried sage leaves
>   2 cups dried, cubed stuffing mix (the crumbled mixes will get too dense)

Demi-Glace

>   1 cup dry white table wine

Place a large, oven-proof fry pan in the oven and preheat to 450°.

1. Slit a 3" pocket into each chop, leaving an inch next to the bone at the top and bottom uncut. Set aside.

2. Sprinkle sugar over the bottom of a small skillet. Turn the heat on low; when the sugar dissolves and begins to color, 5 - 6 minutes, add the onions, stirring to coat the slices with sugar. Cook until the onions turn caramel colored (Watch closely because from caramel to black takes about 45 seconds). Set aside.

3. Heat a small skillet on medium high. Add the pine nuts and, stirring constantly, cook them until they are toasted. Remove from the heat and put the nuts into a medium-sized mixing bowl.

4. Add the stuffing mix and the sage, and make stuffing according to the package directions, using a bit less moisture than called for. Cooking the pork chop adds moisture to the stuffing inside.

5. Open the pocket of each pork chop and put stuffing inside loosely, not packed tight (or put stuffing between two thinner chops). Brush each chop with Dijon Glaze over the top and sides, including over the stuffing that shows. Carefully, with a thick pot holder, remove the hot pan from the oven, and place the chops in the pan, glaze side down. Brush glaze over the top and put the pan back into the oven. Cook thick chops for 6 - 8 minutes and thin chops for 3 - 5. With tongs or a spatula, turn the chops carefully so the stuffing doesn't fall out. Cook the other side, the same amount of time.

6. Remove from the oven, and transfer the chops to a warmed platter for 5 minutes to rest and reabsorb any juice they lose. While they are resting, put the same fry pan on medium low heat, pick out any pieces of stuffing that may have fallen out of the chops, add 1/2 - 3/4 cup stock or white wine, and stirring constantly, simmer until it is smooth and reduced by half, about 5 minutes. If the chops have lost any juice, pour that into the sauce as it simmers. While the Demi-Glace is cooking, heat the caramelized onions on top of the stove, in the oven, or in a microwave.

To serve: Put the chops on warmed dinner plates, ladle sauce over them, and pile each chop with caramelized onion. Serve immediately.

Pork, Lentil, and Mushroom Stew

Stew, another great comfort food, was developed as a solution to tough meat that needed to be tenderized, and as a creative way to extend small quantities of leftover meat. This recipe doesn't start with tough meat, but it does extend leftover pork in what I believe is a healthful, delicious way.

Yield: 4 - 6 servings
Preparation time: 20 minutes. Cooking time: 2 hours

3	cups water
1 1/2	cups lentils
1	cup dried wild mushrooms, re-hydrated in 2 cups water
8	oz. leftover pork, cut into bite-sized chunks (about 2 cups)
3	cups gravy (add canned stock or homemade chicken stock to make the 3 cups, or see next page)
1	large yellow onion, peeled, coarsely (about 1 cup) chopped, and Caramelized (p. 231)
1	carrot, peeled and sliced
3	tbsp. chopped fresh sage, or 2 tsp. dried sage leaves
1	bay leaf, cracked
1/2	lb. button mushrooms, stems trimmed
	kosher salt and cracked pepper

LEFTOVERS
Pork Tenderloin (p. 217) is the recipe that provides this leftover.

This recipe works for leftover beef also.

1. Rinse lentils and sort out pebbles. Fill a 4-quart saucepan with water, add lentils, and cook over medium heat, covered, for 30 minutes. Meanwhile, re-hydrate the dried mushrooms in water. Mix the meat with gravy and set aside to let flavors blend. Caramelize the onions (p. 231).

2. Drain the lentils (save the water) and put them in a large stew pot. Add the mushrooms, with their water, the meat and gravy mixture, and 1 cup of the lentil water. Turn the heat to medium low and begin the incredibly aromatic simmering.

3. Add the carrots and herbs, cover the pan, and simmer for 10 minutes. Uncover, turn the heat down to low, and barely simmer for another 20 minutes. (If you are serving biscuits, this is the time to mix and bake them.) If the stew thickens too much as it simmers, add some of the lentil water.

4. Add the sliced mushrooms and simmer another 15 minutes. Taste the stew (carefully, it's very hot.) Add salt if necessary and 3 turns of freshly ground pepper.

To serve: Ladle the stew into large, warm bowls.

- If there isn't leftover gravy, use 3 cups homemade or canned meat stock thickened with cornstarch paste (2 tbsp. water mixed into 1 tbsp. cornstarch), 1 tsp. dried or 1 tbsp. fresh chopped sage, 1/4 cup red wine, salt and pepper.
- See recipes for Homemade and Modified Canned Stock (p. 108).

Hint #26: If you love the flavor of wild mushrooms as much as I do, this hint will make your day. Some specialty food companies produce powdered wild mushrooms to flavor sauces, soups, etc., but it is very expensive. I make my own by grinding packaged dried wild mushrooms into a fine powder. It stores perfectly in a darkened cupboard and is always ready.

Sausage, Pepper, and Bread Kabobs

Practically every culture has its version of a grilled meal on a skewer. This one is Italian.

Yield: 8 kabobs
Preparation time: 1 hour (plus time to soak wooden skewers)

> 8 metal or wooden skewers (soak wooden skewers in water for 1 hour before using)
> 8 large, mild Italian sausages (fennel flavoring is delicious grilled)
> 3 bell peppers, preferably different colors, stems, seeds, and pith removed
> 1 medium-sized loaf of crusty French or Italian bread

Grilling Marinade
> 2 tsp. minced garlic
> 2 tbsp. minced fresh rosemary, or 2 tsp. dried
> 1/4 tsp. crushed red pepper flakes
> 3/4 cup extra virgin olive oil

1. Cut each sausage into 2" long pieces, each prepared bell pepper into 8 pieces, and the bread into 24, 2" cubes.

2. To make the marinade: combine all ingredients and heat for 5 minutes over medium heat.

3. Alternately thread the skewers with sausage, bell pepper, and bread, then brush each one with marinade. Marinate for 30 minutes (while the grill heats). Grill over low heat coals, turning often, until the sausage is done, about 20 minutes.

Cooking Fresh Vegetables

STEAMED, ROASTED, SAUTÉED, ROASTED GARLIC

Several different methods of cooking vegetables are described in the following recipes. **The most important thing to remember about cooking vegetables is to cook them as little as possible, so that their delicate flavors and vibrant colors will remain intact.** *Cooking at high temperatures keeps the colors from fading and allows the vegetables to cook quickly, so they don't break down and get soft. Blanching raw vegetables sets the color, so it is more important for roasting and sautéing than steaming.*

Harder root vegetables will cook faster if they are julienne-cut (match stick), diced, or thinly sliced. If you want to cook several different vegetables at once, cut the harder vegetables into very small or thin pieces, and they will cook in the same amount of time as softer vegetables cut into larger pieces.

Preparing Vegetables

High Heat Cooking: This term refers to a hard boil for steaming, high temperature for the microwave, 450° for roasting, or medium high heat for sautéing. It does not mean pan-smoking hot.

To blanch vegetables: You will need a large saucepan or pot with 6 cups water and a large mixing bowl filled with ice water (lots of ice in the water). Bring the water in the pan to a hard boil, and dip prepared (washed, peeled if appropriate, tips or stems removed, etc.) vegetables into the boiling water just long enough for it to return to its original hard boil (no longer than 1 minute, maximum). Remove the vegetables with a slotted spoon and plunge them into the ice water for 1 minute to stop the cooking. Transfer the cooled vegetables to a colander and drain. Blanch in small batches (about 2 cups), so the water can reboil quickly. The vegetables are then ready to be sautéed, steamed, roasted, grilled, or added to soups.

Vegetables to blanch: carrots, broccoli, cauliflower, winter roots, winter squashes, string beans, peas, asparagus, Brussels sprouts, cabbage

Vegetables that should not be blanched: bell peppers, chili peppers, potatoes, summer squashes, eggplant, onion, garlic, tomato, radishes

Chiffonade-cut for leafy vegetables: Stack leaves in an even pile. With the leaves facing you horizontally, roll the stack into a tight roll away from you. Cut the roll into slices, as you would with a jelly roll. The result is ribbon or chiffonade slices.

Steamed Vegetables

> **prepared vegetables**
> **minimum amount of water (just enough to provide lots of steam; they shouldn't be immersed)**

Expandable metal vegetable steamers that fit into saucepans or bamboo steamers work best, but if you don't have one of those, this works also:

1. Put water into container. Add vegetables, cover, and steam on medium high until vegetables are just soft enough to pierce with a fork. Microwave works very well.

2. Remove from heat, strain off remaining water, and serve immediately.

3. **For marinated, chilled vegetables:** Prepare an ice water bath while vegetables are cooking, then dip them into it to stop the cooking. Drain and pour marinade over the warm vegetables.

Oven-Roasted Vegetables

> **4 cups raw vegetables**
> **1/4 cup extra virgin olive oil**
> **2 tsp. minced garlic**
> **2 tbsp. fresh chopped herbs, or**
> **2 tsp. dried herb leaves**

> **STOCK BAG**
> Remember your Stock Bag (p. 12).

Preheat oven to 450°. Use a heavy pan which is just large enough to hold the vegetables in a single layer, barely touching.

1. Blanch appropriate prepared vegetables to set color.

2. Put the olive oil, garlic, and fresh herbs into a medium-sized mixing bowl. Stir to blend.

3. Add the firmest vegetables to the oil mixture and toss to coat. With a slotted spoon, transfer them to the roasting pan and cook until they begin to soften, about 10 minutes. Move them around with a spatula to prevent sticking and to expose all sides to the bottom of the pan.

4. Coat the remaining, softer vegetables in the oil mixture and add them to the pan. Roast until the vegetables are cooked and show some browning on all sides, 15 - 20 minutes.

> **Hint #7:** To slice vegetables, lay them on a flat surface, and make a slice on one side to create a flat bottom. That way, the vegetables won't slip out from under the knife!

Sautéed Vegetables

     4-5 cups prepared vegetables
       2 tbsp. olive oil
       **2 tbsp. chopped fresh herb, or 2 tsp. dried
          herb leaves**
          Lemon Oil Drizzle (p. 283)

1. Blanch appropriate prepared vegetables to set color.

2. Heat oil in a skillet or sauté pan. Transfer blanched vegetables
    to the pan, add herbs and sauté, flipping with a spatula to
    prevent sticking, and cook just until they are soft enough to
    prick with a fork. If the vegetables are cut into small shapes,
    this will take less time than you think, maybe 2 - 3 minutes.
    Remove from heat.

3. Drizzle cooked vegetables with Lemon Oil Drizzle and serve
    immediately.

Roasted Garlic

       **1 large head garlic (very firm means
          very fresh)**
       1 tbsp. extra virgin olive oil

Preheat oven to 250°.

1. Remove those outer layers of skin that slough off easily.

2. Cut the tip off the head, and brush the whole head with oil.

3. Put the garlic into an oven-proof, non-reactive container,
    covered loosely with foil. Bake for 35 minutes until flesh
    is soft.

4. Remove from oven, separate cloves, and squeeze roasted
    garlic flesh out of the skin.

> **See Hint #30 (p. 18),
> non-reactive container.**

> **To speed the process by 10 minutes, precook
> the prepared garlic (tightly covered with
> plastic wrap) in the microwave on high heat
> for 1 minute.**

Grilled Marinated Vegetables

Grilled vegetables are really good if they are crisp and browned on the cooked surfaces and not overcooked inside. If you don't have a non-stick coated vegetable grill piece, place a wire baking rack over the grill so the vegetables won't slip through. The marinade contains olive oil, which protects the vegetables from drying out at high temperature.

Yield: 4 servings
Preparation time: 30 minutes. Cooking time: 20 minutes

> 4 **cups prepared vegetables**
> 1 1/4 **cups marinade (recipe follows)**
> 1/4 **cup finely chopped fresh herb for garnish**

Marinade

> 1 **cup extra virgin olive oil**
> 1 **tsp. minced garlic**
> 2 **tbsp. lemon juice**
> 1 **tbsp. minced oregano, basil, or other fresh herb**
> 2 **tbsp. soy sauce (optional)**

STOCK BAG
Remember your Stock Bag (p. 12).

1. Wash, cut, and blanch vegetables if appropriate. The pieces should be about two-bite size that can be turned easily.

2. Marinate the vegetables at room temperature in a zip-type plastic bag or a shallow dish for 30 minutes. Turn them several times to coat thoroughly with marinade.

3. While they marinate, heat the grill to high. Grill the vegetables until they can be pierced easily and have crisp, browned edges on all surfaces, about 20 minutes.

Serve at once or chill for other use.

> • **Japanese eggplant (the small, oblong, seedless variety), red onions, bell peppers, tomatoes, large button mushrooms, summer squash, fennel bulb, and potato grill really well and need little preparation other than cutting.**
> • **See p. 223 for how to prepare vegetables.**

Roasted Bell Peppers

VARIATION: ROASTED BELL PEPPERS WITH VINAIGRETTE (APPETIZER)

Until my good friend and food cohort, Sue Simpkins, taught me how, I dreaded roasting peppers. While we were on a vacation in Italy, where the peppers were just too wonderful to resist, she gently suggested that I was rushing the steaming and peeling them too soon, so the skin didn't come off. Now I sweat them for at least an hour, the skins slide off easily, and I roast peppers and dream about that hilltop kitchen in Tuscany.

Yield: 1 pint
Preparation time: scorching: 15 minutes; steaming: at least one hour; peeling: 10 minutes

> **4 firm, fresh bell peppers (try roasting several colors at once; they look beautiful together) Don't make vinaigrette unless you are serving these as an appetizer.**

Peppers may be roasted directly over a gas element or under the broiler. The object is to scorch the skin all over, cooking the pepper as little as possible in the process. It doesn't take long to scorch them, but they must be turned frequently, so it's a hands-on process.

For the oven: Preheat the oven to broil, setting the top rack as close to the element as possible without having the peppers touch the coils. Place the peppers on a baking sheet and broil, turning them as the skin bubbles and scorches.

For gas stoves: Place the peppers directly on the cooking element. Adjust the flame to about an inch from the peppers. Turn the peppers as they scorch.

1. When all sides are scorched, place peppers in paper or plastic bag, and close the end tight. Let them steam in the bag, at room temperature, for an hour (or all day if you scorch them in the morning and peel them at night).

2. Remove peppers and peel, using a paring knife and rinsing when necessary. Slit open the peppers, remove the seeds and cut out the white pith.

3. Cut the roasted peppers into long sections about 3/4" wide. Drain them on a paper towel.

ROASTED PEPPERS WITH VINAIGRETTE

Put pepper slices in a shallow bowl and pour Basic Vinaigrette (p. 273) over them. Sprinkle 3 tbsp. capers over the top and serve at room temperature.

With or without vinaigrette, roasted peppers store well, covered tightly with plastic wrap and refrigerated, for up to 5 days.

Sautéed Bell Peppers

The secret to this beautiful, tasty recipe is cutting the peppers so that all the pith is removed, then slicing the pieces into very thin strips. You will need a sharp, preferably boning knife.

Yield: 4 servings
Preparation time: 20 minutes. Cooking time: 5 - 6 minutes

> **Prepared peppers wrapped in paper toweling, may be refrigerated up to 2 hours before sautéing.**

1   **each, red, yellow, orange, green, and purple bell pepper (approximately 1 pepper per person)**
1   **tbsp. peanut or pure olive oil**
2   **tsp. fresh grated ginger**
1/4   **tsp. crushed red pepper**
      juice of 1/2 lemon, or juice of 1 lime

1. Cut the peppers in half first, then cut away the stems. Cut the halves into thirds so there are 6 pieces per pepper. Remove the seeds (put them and the stems into the Stock Bag, p. 12).

2. One at a time, lay each piece on a cutting board inside facing up. Lay your palm flat on the piece. Slicing horizontally from right to left, carefully cut away the pith, saving it for the Stock Bag. What remains is flat pieces of pepper, just skin and flesh, about 1/3" thick.

3. Cut those into very thin (julienne-cut) strips.

4. Heat oil in a flat skillet over medium high heat. Add peppers and sauté, moving the pan continuously, until peppers just begin to soften (about 3 - 4 minutes). Add the ginger and pepper flakes, and toss to distribute. Drizzle lemon or lime juice over peppers and serve immediately.

> **Hint #10: Keeping fresh ginger root: Freeze, then peel as much as you need and use a zester to remove the flesh from the frozen root. Or peel and grate the whole root, put extra into a zip-type bag (pressing out all air), and refrigerate for up to a month or freeze for up to two months.**

Sweet and Sour Red Cabbage

You can buy pickled red cabbage ready-made, but this is better! It will keep tightly covered and refrigerated for at least a week.

Yield: 1 quart
Preparation and cooking time: 25 minutes

1	small red cabbage, core removed and thinly sliced
1	red onion, thinly sliced
1/2	medium yellow onion, thinly sliced, core removed
1/2	cup maple syrup
1	tsp. granulated sugar
2	tbsp. olive oil
1/2	cup red wine vinegar
2	tbsp. Balsamic vinegar
1	tsp. crushed red pepper flakes
1	tbsp. crushed fennel seed
1/8	tsp. ground cloves
1/2	tsp. anise flavor
1/2	tsp. kosher salt
1	tbsp. whole grain mustard

1. Steam cabbage and onion with 1/4 cup water in a covered saucepan over medium high heat (or microwave) until cabbage is softened but still crunchy, not more than 5 minutes.

2. Add other ingredients and cook on medium high heat for 5 more minutes, to blend flavors (microwave, 2 minutes). Taste and correct seasoning (it should be tart, spicy, and a little sweet), then cool to room temperature.

3. Store in a glass or plastic container, covered tightly and refrigerated, for up to one month.

Artichokes with Garlic, Basil, and Parmesan

My mother served artichokes as a special treat, with homemade caper mayonnaise. In my best friend's house they were served with drawn butter. When I tasted this version in a restaurant, I was converted instantly. It's tart, tasty, and really brings out artichoke's nutty flavor.

Yield: 4 servings
Preparation and cooking time: 45 minutes

4	big, beautiful green artichokes (maybe 5 so you can have another one tomorrow)
3	lemons
	zest from 1 lemon, chopped
	strained juice from 2 lemons
1 1/2	cups extra virgin olive oil
4	tsp. minced garlic
1	cup finely chopped fresh basil, or 3 tbsp. dried basil leaves
1/2	cup Italian parsley, finely chopped
1/2	cup capers, drained, reserve juice
1/2	tsp. crushed red pepper flakes
1	cup grated Parmesan cheese

You will need a big pot with a lid to cook the artichokes.

1. Prepare the artichokes by pulling off any tough outer leaves, cutting the stem flat to the bottom, and cutting tips off all the leaves with kitchen shears.

2. Put the artichokes upside down into a large pan and cover them with cold water. Squeeze the quartered lemon into the cooking water and then drop the quarters in.

3. Bring the water to a boil, and boil the artichokes, covered, for about 45 minutes, or until they are done (With tongs, pull off one of the outside leaves; if it comes off easily, they're done.) Turn off burner. Remove the artichokes from the pan with tongs, and pour the water down the drain. Return the artichokes, upside down, to the pan, replace the lid, and let the artichokes dry out, drain, and stay warm.

4. While the artichokes are cooking, heat oil in a small saucepan over medium low heat. Add the garlic and zest, and cook for 2 minutes. Add the capers, 1/4 cup of the caper juice, the lemon juice, and the crushed pepper flakes. Simmer for 2 - 3 minutes to set flavors. Remove from heat and add the basil and parsley.

To serve: Put each artichoke in a shallow soup or pasta bowl. Open out the leaves slightly to make more room for sauce. Pour the sauce over the 4 artichokes, and sprinkle the Parmesan cheese onto each one. Serve immediately.

Caramelized Onion

Caramelizing onions produces a depth of flavor that is unique; not quite sweet, but rich. If you are not familiar with them, think of good French onion soup; those caramelized onions are why the soup is so rich tasting. Plain, cooked lentils or a simple pork chop just come alive with a little caramelized onion.

Yield: 3/4 cup
Preparation time: 2 minutes to slice; 15 - 20 minutes to caramelize

> **1 large yellow onion, peeled and sliced into 1/4" slices**
> **1-2 tbsp. granulated sugar**

1. Sprinkle sugar evenly over the entire bottom of a fry pan. Turn heat to medium low, and place onions in pan, in a single layer.

2. Cook, stirring occasionally, until onions are caramel colored, 15 - 20 minutes. Take care not to scorch the onions, as they are not supposed to be fried.

To store: Transfer to non-reactive container and cool to room temperature. Cover tightly and refrigerate until ready to use. They keep this way for one week.

- If you multiply this recipe, use just enough sugar to cover the bottom of the fry pan. Do not multiply the sugar directly with the number of onions. It is very difficult to caramelize more than one layer of sliced onions at a time.
- It is just as easy to caramelize 4 onions as it is 1 (bigger pan, a few more tears). Freeze the extra and it's ready for last-minute dinners (is that redundant?).

Sautéed Apples and Caramelized Onions

This is a wonderful flavor complement to pork, roasted chicken, or game bird. It also makes a fabulous omelette filling with Gruyère cheese.

Yield: 4 servings
Preparation and cooking time: 35 minutes, including caramelizing the onions

> 1 **large yellow onion, preferably Walla Walla Sweet, Vidalia, or Maui, sliced and Caramelized** (p. 231)
> 2 **tbsp. unsalted butter**
> 2 **tart apples, one red and one green (i.e., Granny Smith and Macintosh), cored and sliced with skin on**
> **juice of 1/2 lemon**
> 2 **tbsp. finely chopped fresh sage leaves, or 1 tsp. dried**
> **kosher salt to taste**

1. Put sliced apples in a non-stick skillet, arranged in fan with alternating skin colors. Sprinkle with sage and lemon juice. Cover and steam over medium high heat for 1 minute to soften them slightly.

2. Put the butter into the skillet, moving the pan around to distribute the butter as it melts. Cook uncovered on medium high until the apples begin to brown. Add the caramelized onions and continue to cook for 2 more minutes to heat the onions and blend the flavors.

To serve: Remove the apples and onions with a spatula, or tongs, to arrange them in a fan presentation.

Lentils with Wild Mushrooms and Caramelized Onion

Lentils are healthful and have a great texture, but they are a little bland. So I add the flavors of rich caramelized onions and musty wild mushrooms. French green lentils cook faster and are more tender than the gray-brown ones, but sometimes they are harder to find.

Yield: 6 servings
Preparation and cooking time: 40 - 50 minutes

See Hint #26 (p. 18), wild mushrooms.

2	cups lentils
2 1/2	quarts water
1	large yellow onion, peeled and sliced
1	tbsp. granulated sugar
2	tbsp. olive oil
1/4	lb. fresh wild mushrooms, brushed for dirt, with stem tips cut off, or 1/4 lb. button or crimini mushrooms plus 1/2 cup dried wild mushrooms
2	tbsp. fresh tarragon leaves, minced, or 1 tsp. dried leaves
	kosher salt to taste

If you are using dried mushrooms, re-hydrate them first, and freeze the mushroom water for stock.

1. Wash lentils in a strainer. Put into large saucepan with the water, bring to a boil, and cook on medium heat until soft (20 minutes; I happen to be partial to slightly mushy lentils). Lentils may be cooked a day ahead, drained, covered, and refrigerated.

2. While the lentils are cooking, sprinkle the sugar over the bottom of a non-stick fry pan, put the onion slices over the sugar, and cook on low heat until the onions are caramelized, about 15 minutes. (Caramelized Onions, p. 231)

3. Tear the wild mushrooms into strips, or slice the button mushrooms. Add the oil into the caramelized onions, then add the mushrooms and herbs in the oil. Sauté on medium high heat, stirring often, until the mushrooms are cooked, about 8 minutes.

4. When the lentils are cooked, transfer them to the fry pan with a slotted spoon, and mix it all together. Taste and correct seasoning with salt if necessary.

Caramelized Onion Bread Pudding

VARIATION: COUNTRY SOUFFLÉ

This fluffy golden brown side dish is just different enough to create an impression. And it's pure comfort food!

Yield: serves 6+
Preparation time: 30 minutes. Baking time: 45 minutes

> 2 **large sweet yellow onions (Vidalia, Walla Walla, Maui)*, peeled, halved and sliced 1/4" thick (skins, tops, bottoms into Stock Bag** [p. 12]**)**
> 3-4 **slices stale bread, broken into 1" chunks**
> 3/4 **cup coarsely grated Parmesan, Fontina, or Jarlsberg cheese**
> 4 **eggs, slightly beaten and at room temperature**
> 1 **pint half-and-half**
> 1 **cup milk**
> 1/4 **tsp. crushed red pepper flakes**
> 1 **tsp. kosher salt**
> 1/4 **cup chopped Italian parsley**

*If sweet onion is not available, use large yellow onions and use a little more sugar to caramelize.

Preheat the oven to 375°. You will need a 3-quart, oven-proof souffle dish for the pudding, and a larger pan that will hold it and water.

1. Caramelize the onion (p. 231) and set aside to cool.

2. Butter or spray the baking dish, and put the bread chunks into it. Distribute the onions evenly over the bread, and sprinkle 1/2 cup cheese over the onions.

3. Mix the eggs, half-and-half, milk, pepper flakes, salt, and parsley with a whisk, and pour the mixture over the bread, onion, and cheese. Sprinkle remaining cheese on the top.

To reduce fat, substitute 2% milk for half-and-half, for a total of 3 cups milk

4. Place the baking dish into the larger pan. Pour enough hot water to reach halfway up the sides. Bake for 40 - 45 minutes, or until pudding is puffed, golden brown, and a tester inserted into the center comes out clean. Remove from the oven and serve immediately.

COUNTRY SOUFFLÉ
Substitute 1 cup grated extra sharp cheddar cheese for others, and add 1 tsp. Worcestershire sauce to half-and-half mixture. Sprinkle 1/4 cup grated cheddar over the top of the casserole before baking.

Mother Thomas's Stuffing

*One year my friend Judy gave me this recipe from her late
mother-in-law; that was it! No more experiments, no more
concoctions. This is the purest, simplest, and best stuffing ever.*

Yield: serves 6
Preparation time: 30 minutes

1 1/2	loaves store-bought white bread
1 1/2	cup hazelnuts, chopped and lightly toasted
1	lb. unsalted butter, melted
2	large yellow onions, peeled and chopped
4 - 5	stalks celery, chopped
3- 4	eggs, beaten
	kosher salt and pepper
1/2	cup chopped fresh sage (optional)

1. Cut bread into cubes and dry them on a cookie sheet in the
    oven (250° for 15 minutes).

2. Sauté chopped nuts, onions and celery in butter over medium
    high heat; toss them with the bread cubes, distributing
    everything evenly.

3. Bind stuffing with beaten egg, and season to taste with salt and
    pepper. It should be barely moistened, not at all sticky.

4. Stuff the bird and put extra stuffing in an oven-proof dish.
    Cover with foil and heat at 250° for 30 minutes.

**Never jam stuffing into a turkey or chicken or it
will cook into a gluppy paste. Put it in gently
with lots of air space. Because of the raw egg
against raw poultry, do not stuff the bird until
just before you cook it.**

Oven-Roasted Potatoes

*Potatoes cooked this way will be crisp and golden brown on the
outside and delicately soft on the inside. The flavor varies with
different herbs and oils.*

Yield: 6 servings
**Preparation time: for peeled potatoes, 20 minutes; for unpeeled,
10 minutes**

> 2 lbs. potatoes, washed with skin on or
>   peeled*
> 1/4 cup olive oil
>   1 tbsp. minced garlic
>   1 tbsp. chopped herb, dried work very well
> 1/2 tsp. kosher salt
>   2 tbsp. minced Italian parsley for garnish

*For red-skinned potatoes, Yellow Finns, Yukon Golds, and small
whites, leave skin on; peel russets or other baking potatoes.

Preheat oven to 475°.

1. Cut small potatoes in quarter wedges. Cut peeled baking
   potatoes into 8 wedges.

2. Mix oil, herbs, and salt in a large bowl. Add potatoes and toss
   to coat.

3. Transfer potatoes to a heavy fry pan or, for larger quantities, a
   roasting or sheet pan. Roast for 20 - 25 minutes, turning
   pieces during roasting so all surfaces brown. The smaller the
   potatoes or pieces are, the less time they will take to cook.
   Roasted potatoes will hold in a 120° oven for 30 minutes. After
   that they will dry out.

To serve: Sprinkle with parsley, toss lightly, and serve.

VARIATIONS
Greek: Garlic and oregano with Greek olive oil
French: Garlic and rosemary
Italian: Garlic and marjoram
Mexican: Garlic, oregano, cumin, ground chili pepper, and
   corn oil

**Not sure which potato is a russet or Yukon
Gold? Ask the produce person to identify the
potatoes. They like to share their expertise and
you make a valuable contact for selecting the
freshest produce.**

Pesto Fries

This is a quick, easy accompaniment to barbecued fish or steak, and it really dresses up hamburgers (especially if you put 1 tsp. crumbled gorganzola cheese inside each patty as you make them— the secret thowaway hint of the book!). Pesto fries also are great with grilled fish.

Yield: 4 servings
Preparation and cooking time: 15 minutes

>   **1 package frozen French fry cut potatoes**
>   **that provides 4 servings**
>   **2 tbsp. basil pesto**

1. Cook the potatoes according to your taste and manufacturer's directions (I prefer to broil them).

2. When they are brown and crisp, take them out of the oven and toss them with the pesto.

3. Serve immediately.

Cattle Country Potatoes

VARIATION: SCALLOPED POTATOES

These are a tasty version of scalloped potatoes to serve with hamburgers, hot dogs, or as part of an outdoor barbecue buffet.

Yield: 4 - 6 servings
Preparation time: 40 minutes. Cooking time: 30 minutes

1	**large yellow onion, sliced and Caramelized** (p. 231)
3	**large baking potatoes, peeled and sliced**
3	**slices bacon, cut into small pieces**
4	**oz. sharp Cheddar, grated**
1/4	**cup red wine**
1	**tbsp. minced fresh rosemary**
3/4	**cup chicken stock, preferably Homemade**
1	**cup bottled barbecue sauce**

See recipes for Homemade and Modified Canned Stock (p. 108).

Preheat oven to 350°.

1. Steam potatoes until just soft enough to prick with a fork.

2. Cook bacon until crisp; remove to paper towel with slotted spoon and reserve fat.

3. Brush bottom of 3-quart casserole dish or 9" x 13" pan with bacon fat. Layer half of potato slices on bottom of dish. Cover with layer of onions, bacon, and half the cheese. Drizzle 1/2 cup barbecue sauce over that layer. Repeat, leaving off cheese.

4. Mix wine and rosemary with the stock, and pour it over the potatoes. Sprinkle remaining cheese over the top.

5. Bake for about 30 minutes or until excess moisture is absorbed and cheese is bubbly and brown.

SCALLOPED POTATOES

1	**large yellow onion, sliced and Caramelized** (p. 231)
3	**large baking potatoes, peeled and sliced**
3	**slices bacon, cut into small pieces (optional)**
2	**cups Béchamel Sauce** (p. 301)
	kosher salt and freshly ground pepper to taste
1/4	**cup chopped Italian parsley**

Follow above procedures, 1 through 5, substituting Béchamel for cheese and barbecue sauce. Sprinkle fresh parsley over the top before baking.

Au Gratin Potato Tart

VARIATION: SAUSAGE AND POTATO TART

This tart takes awhile, but it is so pretty and so good that it's worth it, especially for potato lovers.

Yield: 6 servings
Preparation time: 30 minutes with processor to slice potatoes
Baking and cooling time: 50 minutes

5	medium-sized white or red or yellow potatoes
1/2	lb. thinly sliced bacon or pancetta (Italian cured pork) cut cross-wise into thin strips
2	medium onions, peeled and thinly sliced (1 1/2 cups)
1 1/4	tsp. kosher salt
	pinch sugar
1/4	tsp. freshly ground pepper
2	tbsp. olive oil
1 1/2	tbsp. fresh chopped rosemary
1	tbsp. garlic, minced
5	eggs
2	cups heavy cream
	pinch nutmeg
3	cups Gruyere or Jarlsberg cheese, grated

1. Boil potatoes, covered, over high heat, for 5 minutes. Drain, pat dry, and cool slightly.

2. Meanwhile, in 12" oven-proof skillet, cook bacon over moderate heat, stirring continually. Remove to a paper towel with a slotted spoon, and set aside 2 tbsp. of the fat. Coarsely chop cooled bacon.

3. Add onions to the remaining fat. Sprinkle with salt and sugar, then cover the pan and cook the onions over moderate heat, stirring several times, until they are softened and brown, about 25 minutes. Remove onions and set aside.

4. Peel potatoes and coarsely grate; season with salt and pepper.

5. Preheat oven to 350°. Rub reserved 2 tbsp. of fat over the sides of the skillet. Add grated potatoes and evenly press them into the bottom and sides of pan to form a crust. Cook over moderately low heat until the potatoes begin to brown on bottom, about 15 minutes.

6. Heat olive oil, rosemary, and garlic in a small pan, and cook for 3 minutes over moderate heat, stirring often. Remove from heat.

7. In a bowl, beat eggs with cream until blended. Add nutmeg and 2/3 of the rosemary/garlic oil.

8. When potato crust begins to brown, drizzle remaining herb oil over surface. Spread reserved onions over potatoes, then sprinkle the bacon and cheese over the top.

9. Pour egg mixture into potato crust and bake for 40 minutes, rotating pan once, or until the custard is set and golden on top.

10. Remove from oven and cool on a rack for 10 minutes before serving.

SAUSAGE AND POTATO TART
Substitute 1/2 lb. *cooked* bulk sausage for bacon.

Garlic Mashed Potatoes

At the risk of being branded a food heretic, I admit to using instant potato flakes when boiling, ricing, and mashing just isn't in the cards. Roasted garlic and butter pretty well mask that telltale taste of potatoes in a box. But do try it this old-fashioned way, it's really good.

Yield: 4 servings
Preparation time: 1 hour

See recipes for Home-made and Modified Canned Stock (p. 108).

> 2 **whole heads garlic, with any loose, outside skin removed**
> 1 **tbsp. pure olive oil**
> 1/2 **cup vegetable or chicken stock**
> 2 **baking potatoes, peeled and cut into 1" chunks**
> 1 **cup half-and-half or whole milk**
> 3 **tbsp. unsalted butter—softened to room temperature or melted**
> **kosher salt to taste**
> **fresh ground pepper to taste**

Preheat oven to 375°.

1. To roast garlic: Cut the top off the garlic heads so that the cloves show and the top is flat. Brush the heads with oil, put them in a small pan, add stock, and cover tightly with foil. Bake for 35 minutes. Remove from oven and let cool until you can handle them.

2. Meanwhile, put the potatoes into a pot, cover them with cold water (about 2" over the top of the potatoes) and bring the water to a boil. Boil on medium until the potatoes are soft, about 15 minutes. Drain, saving the water.

3. Put the cooked potatoes through a potato ricer or food mill.

4. To remove the cooked garlic from its skin, pull each clove apart from the head, and squeeze it from the bottom into a small mixing bowl, food processor, or blender. When all the cloves are out, add 2 or 3 tbsp. of the potato cooking water to the garlic and purée. Use more water if you need to.

5. Whisk the garlic purée, half-and-half, and butter together, and add to riced potatoes. Mix with an electric mixer until the potatoes are fluffy. If you need more liquid, use the potato cooking water.

6. When the mashed potatoes are the consistency you like, taste and add as much salt and pepper as you wish. Serve immediately.

Note: Finished mashed potatoes will hold for about 30 minutes. After that they begin to collapse, significantly altering the consistency.

If you don't have a ricer or food mill, a hand held masher or an electric mixer will work, but it is difficult to achieve that old fashioned, really fluffy consistency. Do not mash potatoes in a food processor. The force of the blade breaks the gluten molecules apart so much that the result is a very gluey consistency that cannot be rectified.

Potato Pancakes

Draining the potatoes through cheesecloth reduces the starch, enabling the potatoes to cook quickly without getting gluey. Put grated potatoes onto the cloth, form a bundle with the cloth, and squeeze the juice out.

Yield: 8 pancakes
Preparation time: 20 minutes

1/4	cup all-purpose flour
1/4	cup cornmeal
1	cup chopped yellow onion
1/2	tsp. kosher salt
1/2	tsp. crushed red pepper flakes
3	russet potatoes*, coarsely grated (medium blade in food processor), and strained through cheesecloth
1	tbsp. finely chopped thyme or sage leaves, or 1 tsp. dried
2	egg whites, beaten and at room temperature oil for the fry pan

*For an interesting combination, use 2 cups russet and 1 cup sweet potato. With plain russet use thyme, with the combination, use sage.

1. Mix the flour and cornmeal together and set aside.

2. Toss the grated potato with the onion, salt, pepper flakes, and herbs. Mix in the beaten egg whites.

3. Form the potatoes into patties about 4" in diameter and 1/2" high, and dredge each one in the flour mixture.

4. In a heavy skillet on medium heat, pour enough oil to cover the bottom of the pan generously. Fry the pancakes until they are brown and crisp on one side, about 5 minutes, and turn them over and repeat the cooking on the other side. Monitor the temperature of the oil so that the pancakes do not burn before the potatoes are cooked.

Polenta

VARIATION: FRIED POLENTA

There is a difference between the coarse-ground corn meal intended for polenta and the fine-ground corn meal used in corn bread (even though there is a recipe for polenta on most of those boxes). The coarser ground meal often is available in bulk at health food stores. If you can't get it, the finer grind works, but the resulting texture is different from Italian polenta.

Yield: 4 servings
Preparation time: 10 minutes. Cooking time: 30 minutes

> 1 **quart cold water**
> 1 **cup coarse ground corn meal**
> 2 **tbsp. olive oil**
> 1 **tsp. kosher salt**
> 2 **tbsp. heavy cream or butter (not entirely necessary, but good)**
> 1 **cup coarsely grated Parmesan cheese (or other dry, aged Italian cheese)**

1. Put water in 4-quart saucepan. Add corn meal and oil to cold water. Turn on the heat and bring to a boil. Turn heat down to simmer and, stirring quite often, cook the polenta until the moisture is absorbed, about 20 minutes. As the polenta cooks, it spatters as it bubbles. That is why the pan is large. Stirring helps, but if it gets out of hand, reduce the heat slightly. It is done when it is soft enough to roll off a spoon, but stiff enough not to spread out on a plate.

2. Stir in the cream or butter.

3. Sprinkle half the cheese on top. Cover the pan, remove it from the heat and let it sit for 5 or 6 minutes.

To serve: Transfer the polenta to a serving dish or individual plates, sprinkle remaining cheese over the top and serve immediately.

Hint #2: Good Parmesan cheese is so firm that it is difficult to grate. If you heat it in the microwave for a few seconds, it softens enough to grate easily.

FRIED POLENTA

1 cup all-purpose flour for dredging

1. Make as above, and transfer cooked polenta to a glass or plastic-wrap-lined loaf pan. **If you have leftover cooked polenta, reheat it in a covered pan with a little water and transfer it to the loaf pan, then continue to follow this recipe. The cheese isn't crucial**.

2. Cover with plastic wrap and refrigerate for 4 hours.

3. Turn out onto a cutting surface and slice into 3/4" slices. Cut the slices in half to make 2" x 4" rectangles. Dredge each slice in flour, and fry in hot (not smoking) oil until both sides are golden brown and crisp on the edges.

To serve: Transfer to a heated platter or individual plates and sprinkle each slice with grated cheese.

Santa Cruz Hominy

*Hominy, lye-treated corn, tastes more like a grain than corn to me.
It makes a great flavor complement to ham, barbecued meat, or
grilled sausage. Olé!*

Yield: 6 servings
Preparation and cooking time: less than 20 minutes

2	tbsp. corn oil
3/4	cup sliced yellow onion (slice the onion in half, then cut the slices in half)
1	Anaheim pepper, stems and seeds removed, sliced into thin strips
1/2	tsp. crushed red pepper flakes
1	tsp. cumin
3	cups canned white or yellow hominy, rinsed and drained
1/2	tsp. red chili powder (not pure cayenne)
1/2	cup chopped fresh cilantro
1/2	cup Quick Tomato Salsa (p. 287) (if it is watery, drain it)

1. Heat oil in a skillet. Add onions and sliced pepper, and cook until transparent and slightly softened.

2. Mix in the pepper flakes and the cumin. Add the hominy, chili powder, and cilantro and cook, stirring often for 10 minutes. Add the Salsa and cook for 2 more minutes.

Wild Rice Pilaf

VARIATIONS: WILD RICE AND BEAN PILAF, MIXED GRAIN PILAF

I really love grains: rice of all varieties, barley, quinoa, bulgur wheat, etc., separately or in combinations like this one, in which the wild rice flavor dominates. Let your imagination direct you with pilaf; just remember, the stock flavor will make a big difference!

Yield: 6 servings
Preparation time: 10 minutes excluding rice-cooking time
Cooking time: 40 minutes

See recipes for Home-made and Modified Canned Stock (p. 108).

2 tbsp. extra virgin olive oil
1 cup chopped yellow onion
3 cups cooked wild rice (1 cup uncooked)
2 cups cooked brown or long grain white rice (1 cup uncooked)
2 tbsp. chopped fresh tarragon, or 1 tbsp. dried
1 cup vegetable or chicken stock, preferably Homemade

Preheat oven to 275°.

1. In a small fry pan, cook the onion in the oil over medium low heat until it is beginning to brown around the edges.

2. Add the stock and herbs and bring it to a simmer. Remove from heat and set aside.

3. In an oven-proof casserole, mix the grains with a large fork until they are combined. Add the stock and mix again, so that all the grain is moistened.

4. Cover loosely and bake for 30 minutes, until the pilaf is heated through.

WILD RICE AND BEAN PILAF
Add 1 can (about 1 1/2 cups) rinsed, drained red kidney beans, black beans, black eyed peas, pigeon peas, or pinto beans at Step 3.

MIXED GRAIN PILAF
Use 3 or 4 different cooked grains, with 1 dominating (2 cups of one and three cups mixed). Substitute herb of your choice.

Note: You can also use orzo, a pasta the size and shape of grains, as one part of the pilaf.

Jamaican Beans and Rice

VARIATION: CARIBBEAN CHICKEN CASSEROLE

Complex carbohydrates and protein in spades! This can be made ahead and reheated just before it is served.

Yield: 6 - 8 servings
Preparation time: 20 minutes. Cooking time: 20 minutes

1/4	lb. chopped bacon, or 2 tbsp. corn, peanut, or pure olive oil
1	medium red or yellow onion, 1/4" slices
1	tsp. minced garlic
1	red bell pepper, pith and seeds removed, and sliced into strips 1/4" wide
2	tbsp. fresh thyme leaves, or 2 tsp. dried
1	14 1/2 oz. can premium diced tomatoes in purée
1	tsp. Jerk seasoning paste* plus 1/2 tsp. curry powder, or 1 tbsp. Garam Masala Curry Paste® (Resources, p. 340)
1 1/2	pints mixed canned legumes, rinsed and drained (black beans, black eyed peas, pigeon peas, pinto beans, great northern beans, etc. Red kidney beans are too sweet for this dish.)
2	cups cooked long grain rice (1 cup uncooked)
1/4	cup chopped parsley
	kosher salt to taste

°If you can't find Jerk seasoning paste, make your own: 1/2 tsp. Worcestershire sauce, 1/2 tsp. Chinese 5 Spice, 1/2 tsp. ground cumin, 1/4 tsp. crushed red pepper flakes.

In the Caribbean, pork back or bacon fat is used to sauté, adding a distinct taste. If you wish that more authentic flavor, use chopped bacon rather than oil.

Hint #18: Beano®, a product available in most drug stores and many grocery stores, breaks down undigestible proteins before they reach the large intestine (where bacteria break them down, causing gas). A tasteless liquid, Beano® is added after legumes are cooked, just before they are eaten.

1. In a large skillet, heat oil or fry bacon over medium heat until almost done. Add onions and garlic and cook until onion is translucent. Add pepper, thyme, tomato, and seasoning. Simmer for about 5 minutes.

2. Add beans and stir to blend. Simmer for another 5 minutes. Add cooked rice and mix with a fork so it won't get sticky.

3. Taste and correct seasoning with kosher salt if necessary.

4. Sprinkle with chopped parsley and serve.

CARIBBEAN CHICKEN CASSEROLE

Mix 2 tsp. Jerk seasoning with 1/2 cup Dijon Glaze (p. 105). Brush on 8 boneless chicken thighs and 3 boneless breasts, or toss with leftover cooked chicken, add 1 cup chicken stock

Preheat oven to 450°.

1. Bake the glazed chicken for 25 minutes. Turn oven down to 350°. Remove chicken from pan and cool to room temperature, then cut it into bite-sized pieces.

2. Add the stock to the Jamaican Beans and Rice, and transfer to a casserole dish. Mix the chicken into the casserole, cover loosely with foil, and bake 10 minutes. Remove foil and bake an additional 10 minutes.

Refried Black Beans

If you aren't keen on the salty grey blobs of beans served with greasy burritos, try these; they are wonderful.

Yield: 4 servings
Preparation and cooking time: 20 minutes using canned beans

        2 tbsp. pure olive oil
        2 tsp. minced garlic
        4 tsp. finely chopped green onion
        2 cups cooked black beans (if canned,
           thoroughly rinsed and drained)
      1/2 tsp. red chili powder (not pure cayenne)
      1/2 tsp. crushed red pepper flakes
      1/2 tsp. kosher salt
        2 tbsp. chopped fresh mint leaves, or
           2 tsp. dried
        4 oz. chevre (soft, white goat cheese)
      1/3 cup whipping cream
        1 tbsp. chopped fresh mint leaves, or
           1 tsp. dried, for garnish

1. In a non-stick skillet (big enough to hold everything), over medium heat, sauté garlic and onion in oil until they are softened, about 5 minutes.

2. Mix beans with chili powder, chili pepper, salt, and mint. With an electric mixer or processor, chop/mash the mixture until it is soft but still a little chunky. Transfer it to the skillet.

3. Cook the beans at medium high heat, until they have lost some moisture and a crust has formed on the bottom, 6 - 8 minutes.

4. While the beans are cooking, whisk the cream and chevre together into a thick, sour-cream-like sauce.

5. When the crust has formed, slide the beans out of the pan onto a warm serving plate, or divide portions with a spatula and put them onto warmed plates.

To serve: Put a dollop of sauce over the beans, sprinkle remaining chopped mint leaves over the sauce, and serve immediately.

Hint #18: Beano®, a product available in most drug stores and many grocery stores, breaks down undigestible proteins before they reach the large intestine (where bacteria break them down, causing gas). A tasteless liquid, Beano® is added after legumes are cooked, just before they are eaten.

Black Beans with Lime and Cilantro

A quick dress-up for simple black beans.

Yield: 4 servings
Preparation and cooking time: 15 minutes

> 1 tbsp. corn oil
> 1 tsp. minced garlic
> 2 green onions, chopped
> 1 tsp. lime zest
> 1 15 oz. can black beans, rinsed and drained
> 2 tbsp. fresh minced cilantro leaves
> 1/2 tsp. crushed red pepper flakes
> 1 tbsp. fresh lime juice
> kosher salt to taste
> 1/4 cup sour cream at room temperature

1. Drain and rinse beans well, making sure the rinsing water runs clear. Set aside.

2. Put oil into a small saucepan, over low heat, and cook the garlic until it is softened but not colored, about 3 minutes. Add onion and lime zest, stirring to mix. Gently mix in beans, 1 tbsp. cilantro, and red pepper flakes, increase the heat to medium, and cook until the mixture is heated through, 3 - 5 minutes). Drizzle lime juice over the beans, tossing to mix. Taste and add salt to taste.

To serve: Garnish with a sprinkling of remaining cilantro, and add 1 tbsp. sour cream on the side.

Hint #18: Beano®, a product available in most drug stores and many grocery stores, breaks down undigestible proteins before they reach the large intestine (where bacteria break them down, causing gas). A tasteless liquid, Beano® is added after legumes are cooked, just before they are eaten.

White Beans with Onion and Sage

This is very simple, very good. Fresh sage is important.

Yield: 4 servings
Preparation time: 20 minutes, including caramelizing onions
Cooking time: 15 minutes

1	**large yellow onion, peeled, sliced 1/4", and Caramelized** (p. 231)
1/4	**cup chopped fresh sage leaves plus several tops for garnish**
4 - 6	**cups cooked cannellini beans, rinsed and drained**
1	**cup chicken stock**
2	**tbsp. extra virgin olive oil**
1/2	**tsp. crushed red pepper flakes**
	kosher salt to taste

Preheat the oven to 350°.

1. Sprinkle caramelized onions with chopped sage and mix with a fork.

2. Transfer to an oven-proof baking dish. Add the beans, the stock, the olive oil, and the pepper flakes, mixing them together *gently*, to avoid crushing the beans.

3. Taste and correct seasoning with salt if necessary. Bake uncovered for 15 minutes, until the beans have heated through and the flavors have blended.

VARIATION
Substitute 1/4 cup mashed Roasted Garlic (p. 225) for the onion, and sprinkle 1/4 cup coarsely grated Parmesan cheese over the top just before baking.

See Beano® hint on previous page.

Caramelized onion provides a depth to the flavor, but if you are really short on time, it's also very good with sautéed onion.

Green Salads

I love salad, but I have two pet salad peeves: first, pieces so large that they either have to be cut or wedged into my gaping mouth; second, salad plates piled so full that a touch of a fork causes the salad to explode, usually off the plate and onto the table. As you prepare a salad, imagine yourself eating in clean, expensive clothes, with someone whom you would like to impress.

Yield: A generous salad serving is about 2 cups of prepared greens.
Preparation time: 10 minutes

SIMPLE GREENS

1 variety of greens, preferably Bibb, butter, green or red leaf lettuce
salad dressing (see Dressing recipes, beginning p. 273)

MIXED GREENS

See Hint #21 (p. 17), salad dressing.

a mixture of two or three varieties of greens: romaine, butter, spinach, escarole, red or green leaf, chicory, or whatever else is fresh, crisp, and beautiful
fresh herbs
salad dressing

1. Wash, dry, and break up the greens. Toss them together.
2. Pour 1 oz. dressing per serving over the salad and toss.

CAESAR SALAD

Hands down one of America's most popular salads, it also is the most often changed, fixed, and abused. Made simply, with fresh lettuce, this salad is wonderful.

See Hint #2 (p. 15), grating Parmesan cheese.

fresh romaine lettuce only
Caesar Dressing (p. 276)
Homemade Croutons (p. 118)
freshly grated or shaved Parmesan cheese
1 lemon wedge per serving

1. Prepare the lettuce as above and toss it with dressing.
2. Sprinkle croutons and cheese over each serving and garnish with a lemon wedge.

Coleslaw

Tart, crunchy coleslaw with fish or sausage is just plain unbeatable. Shred, don't chop the cabbage, because the longer, thinner strips will provide more flavor than the tiny pieces.

Yield: 4 servings
Preparation time: 10 minutes

1 cabbage, washed
3/4 cup Coleslaw Dressing (p. 277)

1. Cut the cabbage in half, from the top to the core.
2. Cut out the core on each half. Lay each half on a cutting surface, cut side down. Shred or slice the cabbage very thin. When all the cabbage is shredded, cut the slices into edible lengths.
3. Mix the shredded cabbage with Coleslaw Dressing.

Marinated Cucumber Salad

Very traditionally Scandinavian, this salad really brings out the subtle sweetness of cucumber.

Yield: 4 servings
Preparation time: 10 minutes, plus marinating time

1 English cucumber, thinly sliced, or 1 large
regular cucumber, peeled and thinly sliced
1 tbsp. granulated sugar
1/2 cup cider vinegar
1 cup water

1. Place sliced cucumbers in a glass dish in one layer. Sprinkle sugar over the cucumbers.
2. Add vinegar and water and stir gently until the sugar dissolves. Cover with plastic wrap, refrigerate, and marinate for at least 1 hour before serving.

Cucumber, Yogurt, and Mint Salad

VARIATIONS: CURRIED DIP, DILLED CUCUMBER SAUCE

Modified slightly, this salad becomes a refreshing dip for Cumin Flavored Pita Chips (p. 111).

Yield: 4 Servings
Preparation time: 30 minutes. Refrigerating time: 30 minutes

> 1 **English seedless cucumber, peeled and sliced, or 1 large sweet regular cucumber, peeled, seeded, and sliced**
> 1/2 **pint plain yogurt**
> 1/4 **cup sour cream**
> 1 **tsp. lemon juice**
> 3 **green onions, finely chopped**
> 1/4 **cup chopped fresh mint leaves, or 2 tbsp. dried mint leaves**
> 1/2 **tsp. kosher salt**
> 1 **tbsp. chopped fresh mint leaves or parsley for garnish**

1. Place sliced cucumbers in a non-reactive bowl.

2. Mix remaining ingredients except garnish, and pour over the cucumber. Cover with plastic wrap and refrigerate for at least 30 minutes before serving.

To serve: Garnish and serve in shallow bowls or with a slotted spoon.

CURRIED DIP
Add 1 tsp. curry powder or Garam Masala Curry Paste® (Resources, p. 340).

DILLED CUCUMBER SAUCE
Grate the cucumber and substitute chopped fresh dill for the mint, both chopped and garnish.

Hint #30: A non-reactive container is one that will not react chemically to the acid in fruit, peppers, vinegar, or salt. Stainless steel, plastic, and glass are non-reactive. Aluminum and copper are reactive.

Marinated Vegetable Salad

VARIATIONS: MARINATED BEAN SALAD; DILLY CARROTS, CUCUMBERS, AND BEANS

For years, canned vegetables in iceberg lettuce cups was America's sad version of this classic salad. Fortunately those gray, mushy bundles of tinny tasting whatevers have all but disappeared. Now fresh vegetables are always available, and this vibrant, tart, almost crunchy salad can be enjoyed year-round.

Yield: 4 servings
Preparation time: 35 minutes. Marinating time: 1 hour, minimum

> a selection of fresh vegetables*, approximately 2 – 2 1/2 lbs. before stems, peels, etc. are removed (and put into the stock bag)
> 1 cup Vinaigrette of your choice (p. 273-275)
> 1/2 cup chopped fresh herbs, Italian parsley or regular parsley, plus 1 tbsp. for garnish
> 1/2 cup capers (optional)
> 1 15 oz. can white beans, rinsed and drained (optional)

STOCK BAG
Remember your Stock Bag (p. 12).

*Select vegetables for *color, texture* and *shape*, thinking about whether you intend to arrange them in individual salads, present them on a platter, or have them cut into pieces in a salad bowl. If you want to use tomatoes, I recommend cherry or yellow teardrop, but don't blanch or marinate those. Add them at the end.

1. Prepare the vegetables for blanching by peeling, removing stems or ends, and cutting them into the sizes and shapes you wish. Young, small summer vegetables such as string beans, carrots, tiny new potatoes, etc., can be blanched whole, particularly if the salad is served on a big platter.

2. Prepare a large bowl of ice water and set it aside.

3. Separating them by color, blanch the vegetables (except canned beans) separately and a few at a time (see p. 223), and plunge them into ice water to stop the cooking and set their colors. Drain them in a colander.

4. Put the blanched vegetables into a shallow, non-reactive dish (I use zip-type baggies because I can press the extra air out, have the marinade surround vegetables, and take up much less room in the refrigerator).

5. Stir the garlic into the vinaigrette, and pour it over the vegetables. Cover the container with plastic wrap, and refrigerate for at least an hour and up to a whole day before serving.

MARINATED BEAN SALAD

- **1 cup Italian Vinaigrette** (p. 273)
- **3 cloves Roasted Garlic** (p. 255)**, mashed**
- **1/2 cup chopped fresh basil, oregano, or marjoram**
- **1/2 cup chopped Italian parsley**
- **1/2 cup diced fresh tomato (vine ripened or Roma)**
- **2 15 oz. cans rinsed and drained beans (cannellini, red kidney, garbanzo, great northern, pinto, black, pigeon peas, black eyed peas, etc.)**
- **2 cups large sliced green or yellow wax beans (or both), blanched, steamed, rinsed and drained**
- **1/2 tsp. crushed red pepper flakes**
  kosher salt to taste

Mix all ingredients, cover, and marinate the same way.

To serve: Arrange salad greens on plates or platters. Spoon about 1/4 marinade over the greens. With tongs or a slotted spoon, lift the vegetables out of the marinade and arrange them over the greens. Garnish with chopped herbs and capers. Save the marinade to use later as a salad dressing.

To serve in a large salad bowl: Put the vegetables and marinade in a bowl and garnish.

DILLY CARROTS, CUCUMBERS, AND BEANS
1/2 lb. each, thin green or yellow wax beans and carrots, washed
1 long English cucumber
same marinade as p. 258, with 1/2 cup dill pickle juice and 1/4 cup chopped fresh dill sprigs for garnish added

1. Peel and cut the carrots into long sticks, and the cucumber into thin wedges; leave the beans as they are.

2. Blanch the carrots and beans (p. 223); do not blanch the cucumber.

3. Put the vinaigrette into a zip-type bag. Add the vegetables, and press the air out of the bag before you zip it closed. Lay the bag flat in the refrigerator, and chill for 2 or 3 hours before serving. Garnish with dill sprigs.

These are not cooked, so they will last up to 3 days refrigerated.

Chopped Salad

Chopped salad is always a hit in restaurants because it's full of surprises. I'm pretty sure it was created by a cook who couldn't think of anything for dinner and just chopped up all the leftovers in the refrigerator and threw them into a bowl. Guess what, it worked!

Yield: 4 servings
Preparation time: 20 minutes

1	head iceberg or romaine lettuce (the lettuce needs to have body and be crunchy)
12 - 16	leaves of fresh spinach, washed and chiffonade-cut (see box below)
1	cup garbanzo beans, rinsed and drained
1	cup red kidney beans, rinsed, drained, and chopped coarsely
1/2	red onion, sliced very thin and then chopped
1/2	cup chopped green onion
1	cup chopped fresh tomato
1/2	cup finely chopped Italian parsley
1/2	cup finely chopped fresh basil leaves
1	cup Marinated Black Olives (p. 113), chopped
1	cup coarsely grated provolone cheese
1/2	cup crumbled feta cheese
1	cup Caesar Dressing (p. 276), or Italian Vinaigrette (p. 273)

Now look in the refrigerator and see if there is anything else you can add: chicken? fish? pepperoni? ham? a tiny plastic wrap bundle of Parmesan? leftover French fries? a few mushrooms?

1. Chop the lettuce and put it into a large salad bowl.
2. Add everything else, except the feta cheese and the dressing, and toss (I use my hands).
3. Pour the dressing over the salad and toss again. Divide among 4 chilled salad bowls, sprinkle each with feta and serve.

Chiffonade-cut: stack and roll leaves into a cylinder beginning at the wide edge, then cut the cylinder into very thin slices. The resulting strips are chiffonade-cut.

Old-Fashioned Potato Salad

Potato salad is such a revered American tradition that while the idea of new recipes seems terrific, the actual tasting often is disappointing. I don't care for hard boiled egg in potato salad. (At one picnic the hostess proudly proclaimed that there were " 5 eggs to every spud" in her salad. I thought I was going to faint!) This recipe is pretty tart, but it's my family's recipe, so of course I think it's wonderful. See if you agree.

Yield: 4 - 6 servings
Preparation time: 30 minutes, excluding the cooling time for potatoes

> 4 **large baking potatoes, peeled, diced**
> 1/2 **cup Dijon Vinaigrette** (p. 273)
> 1 **cup chopped green onion**
> 1/4 **cup capers**
> 1/4 **cup Italian parsley, chopped, plus**
> **2 tbsp. for garnish**

Dressing
> 3/4 **cup mixed Olive Mayonnaise** (p. 280) **or**
> 3/4 **cup Coleslaw Dressing** (p. 277)

1. **For stove top:** In a large saucepan, cover prepared potatoes by 1" with cold water. Bring the water to a hard boil, cover the pan, turn the heat down to a low boil and cook the potatoes until they can be pierced easily with a fork, about 20 minutes. Drain in a colander. **For microwave:** put the prepared potatoes in a shallow container and cover them with cold water. Cover the container tightly with plastic wrap and cook the potatoes on high heat for 10 minutes. Test for doneness (pierced easily with a fork) and continue to cook if necessary, until they are done. Drain in a colander.

2. While potatoes are still warm, transfer to a serving bowl, and pour vinaigrette over them. Carefully, so the potatoes won't break, mix vinaigrette, chopped onion, capers, and parsley with the potatoes. Cover loosely with plastic wrap and refrigerate to cool, about 45 minutes.

3. Just before you are ready to serve, fold the dressing into the potatoes with a rubber spatula and garnish with remaining parsley.

German Potato Salad

This salad, along with grilled Polish sausage, whole grain mustard, dark rye bread, sliced Muenster cheese, and frosty beer, makes a quick, delicious dinner.

Yield: 4 servings
Preparation time: 30 minutes

> 3 **large baking potatoes, peeled and diced (1"x1")**
> 3/4 **cup chopped yellow onion (1 medium)**
> 4 **slices bacon, cut into small pieces**
> 2 **tbsp. chopped fresh tarragon, or 2 tsp. dried leaves (thyme works also)**
> 2 **tbsp. red wine vinegar**
> 3/4 **cup Dijon Vinaigrette** (p. 273)
> 1/4 **cup chopped Italian parsley**

1. Put potatoes into a large saucepan, and cover by 1" with cold water. Bring the water to a boil, turn the heat to medium low, cover the pan, and cook until just soft enough to be pierced with a fork, about 15 minutes. Drain in a colander, *but don't rinse*.

2. While the potatoes are cooking, cook the bacon and onion until both are cooked but not crisp. Drain on paper towel. Put the drained potatoes, the parsley, and the bacon and onion into a salad bowl.

3. Heat the Vinaigrette with the vinegar and tarragon in a small saucepan or microwave. Pour the heated dressing over the potato mixture and toss gently with a fork, taking care not to break up the potatoes.

4. Serve warm or at room temperature.

New Potato Salad, French Style

This is a very quick, easy, and pretty version of potato salad. Because it does not contain mayonnaise, it does not need to be refrigerated. With Low-Fat Vinaigrette (p. 274), it is a delicious, low-fat salad.

Yield: 4 servings
Preparation time: 10 minutes. Cooking and cooling time: 45 minutes

> 2 **lbs. red-skinned potatoes, sliced, with skin on**
> 1 **tbsp. fresh tarragon leaves, chopped**
> 3/4 **cup Dijon Vinaigrette** (p. 273), **or Low-Fat Vinaigrette** (p. 274) **with 1 tsp. Dijon mustard added**
> 2 **tbsp. capers**
> **fresh tarragon sprig tips for garnish**

1. In a covered skillet over medium heat with 1 cup water added, poach sliced potatoes for 5 - 10 minutes until they are barely soft. **For microwave:** place sliced potatoes in a shallow container with 1/2 cup water. Cover tightly with plastic wrap and cook on highest temperature for 3 - 4 minutes, until potatoes are barely soft.

2. Drain. With a spatula, carefully transfer the potatoes to a platter.

3. Mix tarragon leaves and capers into the vinaigrette and pour over hot potatoes. Cover loosely with plastic wrap, refrigerate if you are in a hurry, and cool to room temperature.

To serve: Serve at room temperature, garnishing each serving with a tarragon tip.

Roasted Potato and Sausage Salad

This is really good with dark rye bread and Muenster or Edam cheese.

Yield: 4 servings
Preparation time: 30 minutes

> 2 **cups leftover Roasted Potatoes** (p. 237)**, cut into bite-sized chunks, at room temperature**
> 3/4 **cup match-stick-cut summer sausage or 4 oz. Polish sausage, sliced, browned, and cooled to room temperature**
> **1/2 cup minced fresh Italian parsley**
> 2 **green onions, finely chopped**
> 1/2 **cup Dijon Vinaigrette** (p. 273)
> 4 **cups mixed salad greens**
> 1/4 **cup coarsely grated Parmesan cheese**

1. Put potatoes into serving bowl. Add parsley, onion, and 1/4 cup vinaigrette and toss until coated. Add meat and toss again.

2. Toss salad greens with remaining vinaigrette, and distribute them among 4 salad plates. Place the potato mixture on top of the greens and sprinkle each serving with grated cheese.

Hint #2: Good Parmesan cheese is so firm that it is difficult to grate. If you heat it in the microwave for a few seconds, it softens enough to grate easily.

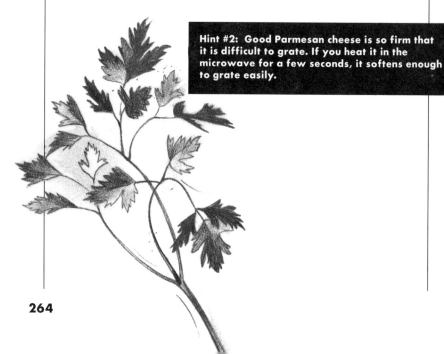

Rice Salad

VARIATIONS: BEANS AND RICE SALAD, WILD RICE SALAD

The first rice salad had to have been a very clever cook's use of leftover rice. This recipe is good, but don't stop here. Rice salad is a wonderful vehicle for cleaning out the refrigerator.

Yield: 4 servings
Preparation time: 25 minutes

STOCK BAG
Remember
your Stock
Bag (p. 12).

4	**cups cooked rice (half should be white, the rest can be a blend) (2 cups uncooked)**
1/2	**cup finely chopped green onions**
2	**green onions, cut diagonally into thin slices**
1	**cup frozen peas, thawed**
1/4	**cup minced red onion**
2	**bell peppers of different colors, stems and pith removed, and sliced very thin, then cut into 1" strips**
1	**cup chopped tomato**
2	**cups chopped fresh vegetables; cooked if appropriate (use 2 or 3: mushrooms, zucchini, string beans, corn, etc.)**
1/4	**cup chopped fresh parsley or cilantro**
2	**tbsp. chopped fresh herb, or 2 tsp. dried herb leaves**
3/4	**cup Vinaigrette of your choice** (p. 273-275)

1. Put rice into large salad or mixing bowl. Add other ingredients except green onions and dressing. Mix thoroughly.

2. Pour dressing over salad and mix again. Garnish with onions.

BEANS AND RICE SALAD

1. Add 1 cup thoroughly rinsed and drained legumes such as: red kidney beans, black beans, black eyed peas, champion peas, pinto beans, etc.

2. Add 1 tsp. Jerk seasoning (See Resources, p. 340 or Jamaican Beans and Rice, p. 249) to Honey Mustard Dressing (p. 277).

WILD RICE SALAD

Substitute cooked wild rice, eliminate peas and vegetables, add
1/2 cup toasted pine nuts or roasted Mexican Pumpkin Seeds
(p. 110), add 1 cup sliced fresh mushrooms, and use Ginger
Sesame Vinaigrette or Dijon Vinaigrette (p. 273).
Garnish with pumpkin seeds.

Pasta Salad

The trick to this delicious version of pasta is to let one flavor dominate, either through a few ingredients combined with one herb in the dressing, or a blend of herbs and one primary ingredient. Too much flavor destroys the subtlety of the pasta.

Yield: 2 servings
Preparation time: 20 minutes

See Hint #2 (p. 15), grating Parmesan cheese.

3	cups cooked and drained pasta*
1/4	cup chopped and pitted calamata olives (or sliced black olives)
1	cup chopped ripe tomato
1/2	cup (approximately) Roasted Bell Pepper (p. 227), chopped
1/2	cup chopped green onion
1	tbsp. chopped Italian parsley
2	tbsp. chopped fresh basil
1	tsp. capers with juice
1 1/2	oz. chopped feta cheese
	cracked pepper to taste
1/2 - 3/4	cup Italian Vinaigrette (p. 273) or Caesar Dressing (p. 276)
1	tbsp. grated Parmesan per serving for garnish
	mixed salad greens

*Use a shaped pasta that will trap the dressing and herbs, such as sea shells or rotini. Smooth pastas end up pretty tasteless after an hour or so.

Mix all the ingredients, except the Parmesan cheese, and let flavors set for 15 minutes.

To serve: Spoon over mixed greens and sprinkle Parmesan over the top.

Santa Fe Salad

VARIATION: SANTA FE FAJITAS

This salad was designed for leftover grilled flank steak. If you make it from scratch, add 1 1/2 hours to grill and cool steak.

Yield: 4 servings
Preparation time: 40 minutes

LEFTOVERS
See Barbe-
cued Flank
Steak (p. 204).

- 6 - 8 oz. leftover flank steak, in very thin slices
- 1/3 cup Red Chili Sauce (p. 298)
- 8 oz. washed and torn mixed greens (p. 254)
- 1/2 cup coarsely chopped green onion
- 3/4 cup coarsely chopped cilantro
- 3/4 cup black beans, rinsed and drained
- 1/2 cup finely chopped, fresh Anaheim pepper,
- 2 avocados, peeled
- 1 tsp. lime juice
- 1 large red bell pepper, stem and pith removed and cut into thin strips
- 4 very thin slices red onion
- 1 cup fresh corn kernels
- 4 Roma tomatoes cut into thin wedges, or the equivalent amount of other ripe tomato
- 8 tbsp. grated Monterey Jack cheese
- 4 tbsp. crumbled feta or chevre cheese
- 8 tbsp. sour cream
- 1/2 pint Quick Tomato Salsa (p. 287)
- 1 cup Lime Cumin Vinaigrette (p. 274)

1. Pour red chili sauce over steak strips and set aside.

2. In a large mixing bowl, toss the salad greens, cilantro, black beans, pepper and chopped onions with 1/2 cup vinaigrette. Place on salad plates.

3. Slice avocado into long, thin slices. Drizzle with lime juice.

4. Arrange the steak strips, avocado slices, bell pepper strips, red onion slices, corn, and tomato wedges on the lettuce mixture. Drizzle remaining dressing over the salads.

5. Sprinkle the grated and crumbled cheese over the salads. Add dollops of sour cream and Salsa to each plate.

SANTA FE FAJITAS

For Santa Fe Fajitas, eliminate mixed greens. Wrap other ingredients in flour tortillas.

Seafood Salad

The key to this salad is lots of seafood, separated rather than mashed, with a little lime juice or lemon juice drizzled over it. The mayonnaise just barely binds it and should not overpower the delicate flavor of the seafood.

Yield: about 1 quart
Preparation time: 30 minutes

2	cups cooked seafood
1	cup finely diced cucumber (seeds removed)
	juice of 1/2 lemon, or 1 lime
2	tbsp. finely sliced and then chopped red onion, or chopped green onion
2	tbsp. chopped Italian parsley
1/2 - 3/4	cup mayonnaise-based dressing (Tartar Sauce [p. 281], **Coleslaw Dressing** [p. 277], etc.)
2	tbsp. cream or half-and-half (to cut the thickness of mayonnaise if necessary, could use caper juice)
1/4	cup capers, drained
1/2	tsp. crushed red pepper flakes
1	tbsp. chopped fresh herb, or 1 tsp. dried herb leaves

1. Flake seafood (if appropriate, obviously not shrimp or scallops) with a fork to create small pieces.

2. Add cucumber, mix together with a fork, and squeeze citrus juice over, tossing gently.

3. Add other ingredients and mix gently with a fork. Taste and correct seasoning with kosher salt if necessary. Cover and chill slightly before serving.

> **Seafood combinations work really well in this salad (shrimp and scallops, smoked salmon and lobster, etc.)**

Lamb and Chevre Salad

This is a salad for leftover Lamb (p. 210). You could buy and cook lamb especially for the salad, but it becomes a very expensive item.

Yield: 4 servings
Preparation time: 40 minutes

8	**oz. sliced leftover Lamb** (p. 210)
8	**oz. Demi-Glace** (p. 107) **from roasted lamb**
3	**tsp. olive oil**
3	**tsp. sherry vinegar**
11/2	**tbsp. granulated sugar**
1/4	**cup water**
1/2	**tsp. crushed red pepper flakes**
6	**oz. thinly sliced fresh fennel**
3	**oz. chevre, marble-sized chunks**
3	**oz. thinly sliced fresh mushrooms**
6	**oz. fresh, crisp mixed greens (butter, lettuce, red or green leaf, arugula, chicory, watercress)**
3/4	**cup Dijon Vinaigrette** (p. 273)
3	**oz. chevre, formed into four 2" circles**
1/4	**cup toasted bread crumbs**
2	**tbsp. unsalted butter or olive oil**

LEFTOVERS
See Roasted Lamb (p. 210). Buy enough for this terrific salad.

1. If there is any rosemary in the Demi-Glace or in the roasting pan, strain it out.

2. Mix olive oil, vinegar, sugar, water, and pepper flakes with the Demi-Glace in a small saucepan.

3. Bring the mixture to a boil on medium heat, and add fennel. When the fennel has cooked for 1 minute, remove it with a slotted spoon and set aside.

4. Remove the sauce from the heat and add mushrooms. Marinate for 2 - 3 minutes. Remove the mushrooms with slotted spoon and set aside.

Until salad spinners were invented there were lots of suggestions for drying greens, some more bizarre than others. My sister was told to tie them in a kitchen towel and spin it in the dryer on no heat cycle; my aunt used to wave towel-wrapped greens in huge circles over her head; a neighbor lined her refrigerator drawers with paper towels. Here's to simple spinners!

5. Reheat sauce and pour over the lamb. Marinate for 3 minutes, and pour sauce off. Reserve for another use (see box this page).

6. Toss greens with Dijon Vinaigrette. Place them on entrée size plates. Sprinkle fennel and mushrooms on greens. Arrange slices of lamb over the top.

7. Dredge cheese rounds in bread crumbs. Sauté on high heat until brown on both sides, about 2 minutes. Place a cheese round on each salad and serve immediately.

Freeze the reserved sauce for soup, risotto, or pasta, or sauté 1 cup sliced mushrooms, pour the sauce over them and serve with Crostini (p. 119) as an hors d'oeuvre.

Asian Chicken Salad

This versatile salad is great with leftover cooked or chilled smoked chicken, fish, shrimp, or crab. Try different vegetable combinations, thinly sliced. If you have a very fine Asian shredder, make a nest of carrots. Add sliced almonds or canned chow mein noodles or pickled ginger or fresh tangerine sections or . . .

Yield: 4 servings
Preparation time: 20 minutes

8	oz. cooked Chicken (p. 167) **or smoked chicken breast, sliced in 2-3" pieces**
3/4	cup Ginger Sesame Vinaigrette (p. 275)
4	oz. mixed greens (see Mixed Greens Salad, p. 254), **broken into bite-sized pieces**
2	oz. shredded Napa Cabbage
1	red bell pepper, seeded, pith removed, thinly sliced
1/4	cup sliced water chestnuts, or bamboo stalks, or julienne-cut jicama
1	stalk celery, thinly sliced 1/4" diagonal cut
2	green onions, sliced on the diagonal into 3/4" lengths
1/4	cup toasted sesame seeds

1. Put the chicken into a small container, and pour 1/4 cup dressing over it to marinate while the rest of the salad is being prepared.

2. In a large bowl, mix Napa cabbage with greens. Add red bell pepper, sliced water chestnuts, and celery. Toss with additional remaining vinaigrette, and transfer to chilled salad plates.

3. Arrange the marinated chicken pieces over the greens, then sprinkle with green onion and toasted sesame seeds.

SALADS

Watermelon, Jicama, and Radish Salad

This is one of the prettiest salads ever, and delicious with Mexican, Caribbean, or other spicy foods.

Yield: 4 - 6 servings
Preparation time: 30 minutes, including making the vinaigrette

> 1/2 **medium-sized seedless watermelon**
> 1 **medium jicama, peeled**
> 6 or 8 **radishes**
> 1/2 **cup chopped fresh cilantro**
> 1/2 **cup Lime Cumin Vinaigrette** (p. 274)

1. Peel, seed, and julienne cut (2" long) the watermelon (about 2 1/2 cups). Put it in a large transparent bowl. Julienne cut (1" long) the jicama (about 1 1/2 cups) and add it to the watermelon. Thinly slice the radishes, then slice again into half circles, and add them to the watermelon and jicama.

2. Add the cilantro and mix gently, taking care not to break the melon.

3. When you are ready to serve, pour Lime Cumin Vinaigrette over the salad and toss again.

To serve: Serve with a slotted spoon.

If you can get yellow watermelon, add it along with the pink; it's gorgeous!

Vinaigrette

This is a basic vinaigrette formula that can be modified almost endlessly by adding flavors such as herbs, spices, or Dijon mustard, and by changing oils and vinegars. Matching oils to vinegars is important, particularly because extra virgin olive oils from different countries taste very different, and a mismatch can be an expensive mistake.

Yield: 1 1/4 cup
Preparation time: 5 minutes for basic Vinaigrette; 10 minutes for the most complicated

> 2 tbsp. red or white wine vinegar (Balsamic, sherry, fruit, or rice vinegar may be substituted)
> 1/2 cup extra virgin olive oil
> 1/2 cup pure olive oil
> 1/4 tsp. kosher salt
> fresh coarsely ground pepper to taste

Mix or whisk ingredients until completely blended.

VARIATIONS

Dijon Vinaigrette: Add 2 tsp. Dijon mustard.

Blue Cheese Vinaigrette: Use red or white wine vinegar, add 2 tbsp. crumbled blue cheese, and mix with a fork.

Pesto Vinaigrette: Use white wine vinegar, add 2 tbsp. pesto.

Tomato Vinaigrette: Use Balsamic vinegar, add 1/4 cup tomato purée (not tomato sauce).

Salsa Vinaigrette: Use red wine vinegar and only pure olive oil. Add 1/4 cup tomato salsa, 1/2 tsp. ground chili powder, 2 tsp. lime juice, and 1/2 tsp. crushed red pepper flakes.

Italian Vinaigrette: Use Balsamic vinegar, add 1 tbsp. Italian herb mix.

Herb Shallot Vinaigrette: Use Balsamic vinegar, add 2 tbsp. chopped fresh herb (one variety), 2 tsp. finely chopped shallot.

Orange Shallot Vinaigrette: For vinegar use 3 tbsp. *unseasoned* rice vinegar. Add 1/4 cup fresh orange juice, 1 tbsp. finely chopped orange zest, 1 shallot finely chopped, 1/4 tsp. crushed red pepper flakes. For oil use 3/4 cup olive oil.

Lime Cumin Vinaigrette: 2 tbsp. lime juice, 1 tbsp. lemon juice, 1/2 tsp. cumin, 1/2 tsp. red chili powder, 1/2 tsp. kosher salt, 1/3 cup peanut oil, and 1/3 cup pure olive oil.

Chutney Vinaigrette: For vinegar use 3 tbsp. *unseasoned* rice vinegar, add 1/2 cup chutney.

Lemon Oil Vinaigrette: Substitute 3 tbsp. fresh lemon juice for vinegar.

Low-Fat Vinaigrette

Keeps for up to two weeks covered in refrigerator.

Yield: 1 cup
Preparation time: 5 minutes

> 1 **cup chicken or vegetable stock**
> 2 **tbsp. red wine vinegar**
> 1 **tbsp. pure olive oil**
> 1/2 **tsp. minced garlic**
> 2 **tsp. fresh tarragon leaves, chopped, or 1 tsp. dried**
> 1 **tsp. Dijon mustard**

Combine all ingredients.

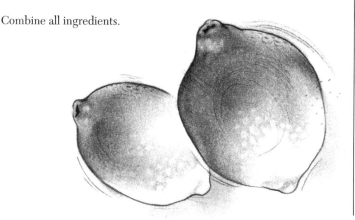

Pineapple Mint Vinaigrette

This recipe works best with fresh mint.

Yield: 1 1/2 cups
Preparation time: 10 minutes

        3 tbsp. fresh mint leaves, finely chopped
      1/2 cup extra virgin olive oil
        1 tbsp. fresh lime juice
        1 tbsp. *unseasoned* rice vinegar
        1 tbsp. fresh cilantro, minced
        2 medium shallots, peeled and minced
      1/2 cup fresh pineapple, minced with juice
        2 tsp. minced garlic
      1/2 tsp. crushed red pepper flakes
          kosher salt to taste

Mix all ingredients. Let flavors set for 30 minutes.

Ginger Sesame Vinaigrette

This is a wonderful sauce for pasta (see Spicy Vermicelli Noodles, p. 149) or a dip for cooked shellfish or raw oysters.

Yield: 1 pint
Preparation time: 15 minutes

        2 tbsp. granulated sugar
      1/2 cup soy sauce
      1/2 cup *unseasoned* rice vinegar
        1 tsp. pure sesame oil
      1/2 cup peanut oil
        2 tbsp. grated fresh ginger
        1 tbsp. lime juice
      1/2 tsp. crushed red pepper flakes
      1/4 cup green onion, sliced diagonally (about
          3/4" long and 1/4" thick)
      1/4 cup finely chopped fresh cilantro (optional)

Combine all ingredients and mix thoroughly. Let flavors set for
    10 minutes before serving.

Seafood Marinade: Add cilantro. Pour half over seafood before
    it's cooked and the remainder afterward.

Caesar Salad Dressing

VARIATION: RED CHILI DRESSING

A taste for anchovy is personal, sometimes even a little bit touchy.
For me, a Caesar Salad (p. 254) without anchovy just isn't.

Yield: 1 pint
Preparation time: 15 minutes

>   2 tsp. garlic, minced
>   2 tsp. anchovy paste, or 2 anchovies
> 2 1/2 oz. lemon juice
>   1 egg, or 1/4 cup egg substitute
> 1 1/2 tsp. Worcestershire sauce
>   1/4 cup extra virgin olive oil
> 1 1/2 cup pure olive oil
>   1/2 tsp. coarse ground pepper
>   1/4 tsp. kosher salt

1. Process garlic, anchovy, lemon juice, egg, and Worcestershire
    sauce until thoroughly blended.

2. Gradually add oil, whisking or processing until the dressing
    emulsifies and thickens slightly. Add salt and pepper and
    stir again.

RED CHILI DRESSING

>   2 tsp. garlic
>   juice from 1 lime
>   1 egg, or 1/4 cup egg substitute
>   1/2 tsp. ground cumin
>   1/2 tsp. ground red chili powder (not pure
>   cayenne)
>   1/2 tsp. kosher salt
>   1/2 tsp. crushed red pepper flakes
>   1/4 cup peanut oil
> 1 1/2 cups corn oil

Process ingredients as above.

Honey Mustard Dressing

VARIATION: CURRIED HONEY MUSTARD DRESSING

There are some very good bottled honey mustard dressings; most of them are just a little too sweet for my taste. If you find one you like and it's too sweet, try adding a little rice vinegar.

Yield: 1 3/4 cups
Preparation time: 10 minutes

- 1/4 cup warm water
- 2 tbsp. honey
- 1/8 tsp. allspice
- 1 tbsp. plus 1 tsp. mustard powder
- 1/4 cup Dijon mustard
- 1/4 cup *unseasoned* rice vinegar
- 1 cup pure olive oil
- 1/4 tsp. crushed red pepper flakes

Mix honey in water, then add other ingredients, whisking continually. Let flavors set up for 5 minutes before serving.

CURRIED HONEY MUSTARD DRESSING

Add 1 tsp. curry powder or Garam Masala Curry Paste® (see Resources, p. 340).

Coleslaw Dressing

By reducing the caper juice to 1/2 tsp., this turns into a good tartar sauce.

Yield: 1 cup
Preparation time: 10 minutes

- 1 cup Homemade Mayonnaise (p. 279)*
- 1 tsp. Dijon mustard
- 1/4 cup capers, drained
- 1 tbsp. caper juice
- 1/4 cup finely chopped green onion
- 1/2 tsp. crushed red pepper flakes

*If you do not use homemade, I recommend Hellmann's® or Best Foods® (same manufacturer).

Combine all ingredients and let flavors set up for 10 minutes.

Flavored Butters

Flavored butter may be served as a spread or used at room temperature as a "sauce" over seafood. Make up your own favorite flavors.

Yield: 1/4 lb. butter
Preparation time: 5 minutes

> **1/4 lb. butter, at room temperature**
> **2 tbsp. chopped fresh herb, or 1 tsp. dried or ground herb**

1. In a processor, pulse 5 or 6 times to blend. If you pulse too much, the butter will turn whatever color the herb or spice is.

2. Chill until it is spreadable or until you wish to serve it. Flavored butters will keep frozen for several months, or covered and refrigerated for several weeks.

VARIATIONS
Coriander Butter: 1 tsp. ground coriander (cilantro seeds)

Cilantro Butter: 2 tbsp. minced fresh cilantro or 1 tsp. dried leaves

Cumin Butter: 1 tsp. ground cumin

Lime Chili Butter: 1 tsp. ground chili powder plus juice of 1 lime

Try flavored butter on the toast under poached eggs. Yum!

Homemade Mayonnaise

Really, this is so easy, and it makes such a difference! With a blender or processor, mayonnaise takes 2 - 3 minutes to make, and the taste is completely different from whatever kind you can buy at the store. Just try it, you'll see.

Yield: 1 pint
Preparation time: 5 minutes

> 2 tbsp. white wine vinegar
> 1 egg
> 1 tsp. Dijon mustard
> 1/4 cup extra virgin olive oil
> 1 3/4 cup no-cholesterol oil
> 1/4 tsp. crushed red pepper flakes
> kosher salt to taste

Note: If you add fresh green herbs before the final 1 or 2 pulses, the mayonnaise will be green.

1. Put vinegar, egg, and Dijon mustard into a processor or blender and blend.

2. With machine on, slowly add olive oil first, then other oil, blending or processing until ingredients emulsify into mayonnaise. Stop adding oil when the consistency is what you want. If you need more oil than the recipe calls for, use it, as oils vary.

3. Add pepper flakes and herbs or extras, and pulse 2 or 3 more times.

4. Season to taste with salt.

Store mayonnaise, refrigerated, in covered glass or plastic container. It will last several weeks before it begins to separate.

VARIATIONS
Dijon Mayonnaise: Add 1/4 cup Dijon instead of 1 tsp.

Pesto Mayonnaise: Add 2 tbsp. pesto for the last 30 seconds of blending. This mayonnaise is green.

Herb Mayonnaise: Add 2 tsp. dried, or 2 tbsp. minced fresh herbs, during the last 1 or 2 pulses.

Wasabi Mayonnaise: Use *unseasoned* rice vinegar and add 1 tbsp. wasabi horseradish, 1 tsp. fresh lime juice, and 2 tsp. grated fresh ginger. The wasabi turns this mayonnaise a lovely pale green.

Curry Mayonnaise: Add 1 tsp. curry powder, and stir in 1/4 cup mango chutney at the end.

Red Chili Mayonnaise: Add 1 tsp. ground red chili pepper, and stir in 1/4 cup tomato salsa at the end.

Mixed Olive Mayonnaise: Add 6 oz. drained pimento-stuffed green olives (cheapest grade called "olive salad mix"); 6 oz. drained, pitted Calamata olives (Resources, p. 340) or Marinated Black Olives (p. 113); 1 tsp. minced garlic; 2 tbsp. green olive mix juice; 1/2 tsp. crushed red pepper flakes. Pulse to mince olives and mix ingredients.

> **Store pesto, mayonnaise, salsas, chutneys, etc., with the least amount of air possible between the food and the lid. Mold spores live in that air.**

Cajun Tartar Sauce

Really good with chilled shrimp or crayfish!

Yield: 1 pint
Preparation time: approximately 10 minutes (if the mayonnaise is already-made)

> 1 cup **Homemade Mayonnaise*** (p. 279)
> 1 tsp. **Dijon mustard (if you don't have Dijon, don't substitute hot dog mustard, just leave it out)**
> 3/4 cup **chunky Salsa (drained if fresh)**
> 1/4 cup **capers with 1 tsp. caper juice**
> 1/4 cup **minced Italian parsley**
> 1/2 tsp. **paprika**
> 1 tsp. **Worcestershire Sauce**
> 1/2 tsp. **crushed red pepper flakes**

*If you do not use homemade, I recommend Hellmann's® or Best Foods® (same manufacturer).

Combine ingredients and let flavors set for 5 - 8 minutes. Add more red pepper if necessary.

Red Chili Tartar Sauce

VARIATION: CREAMY RED CHILI DRESSING

A south-of-the-border version of the old standby.

Yield: 1 1/2 cups
Preparation time: 10 minutes

> 1/4 cup **mild tomato salsa**
> 3/4 cup **mayonnaise**
> 1/2 tsp. **ground cumin**
> 1 **4 oz. can chopped mild green chilies**
> 1 tbsp. **white vinegar**
> 1/4 tsp. **dehydrated red pepper flakes**

> **Store pesto, mayonnaise, salsas, chutneys, etc., with the least amount of air possible between the food and the lid. Mold spores live in that air.**

Combine all ingredients and let flavor set up for 10 minutes before serving.

CREAMY RED CHILI DRESSING
Reverse the quantities of salsa and mayonnaise.

Crème Fraîche

VARIATIONS: MOCK CRÈME FRAÎCHE, CRÈME FRAÎCHE SWIRLS

There are several commercially made crème fraîche products available at specialty food markets. This one works fastest with heavy whipping cream and 4% buttermilk (not a low-fat item!).

Yield: 5 oz.
Preparation time: 5 minutes. Curing time: 6 hours

> **4 oz. ultra-pasteurized whipping cream**
> **1 tbsp. buttermilk**

1. Mix the cream and buttermilk in a glass container. Cover loosely, to protect it from dust, etc., and let it cure at room temperature for 6 plus hours.

2. Cover tightly and refrigerate until needed. Refrigerated it will store for 1 week.

Option: Add minced fresh herbs: cilantro, basil, mint, etc.

MOCK CRÈME FRAÎCHE
> **1/3 cup sour cream**
> **1 tbsp. milk**
> **1 tbsp. powdered sugar**

Whisk milk and sugar into sour cream and serve.

CRÈME FRAÎCHE SWIRLS
Put it into a plastic bottle and squeeze swirls onto soup or sauce, as a garnish. For Swirls, the Crème Fraîche must be almost too thick to pour.

> **Hint #22: Swirls made in sauces add a special touch that makes you look like a pro. All you need is a plastic bottle with a 1/8" open tip lid (drug stores carry them for travel cosmetics). Suggestion: practice on a plain plate. Put the sauce into the container and squeeze swirls to your heart's content. For "bleeding hearts": squeeze dots about 1" apart on top of sauce. In one movement, pull the tip of a paring knife, skewer, or toothpick through and slightly beyond each dot. For fleur-de-lis, squeeze straight, horizontal lines across the sauce about 1" apart. Using the tip of a sharp paring knife, skewer, or toothpick, pull vertical lines through the horizontal lines, alternating from top to bottom, then from bottom to top.**

Lemon Oil Drizzle

VARIATION: LEMON CAPER SAUCE

This incredibly simple sauce transforms cooked vegetables. The lemon brings out subtle flavors and the oil provides just enough sheen. I add the salt, pepper, herbs, or capers just before or as I put it on the vegetables.

Yield: 1 cup (16 servings); portion size: 1 tbsp. per serving
Preparation and cooking time: 5 minutes

> 7 oz. extra virgin olive oil
> 1 oz. fresh lemon juice, strained for seeds
> 1/8 tsp. kosher salt
> 1/8 tsp. cracked black pepper

Add the lemon juice to the oil and mix. Add the salt and pepper
    (herbs, capers, etc.) and drizzle over steamed vegetables.

LEMON CAPER SAUCE

> 2 tsp. fresh Italian parsley, finely chopped
> 2 tbsp. capers
> 1/4 tsp. crushed red pepper flakes

Add capers, herbs, and pepper flakes. Let flavors set up for
    5 minutes before serving.

> **Make a pint or so at a time and keep it in the refrigerator. Microwave it for 10 seconds to liquefy the oil.**

Garlic Oil Parsley Sauce

This is a simple and elegant sauce for plain pasta (with grated Parmesan on top) or pastas with particularly flavorful fillings, or for steamed potatoes, or as a sauce for cooked vegetables.

Yield: 3/4 cup
Preparation and cooking time: 5 minutes

> 1/2 cup extra virgin olive oil
> 2 tsp. minced garlic
> 1/4 tsp. crushed red pepper flakes
> 1/2 cup Italian parsley, minced

In a small skillet over medium low heat, cook garlic and pepper
    flakes in oil until the garlic is softened, about 4 minutes.
    Add parsley and stir until mixed. Remove from heat.

Sun-Dried Tomato Pesto

Covered and refrigerated, this pesto will keep for months. It makes a great cracker spread; it adds instant thickness to tomato sauce; it's a wonderful flavor for Dijon Glaze (p. 105); and it really adds flavor to sandwiches or scrambled eggs. I also mix it with a little chicken stock and toss it with pasta. Instant entree!

Yield: 1 pint
Preparation time: about 10 minutes

1	3 oz. package dehydrated or sun-dried tomatoes
1/4	cup water
2	tsp. minced garlic
3	tsp. dried basil leaves
3/4	cup extra virgin olive oil
1/8	tsp. crushed red pepper flakes
	kosher salt to taste

1. In covered saucepan on medium high, cook tomatoes and water until the tomatoes have absorbed the liquid and softened, about 3 minutes, or microwave on high.

2. Transfer to processor bowl and add other ingredients, except salt.

3. Pulse until it becomes a paste with some texture, almost but not quite puréed. Add salt to taste.

4. Put in a covered glass or plastic container and refrigerate.

Store pesto, mayon-naise, salsas, chutneys, etc., with the least amount of air possible between the food and the lid. Mold spores live in that air.

Greek Marinade

This is a wonderful marinade for fish, shellfish, or chicken.

Yield: 1/2 pint
Preparation time: 20 minutes, including flavor set up time

> 3/4 cup Greek olive oil
> 2 tbsp. red wine vinegar
> 1 1/2 tsp. minced garlic
> 1 tbsp. chopped fresh oregano leaves, or
>   1 tsp. dried
>   juice of 1/2 lemon

Note: If you add 1/2 cup water or vegetable stock, this makes a
good salad dressing, especially if you have some feta cheese to
crumble over the salad greens.

Blend all ingredients and let flavors set up for 15 minutes. Store,
covered, in glass container.

Moroccan Marinade (Moroccan Spice Paste)

If you can't get Garam Masala Curry Paste® (Resources, p. 340), this is a good substitute. See Moroccan Chicken and Moroccan Curry Sauce (p. 296). It also is a good basting sauce on grilled or baked chicken, pork, flank steak, prawns, halibut, Chilean Sea bass, or other firm- fleshed, white fish.

Yield: 1 cup
Preparation time: 10 minutes

1	tsp. paprika
1/2	tsp. ground cumin
1	tsp. turmeric
1/4	tsp. ground anise seed
1/2	tsp. ground ginger
1	tsp. curry powder
1/2	tsp. crushed red pepper flakes
1/2	tsp. kosher salt
1/2	cup peanut oil or pure olive oil
4	tbsp. fresh cilantro, chopped, or 2 tsp. dried cilantro leaves*
1	tbsp. fresh lemon juice (for fish)

*This paste will keep in a sealed plastic bag, refrigerated, indefinitely. If you intend to keep it on hand, use dried cilantro.

1. Process all ingredients except cilantro and lemon juice in a processor or blender until it becomes a paste.

2. To use as a marinade: In the cooking pan, brush meat, poultry, or seafood with paste on all sides. Cover loosely with plastic wrap and let stand at room temperature for 30 minutes.

3. Cook fish or meat at high temperature (p. 14) and remove to warmed platter.

To finish the sauce: Add 2 tbsp. of olive oil or butter or stock to the pan and add cilantro and lemon juice for fish. Heat and pour over sliced meat or fish. Serve immediately.

Quick Fruit Chutney

Almost homemade, fresh tasting chutney in minutes!

Yield: 1/2 pint
Preparation time: 10 minutes

> 1 jar prepared fruit chutney
> 1 pear, cored and diced
> 1 small can crushed pineapple, strained
> 1/4 tsp. crushed red pepper flakes (unless
> the prepared chutney is labeled "hot")

Mix the pear, pineapple, and pepper flakes into the chutney.
Let flavors set up for 5 minutes.

Quick Tomato Salsa

This recipe is very close to homemade!

Yield: 1 pint
Preparation time: 5 minutes

> 1 pint store-bought salsa, mild
> 1 fresh, ripe tomato, chopped
> 1/4 cup chopped fresh cilantro
> 1/4 tsp. crushed red pepper flakes
> 2 tsp. lime juice

If salsa is the fresh type from a refrigerated case, strain out excess
juice. Add remaining ingredients, mix, and serve.

Hint #30: A non-reactive container is one that will not react chemically to the acid in fruit, peppers, vinegar, or salt. Stainless steel, plastic, and glass are non-reactive. Aluminum and copper are reactive.

Store pesto, mayonnaise, salsas, chutneys, etc., with the least amount of air possible between the food and the lid. Mold spores live in that air.

Cranberry Chutney

When my daughter, Mari, brought this to Thanksgiving one year, it usurped the throne formerly held by our old standby cranberry orange, and it will be at our family table for many generations to come.

Yield: 1 quart
Preparation time: 20 minutes; cooking time: 25 minutes plus cooling

1/2	cup berry or cider vinegar
2 1/4	cups brown sugar
1/2	tsp. ground cinnamon
1/4	tsp. ground allspice
1/4	tsp. ground cloves
1/2	tsp. ground ginger
1	tsp. curry powder
2	tbsp. orange zest, chopped
2	juice oranges, sliced and cut into 8ths, with skin on and seeds removed
2	tbsp. lemon zest, chopped
2	lemons, sliced and quartered, with skin on and seeds removed
1	Granny Smith apple, peeled, cored, and coarsely chopped (processor)
6	cups fresh cranberries, coarsely chopped (processor)
1/2	cup golden raisins
1/2	cup dried apricots or peaches, coarsely chopped (processor)
1/2	cup chopped walnuts or almonds

1. Put all ingredients except nuts into a saucepan. Simmer on low heat until sauce thickens and fruit is softened and blended, about 20 minutes. Transfer to a non-reactive container, add nuts and let cool to room temperature.

2. If it is made ahead, store refrigerated in a tightly covered glass or plastic container.

3. Serve at room temperature.

- **This sauce will store refrigerated in an airtight container for several months. It's wonderful with grilled Italian sausage!**

- **Store pesto, mayonnaise, salsas, chutneys, etc., with the least amount of air possible between the food and the lid. Mold spores live in that air.**

Fresh Mango Tomatillo Salsa

This salsa is wonderful with grilled seafood, pork chops, or chicken.

Yield: 5-6 cups
Preparation time: 20 minutes

6	cups fresh tomatillos, or 1 14 oz. can
1/2	cup unsweetened pineapple juice
1/4	cup unseasoned rice vinegar
1	tsp. minced garlic
1/2	tsp. crushed red pepper flakes
1/2	cup chopped fresh cilantro leaves
1	tsp. cumin
2	limes, juiced
1/4	cup minced red onion
3	ripe, firm mangoes, peeled, pitted and diced
1/2	cup green and red bell pepper, pith removed and finely chopped

1. If you are using fresh tomatillos, peel and cut them into chunks. Steam the chunks in a small, covered pan (or glass dish for microwave) until they are soft, 5 minutes on stove; 3 minutes in microwave.

2. Put tomatillos, pineapple juice, vinegar, garlic, pepper flakes, cilantro, cumin, and lime juice in the processor, and pulse to blend, but do *not* purée.

3. Combine the red onion, mangoes, and bell peppers in a non-reactive bowl, and stir in the processed mixture.

4. Cover with plastic wrap and refrigerate until ready to serve.

Hint #30: A non-reactive container is one that will not react chemically to the acid in fruit, peppers, vinegar, or salt. Stainless steel, plastic, and glass are non-reactive. Aluminum and copper are reactive.

Tropical Fruit Salsa

Mango, peach, nectarine, or pear substitute nicely for the papaya.

Yield: 3 cups
Preparation time: 45 minutes plus refrigeration time

> **3/4** cup finely diced fresh pineapple or orange
> **1** medium *ripe* papaya, peeled, seeded, diced into 1/4" cubes (1 cup)
> **1** cup peeled, seeded cucumber diced into 1/4" cubes
> **1** Anaheim chili pepper, seeded and minced
> **1/4** cup red onion, finely diced
> **1** tbsp. granulated sugar
> **1** tbsp. *unseasoned* rice vinegar
> **2** tbsp. fresh lime juice
> **1/2** tsp. kosher salt
> **3** tbsp. minced fresh cilantro leaves, or 2 tsp. dried
> **3** tbsp. minced fresh mint leaves, or 2 tsp. dried
> **1/2** tsp. crushed red pepper flakes (optional)

1. Combine first five ingredients in a non-reactive bowl, and toss them gently with a fork.

2. In a separate bowl, mix the remaining ingredients. Let the flavors blend for 5 minutes, then taste. Correct the seasoning with lime juice or salt.

3. Pour the liquid over the chopped fruit and vegetable, cover with plastic wrap and refrigerate for at least 2 hours.

   Serve at room temperature.

Store pesto, mayonnaise, salsas, chutneys, etc., with the least amount of air possible between the food and the lid. Mold spores live in that air.

Hint #30: A non-reactive container is one that will not react chemically to the acid in fruit, peppers, vinegar, or salt. Stainless steel, plastic, and glass are non-reactive. Aluminum and copper are reactive.

Italian Tomato Salsa (Salsa Cruda)

This is an Italian salsa, not Mexican. In Italy it is served on grilled bread, called bruschetta. It is wonderful that way and on Crostini (p. 119).

Yield: 1 pint
Preparation time: 15 minutes. **Marinating time:** 30 minutes

- 1 medium or 2 small semi-green tomatoes, diced (about 3/4 cup)
- 1 yellow tomato, diced (optional; it's beautiful if it's available)
- 1 ripe red tomato, diced
- 1 stalk celery, chopped fine
- 1/4 cup coarsely chopped yellow onion (1 small onion)
- 1/2 cup chopped fresh basil, oregano, or marjoram leaves, or 2 tbsp. dried leaves
- 2 tbsp. finely chopped Italian parsley (if it's not available, leave it out; don't use regular parsley)
- 1 tbsp. fresh lemon juice
- 1/2 tsp. crushed red pepper flakes
- 1 tbsp. extra virgin olive oil
- 2 tbsp. drained capers
- 1 tbsp. caper juice

Combine ingredients in non-reactive bowl. Let flavors set for 30 minutes before serving. Serve this salsa with a slotted spoon.

This is OK on the second day. From then on, add it to soup or sauce, or toss it.

291

Quick Tomato Sauce

VARIATIONS: LIGHT TOMATO SAUCE, SUN-DRIED TOMATO SAUCE

This is my 5-minute homemade alternative to Paul Newman or Chef Boyardee®. For variety, add capers, marinated black olives, sliced mushrooms, roasted or sautéed bell pepper, sautéed eggplant, chopped zucchini, etc.

Yield: 1 pint
Preparation and cooking time: 10 minutes

> 2 **cloves fresh garlic, minced, or 1 tsp. dehydrated**
> 2 **tbsp. extra virgin olive oil**
> 1 **14 1/2 oz. can premium diced tomatoes in purée**
> 1/2 **cup red wine**
> 1/2 **cup Italian parsley, finely chopped**
> 1/4 **cup finely chopped fresh basil, oregano, or marjoram, or 1 tbsp. dried leaves**
> 1/4 **tsp. crushed red pepper flakes**
> **kosher salt to taste**

For low fat, reduce the olive oil to 1 tbsp.

1. Put the garlic and oil into a cold saucepan. Turn heat to medium low and cook until garlic softens and just starts to color, 3 - 5 minutes. Add all other ingredients but salt.

2. Simmer for 3 - 4 minutes and taste, particularly for the "heat" from the chili peppers. Add salt and correct seasoning if necessary.

LIGHT TOMATO SAUCE
Eliminate Italian parsley and substitute vegetable stock for wine.

SUN-DRIED TOMATO SAUCE
Add 1/4 cup Sun-Dried Tomato Pesto (p. 284), or chopped sun-dried tomatoes from a jar, or re-hydrate dried tomatoes (microwave works fast), chopped.

> **Do not overcook garlic. At first the heat releases the acid and makes the garlic mellow and rich. The next step (when the garlic browns) is bitter and bad-breath causing. If garlic browns, throw it out.**

Creamy Tomato Sauce

This is a very easy, basic creamy tomato sauce. For variety, add different herbs .

Yield: 1 1/2 pints
Preparation and cooking time: 10 minutes

- 1   14 1/2 oz. can *crushed* tomatoes in purée
- 1   tsp. lemon juice
- 1/2   tsp. kosher salt
- 1/8   tsp. crushed red pepper flakes
- 1/4   cup finely chopped fresh herb (basil, marjoram, tarragon), or 1 tbsp. dried leaves (not ground)
- 1/2   cup heavy cream

1. Combine all ingredients except cream, in non-reactive saucepan. Heat to a low simmer and cook for 3 - 4 minutes, until flavors blend.

2. Add cream and simmer until sauce thickens slightly.

- **What is a non-reactive pan anyway? See Hint #30, p. 18.**
- **If you can't find crushed tomatoes, put diced   tomatoes in purée in the processor and crush them.**

Puttanesca Sauce

Puttanesca is similar to marinara sauce, but it is tart and spicy. It should be "hot" enough to establish a bite, but the pepper should not overpower the delicate flavor of the herbs.

Yield: 4 - 6 servings
Preparation and cooking time: 20 minutes (If you are pitting the olives, add 10 minutes.)

> 1/4 **cup extra virgin olive oil (for low-fat, use 2 tsp.)**
> 2 **tsp. finely minced garlic**
> 1 **14 1/2 oz. can premium diced tomatoes in purée**
> 3/4 **cup calamata olives, pitted and chopped** (Resources, p. 340)
> 1/2 **bunch Italian parsley, leaves only, finely chopped, or 2 tbsp. dried**
> 1 **bunch fresh basil, chopped, or 3 tbsp. dried**
> 1/2 **tsp. crushed red pepper flakes**
> 1/3 **cup capers plus 2 tbsp. caper juice kosher salt to taste**
> 1 **anchovy, minced, or 1 tsp. anchovy paste (optional)**

1. Heat garlic in olive oil on low, until it softens and releases acid, about 3 minutes.

2. Add tomato, olives, parsley, and basil. Simmer until herbs are absorbed and softened, 5 more minutes. Add crushed pepper, capers, and anchovy.

3. Simmer for 5 minutes until flavors have set. Taste for "heat"; if it doesn't taste spicy enough for you, add 1/4 tsp. crushed pepper flakes and let the sauce sit over warm heat for 5 more minutes. Taste again, and then add salt if necessary.

With pasta: Ladle about 1/2 cup over the top of cooked, slightly oiled pasta, and serve with grated Parmesan. (Use less sauce than with marinara).

As a side sauce for chicken or fish or a spread for bruschetta: Heat or use at room temperature.

Keeps tightly covered in the refrigerator for two weeks.

Fresh Tomato Sauce

This is a very light sauce that complements seafood and pasta, especially ravioli or tortellini.

Yield: about 2 cups
Preparation time: 15 minutes

>   1/3 cup extra virgin olive oil
>   3 cloves garlic, thinly sliced or minced
>   2 cups ripe, coarsely chopped tomatoes*
>   1/2 cup chopped fresh basil
>   1/2 tsp. crushed red pepper flakes
>   1/4 cup tomato purée
>   kosher salt to taste

*If tomatoes are not vine-ripened, use Romas.

1. Put oil and garlic in a saucepan over medium low heat, and cook garlic until it softens and releases acid (3 minutes).

2. Add tomatoes, basil, peppers, and purée, and simmer for 5 minutes.

If you like garlic, I suggest you buy a garlic slicer gadget made by Acea® (about $8). It slices garlic cloves paper thin in seconds, and it is very easy to clean!

Moroccan Curry Sauce

I have never been to Morocco and I made this up on a hunch after I watched Humphrey Bogart in The Maltese Falcon. *All I know is that the title sounds romantic and the sauce tastes like I think Moroccan sauces might. It is delicious with poultry or rabbit, and also is wonderful over couscous.*

Yield: 1 1/2 pints
Preparation time: 20 minutes

2	tbsp. pure olive oil
1	medium yellow onion, cut in half and sliced 1/4" thick
1/2	tsp. allspice
1	green pepper, seeded, pith removed and sliced into thin strips
2	cups stock (chicken, vegetable, or meat)
1	14 1/2 oz. can premium diced tomatoes in purée
2	tbsp. **Garam Masala Curry Paste**® (Resources, p. 340) **or Moroccan Marinade** (p. 286)

1. In a small skillet over medium heat, sauté onion slices in oil until they are translucent, 5 - 6 minutes. Sprinkle the allspice over the onions, then add the pepper slices and continue to sauté until the peppers begin to soften slightly.

2. Add the stock, tomatoes, and spice paste, turn the heat down to low, and simmer for 10 minutes, to reduce the moisture and thicken the sauce.

See recipes for Home-made and Modified Canned Stock (p. 108).

Spicy Caribbean Sauce

*Jerk seasoning usually is very spicy, so if you haven't tasted it
before, go slowly. Use as a sauce on or marinade for poultry,
seafood, or meat.*

Yield: 1 1/4 cup
Preparation and cooking time: about 20 minutes

See recipes
for Home-
made and
Modified
Canned Stock
(p. 12).

> 1 cup chicken stock, preferably Homemade
> 1 tbsp. chopped red onion
> 3 tbsp. water
> 2 tsp. cornstarch
> 1/2 cup crushed pineapple, unstrained
> 1 tsp. orange juice concentrate
> 1 tbsp. grated ginger
>   zest and juice from 1 lime
> 1 tbsp. Pickapeppa® sauce or 1 tsp. Jerk
>   seasoning paste
> 1 tsp. curry powder or Garam Masala
>   **Curry Paste**® (Resources, p. 340)
> 1 green onion, chopped finely

1. Put stock and onion into a small saucepan and bring to a low
    boil. Cook the onion for about 1 minute.

2. Meanwhile, add water to the cornstarch and stir into a smooth
    paste. Add the paste to the stock and cook, uncovered, until it
    clears and thickens slightly.

3. Add remaining ingredients and simmer for 5 more minutes.
    Remove from heat and cool to room temperature.

Store refrigerated in a tightly covered non-reactive container.

**Freeze extra sauce in a zip-type bag. For
instant "Jerk" rice, scoop out 2 tbsp. of frozen
sauce from the bag and stir it into cooked rice.**

Red Chili Sauce

This sauce is flavorful and a little spicy, almost like a Mexican chutney. It's wonderful served over Dijon-Glazed Chicken (p. 167), with Grilled Pork Chops (p. 217), Barbecued Flank Steak (p. 204), or ground beef, or as a sauce with fajitas or quesadillas.

Yield: 2 cups
Preparation time: 34 minutes

2	red dried ancho or poblano chilies, stemmed and seeded
1 1/2	cups water
2	tbsp. corn oil
1/4	cup chopped yellow onion (about 1 small onion)
3	tsp. minced garlic (about 3 cloves)
3/4	cup fresh tomatoes, coarsely chopped (3 small, or 1 large)
1	14 1/2 oz. can premium diced tomatoes in purée
1	tsp. ground cumin
1	tsp. powdered unsweetened chocolate
1	tbsp. minced fresh oregano leaves or 1 tsp. dried leaves
1	tbsp. tamarind paste (optional) (Resources, p. 340)*

*Tamarind paste provides a tart/sweet, slightly fruity flavor. A suggested substitute for tamarind paste in this sauce is 2 fresh tomatillos, peeled, chopped, and steamed to soften, plus 1/2 tsp. honey.

1. Place chilies in a small, oven-proof skillet and roast for 8 minutes in a 350° oven. Check them while they are roasting, and shake the pan if they are getting black. Remove from the oven and set aside so the pan will cool.

2. Put the water in a saucepan, add the roasted chilies, and simmer covered until they are re-hydrated, about 15 minutes (microwave, 5 minutes, but not in that pan!).

3. In the same skillet, heat the corn oil to medium and cook the onion and garlic until softened and translucent, about 5 minutes.

4. Purée the chilies and cooking water in the processor. Add the canned and fresh tomatoes, onion, garlic, cumin, chocolate, oregano, and tamarind (optional). Pulse process until the mixture is thoroughly blended but still coarsely textured.

6. Return the sauce to the saucepan and simmer for 15 minutes, or until the sauce is reduced to about 1 pint, and is as thick as bottled salsa. Taste. If it is not "hot" enough, add crushed red pepper flakes, 1/4 tsp. at a time, waiting for at least 5 minutes after each addition.

Covered and refrigerated, this sauce will keep for several days.

- **See Hint #12 (p. 15), chili peppers.**
- **Wash and dry your hands thoroughly after handling chili peppers, or use rubber gloves.**

Black Bean Sauce

This sauce is very Tex-Mex or Pacific Rim. The mustiness of the fermented black bean combined with the tart goat cheese and lime is just wonderful. Serve it over Dijon-Glazed Chicken Breasts (p. 167) or Fish (p. 182), with Chili Corn Fritters (p. 165), or Quesadilla (p. 175). Serve Tomato Salsa (p. 287) on the side.

Yield: 1 pint
Preparation and cooking time: 25 minutes

> 2 **tbsp. fermented black beans, or 1 tbsp.**
> **prepared Chinese black bean garlic sauce**
> **(Asian section of grocery store)**
> (Resources, p. 340)
> 1/2 **cup canned black beans, rinsed**
> 2 **tsp. lime zest**
> 1 **tbsp. lime juice (juice from one lime)**
> 2 **cups chicken stock**
> 1 **tsp. red chili powder**
> 1/2 **cup heavy cream**
> 1 **oz. chevre**
> 1/2 **tsp. crushed red pepper flakes**
> 1/4 **cup minced fresh cilantro, optional**

1. Rinse fermented beans several times, and soak for at least 1 hour. Rinse again thoroughly, drain, and purée with canned beans and a little stock, gradually adding more until a smooth purée is formed.

2. Transfer to saucepan, stir in lime zest and bring to low boil, simmering for 5 - 6 minutes.

3. Add chevre, cream, and crushed pepper flakes, and simmer until the sauce thickens and flavors have thoroughly set up, about 5 - 8 minutes.

4. About 5 minutes before serving, stir in cilantro.

If you put red chili powder in a single layer in a non-stick skillet and cook it just until it begins to brown around the edges (5 minutes) then remove it immediately from the heat, it will take on a smoky flavor. (Make a funnel with paper to get it back into its jar.)

Béchamel Sauce

This is basic white sauce or cream sauce. (It's the one that Mrs. Cleaver mixed with a can of tuna and grated yellow cheese, and then poured over white bread toast. Yummmmmy!) If you skip the tuna/cheese treatment, this is the base sauce for almost all white (or non-tomato) sauces.

Yield: 1 pint
Preparation time: less than 10 minutes

> **3 tbsp. unsalted butter or margarine**
> **2 tbsp. all-purpose flour**
> **2 cups warm milk**
> **1/8 tsp. ground nutmeg (eliminate this if the finished sauce will be used for fish)**

1. In a saucepan over low heat, melt the butter. Sprinkle the flour over the butter and cook, stirring often, for 2 - 3 minutes, until the flour just begins to turn brown. If the heat is too high, the flour will burn and the sauce won't work. If the flour is not cooked enough, the sauce will taste chalky.

2. Add the warm milk slowly, stirring constantly until the sauce is a smooth, creamy consistency. Stir in nutmeg.

Three Cheese Sauce

This is a wonderful white sauce for pasta. In Italy, it is used regularly in lasagne.

Yield: 3+ cups
Preparation time: 20 minutes, including time to make Béchamel

> **1 cup Béchamel Sauce** (p. 301)
> **1/2 cup coarsely grated Parmesan cheese**
> **1/2 cup provolone cheese, grated**
> **4 oz. fresh mozzarella, cubed**
> **1/2 tsp. crushed red pepper flakes**
> **1/2 - 1 cup vegetable or chicken stock**

If you can't get fresh mozzarella, substitute 1/2 cup Fontina or Jarlsberg, coarsely grated.

1. Heat Béchamel in a saucepan. Add cheeses, one at a time, stirring to mix thoroughly, creating a very smooth texture. Add pepper flakes and stock, and let flavors set for at least 5 minutes.

2. Correct seasoning with salt.

Apple Pie

If you are an experienced pie maker, you probably have a favorite pie crust recipe. If you are not and want to be, I suggest that you read Baking, *by Jim Dodge, or* The Fannie Farmer Baking Book, *by Marion Cunningham.*

Yield: 1 9" pie
Preparation time: 20 minutes. Cooking time: 1 hour including cooling

1 1/2	lbs. tart apples (5 cups), peeled, cored and sliced 1/3" thick
1	tbsp. lemon juice
1 1/2	cups plus 1 tbsp. granulated sugar
1/4	cup all-purpose flour
2	tsp. cinnamon
2	tbsp. unsalted butter
1	recipe pie dough, enough for 2 crusts egg wash (egg white beaten with 1 tbsp. water)

Preheat oven to 425°.

1. Put apple slices into a large mixing bowl. Drizzle lemon juice over the apples and toss with your hands to distribute the juice.

2. In a small mixing bowl, thoroughly mix 1 1/2 cups sugar, flour, and cinnamon. Sprinkle over the fruit and toss with a wooden spoon until all the fruit is coated.

3. Roll half the pie dough into a 10" circle and line the pie pan. If you are using frozen pie dough, sprinkle the bottom with 1 tbsp. sugar to compensate for the saltiness of the dough.

4. Add the apple mixture and dot with butter.

5. Roll out the top crust and carefully place it over the apples. Press crust edges together. Cut off excess dough and crimp the edges all around with the ends of two fingers or with the tip of a teaspoon handle.

6. Prick the top crust several times with a dinner fork and brush with egg wash. Put the pie pan on a pie circle or larger pan (to catch any syrup drippings), and bake for 10 minutes. Turn the oven down to 375° and continue baking for 30 - 35 minutes, until the top is golden brown, and syrup is bubbling around the edge. If the edges begin to brown too much before the pie has cooked, cover them loosely with foil or pie edge savers.

7. Cool to room temperature on a baking rack.

- If you are feeling creative, roll out dough scraps and cut out apples or leaves to decorate the top crust. They stick with egg wash.

- If you haven't learned the art of the flaky pie crust and this is an important occasion, buy refrigerated or frozen crust and put your energy into fabulous filling. P.S. Transfer the ready-made dough to your own pie pan and say nothing!

Tart Dough

Because finished tart crusts are intended to stand up without the support of a standard pie dish, they need to be firm, like shortbread. That is achieved with the addition of egg yolk in most recipes, or with added butterfat, as in this recipe. If you want to produce a flaky, delicate texture, really chill everything used, including the ingredients and utensils, to thwart the stretching of the gluten in the flour. Baked tart shells freeze well if carefully wrapped.

Yield: one 9" tart shell
Preparation time: 10 minutes plus chilling time

> 3/4 **stick chilled unsalted butter, diced**
> 1 **tsp. sugar (for sweet dough; for appetizer or quiche, omit)**
> 1 **tiny pinch kosher salt**
> 3/4 **cup all-purpose flour**
> 1 **tbsp. whipping cream**
> 1 **tbsp. ice water**

1. Put the butter, sugar, salt, and flour in the processor bowl. Process until well blended (it will look like golden yellow cornmeal).

2. Sprinkle the cream and water over the flour mixture, and pulse or blend until the dough first forms into a ball. Put it on a floured surface and pat it into a flat circle.

3. Roll the dough into a 10"+ circle, and lift it onto the tart pan. Press the dough against the bottom edge and around the sides. Fold over the top edges and press the sides. The dough should stick up slightly from the sides as it will shrink while it cooks.

4. Prick the bottom all over with a fork, and put the shell in the freezer for 15 minutes.

5. Preheat the oven to 400°. Line the tart shell with parchment or foil and put pie weights (or rice, dried beans, or barley. A good way to roast barley; another secret hint!) on it to keep it from bubbling. Put the tart into the oven and bake for 15 - 20 minutes, almost but not quite done. Remove the foil and weights, pat down any bubbles, and continue to cook until the shell is golden brown, about 8 more minutes. Cool on a wire rack.

Rustic Fresh Fruit Tart

If you don't have a tart pan with a removable bottom, use a traditional pie pan and crimp the crust edge down, so that the tart sides will be about 1" high. Fruit should be perfectly ripe and firm.

Yield: 6 servings
Preparation time: 15 minutes. Baking time: 40 minutes

Crust
One 9" Tart or Pie Pan
> 1 recipe Tart Dough (p. 304) , or
> 1 prepared crust for 9" pie

6 Individual, Small Tarts
> 2 recipes Tart Dough (p. 304) or
> 4 prepared crusts for 9" pies

Filling
> 2 medium to large pears, or 4 or 5 plums or
> Italian prunes depending upon size, or
> 3 large nectarines or peaches, or 3 golden
> delicious apples
> 2 tsp. all-purpose flour
> 2 tsp. orange zest
> 1/8 tsp. cinnamon
> 2 tbsp. orange juice
> 1 tsp. cornstarch
> 1 tbsp. granulated sugar
> 2 tbsp. powdered sugar for dusting

Preheat oven to 400°.

1. Prepare the tart dough and roll into a circle 2" larger than the tart pan. Lift it carefully into the tart pan pressing it onto the sides and into the corners, but not the bottom.

2. Roll the edge of the dough a little bit above the pan, as it will shrink down while it cooks. Prick the bottom in 5 or 6 places with a fork.

3. Sprinkle the flour and then the orange zest and cinnamon over the bottom of the tart shell.

4. Peel, halve, and core the fruit. For apples, steam them for 2 minutes to soften slightly.

5. Slice the fruit into thin slices, and carefully place the slices over the bottom of the crust, beginning at the outer edge, overlapping slightly as you move around. Fill in the center with slices close together.

6. Mix the orange juice with the cornstarch to form a paste. Brush it over the fruit and sprinkle with sugar.

7. Bake the tart about 40 minutes or until the crust is brown and the juice has turned to shiny syrup.

8. Cool on a baking rack until ready to serve. Sift powdered sugar over the whole tart, including the crust, just before it is served (the sugar will dissolve over the fruit and show only on the edge).

Note: This dessert is best served slightly warm. If the tart is cooked ahead, keep it at room temperature and warm at 350° for 5 minutes.

Individual tarts: If you do not have individual tart pans, you can cook the tarts on a parchment-covered sheet pan. Roll the dough into 6" circles. Place the circles on the parchment and sprinkle the flour and orange zest inside the circle, to about 3/4" from the edge. Prepare the fruit and cool it if you have steamed it. Place a sliced fruit half in the center of each circle, or arrange the slices so that they take the shape of a fruit. Crimp dough edges, and press them in slightly so that they are hugging the fruit. Follow Steps 5 - 8.

Tarte Tatin

Tarte tatin is a classic luncheon dessert in the French countryside, where it is made and served immediately. You may cook it ahead (an hour or so) through Step 6, and then hold it at room temperature until just before it will be served. Reheat it in a 350° oven for 6 or 7 minutes, then continue with Step 8.

Yield: 4 servings
Preparation and cooking time: 45 minutes

> 1 **recipe pie crust dough (for one crust), or refrigerated pie dough**
> 3 **tbsp. unsalted butter**
> 2 **large, tart apples (Granny Smith, Gravenstein, Macintosh, or Golden Delicious)**
> 3/4 **cup granulated sugar (1/2 cup for Golden Delicious)**
> 4 **oz. Grand Marnier or Calvados**
> 1/2 **cup heavy cream**

You need a heavy 9" oven-proof skillet. If yours does not have a metal handle, a wooden or hard plastic handle may be covered with double aluminum foil to protect it from the oven heat.

Preheat oven to 375°.

1. Using 1 tbsp. of butter, cover the bottom of the skillet. Sprinkle half the sugar over the butter.

2. Peel, core, and cut the apples into quarters, then into eighths. Pack the pieces into the bottom of the skillet so that it is completely covered. Sprinkle the remaining sugar on top.

3. Melt remaining butter and pour over apples.

4. Cook on top of stove, over medium heat, for 20 minutes or so, until the sugar is caramelized to a pale brown.

5. While the apples are cooking, roll out pastry to 1/4" thickness. Remove the pan from the heat and place the pastry on top of apple mixture in skillet, tucking pastry edges down inside.

6. Put the skillet into the preheated oven and bake for 30 minutes, or until pastry is golden brown.

7. Place a serving plate upside down over top of pan and turn the tarte over onto the serving dish. Carefully replace any apple pieces that stayed in the pan.

8. Put the pan on medium high heat and pour Grand Marnier and cream into caramelized sugar residue. Scrape and stir while mixture is thickening. Pour sauce over each serving.

Berry Tart

VARIATION: LEMON TART

This is very easy to make, the ultimate last-minute summer dessert. But, it will only be as good as the lemon curd and the berries, which must be fresh, succulent and sweet.

Yield: 6 servings
Preparation time: 15 minutes excluding crust preparation
Cooking time: 15 minutes

>   1 9" cooked tart shell (p. 304) or 6 cooked
>   tart shells
>   1/2 pint lemon curd
>   1 pint fresh berries, cleaned (avoid washing if
>   possible) and stemmed
>   powdered sugar for dusting

1. While the shell is still warm, spread the lemon curd with a rubber spatula over the bottom of the crust. Cool to room temperature.

2. Cover the lemon curd with berries, piling the whole pint as high as necessary. For strawberries, arrange slices around the edge of crust, with the tips pointing out. Arrange the next row with the berry points between the two above it, continuing that way until the circle reaches the center.

3. Just before you serve the tart, sift the powdered sugar over the top, covering the berries and the outside edge of the tart.

LEMON TART

>   1 9" cooked tart shell or 6 cooked tart shells
>   1/2 pint lemon curd, room temperature
>   1 cup whipped cream or Crème Fraîche (p. 282)

1. Cool crust completely.

2. In a medium-sized mixing bowl, fold whipped cream or Crème Fraîche into lemon curd.

3. Fill shells and garnish with candied lemon zest or shaved chocolate curls.

Candied lemon zest: Boil lemon zest for 1 minute in 1/2 cup water mixed with 1/2 cup sugar. Drain and cool on waxed paper. Roll in granulated sugar and let them dry out for 1 hour.

Fruit or Berry Crisp or Cobbler

I make a doubled recipe of topping and freeze it in a zip-type bag so I can make crisp, quickly. Biscuit mix (1/2 cup) may be substituted. Almost any fruit or berry works.

Yield: 6 servings
Preparation time: 35 minutes. Baking time: 30 - 40 minutes

Fruit Filling

- 6 **cups prepared fruit,* pitted and sliced if necessary**
- 2 **cups sugar (approximate; sweetness varies with the particular fruit)**
- 2 **tbsp. Minute Tapioca®**
- 1 **tsp. grated lemon or orange zest**
- 1 **tbsp. lemon juice**

Crisp Topping

- 1/2 **cup brown sugar, firmly packed**
- 1/2 **cup all-purpose white flour**
- 1/2 **cup oatmeal (not instant)**
- 1/2 **tsp. ground cinnamon**
- 1/4 **tsp. kosher salt**
- 4 **tbsp. butter, melted**

*Apples, apricots, peaches, nectarines, berries, plums, rhubarb (rhubarb may need more sugar than other fruits).

Preheat oven to 425°.

1. Put fruit into a large mixing bowl, and sprinkle lemon juice over it. Add sugar, tapioca, and zest, and toss until mixed. Let the tapioca set up for 15 minutes. Spread it evenly into an 9" square baking pan (non-stick or lightly buttered).

2. Mix dry topping ingredients in a small bowl; add melted butter and hand mix until it is well combined.

3. Sprinkle topping over prepared fruit and press it down gently. Bake for 15 minutes. Reduce heat to 350° and continue baking; bake until topping browns and fruit is tender when pierced, 30 - 40 minutes.

Serve warm or at room temperature.

Cobbler Topping
- 1 1/2 cups Krusteaz® scone mix*
- 2 tsp. granulated sugar
- 1 tsp. grated orange zest
- 1/4 cup heavy cream
- 1/2 tsp. vanilla extract
- 2 tbsp. powdered sugar for garnish

*This brand does not require egg added; biscuit mix may be substituted.

Preheat oven to 400°.

1. While the fruit is setting up, put scone mix, granulated sugar, and zest in a bowl. Mix the vanilla with the cream and then into the scone mix, blending with a fork until the mix is just moist.

2. On a floured surface, pat or very gently roll the batter into a rectangle which is about 1/2" thick and the approximate size of the cobbler pan. (For individual cobblers, cut out rings with a cookie biscuit cutter. If you need to reform the dough to make all of the circles, do, *but not more than twice*.)

3. Transfer berries to a 9" x 9" pan or ramekins, and place dough over the top of the berries.

4. Bake for 25 - 30 minutes, until top is browned and dough is cooked.

To serve: Sift powdered sugar through a strainer onto the cobbler to dust the top.

Cobblers have flaky biscuit tops baked over filling. Crisps have crumbly tops. Both adapt well to individual as well as large containers.

Warm Berries in Currant Sauce

One warm summer day on Salt Spring Island in Canada, I ate morning-picked blackberries this way with thickened fresh whipping cream over the top. I don't ever remember a luncheon dessert that tasted this scrumptious.

Yield: 4 servings
Preparation time: 5 minutes. Cooking time: 15 minutes

> **7 cups fresh or individually frozen blackberries**
> **1 cup currant jelly**

Preheat oven to 250°.

1. For fresh berries: Place in one layer on a baking sheet and distribute spoonfuls of jelly around them. Bake for 15 minutes, until the berries and jelly blend.

2. For frozen berries: Put the berries in a 9" x 12" pan. Heat the jelly (microwave works) separately and pour it over the berries. Bake them for 15 minutes, until the berries heat through and blend with the jelly.

To serve: Put the berries and juice in bowls and serve with thickened whipping cream flavored with a tiny bit of almond extract or Grand Marnier liqueur, or serve over vanilla ice cream.

Strawberries with Sour Cream and Brown Sugar

In Washington, the strawberry season is less than a month long, but the berries are deep red all the way through, very sweet, and incredibly juicy. So we eat strawberries for dessert a whole lot between mid June and mid July.

Yield: 4 servings
Preparation time: 10 minutes

Don't soak berries; it just dilutes the flavor, and a speck of missed dirt won't hurt anyone.

> **3 dozen (or so) ripe strawberries**
> **4 tbsp. sour cream**
> **4 tbsp. brown sugar (for variety, substitute powdered sugar)**

1. Put 1 tbsp. sour cream and 1 tbsp. sugar in the center of each dessert plate.

2. Wipe any dirt off the berries with a wet paper towel. Leaving the green crown and stems on, place the berries around the edge of each dessert plate.

Grapes with Sour Cream and Brown Sugar

Brown sugar creates marbled swirls through the sour cream.

Yield: 4 servings
Preparation time: 10 minutes. Chill time: 30 minutes

> **3 cups seedless green grapes**
> **1/2 cup sour cream, at room temperature (low fat works fine)**
> **1/2 cup plain yogurt (low-fat works fine)**
> **1/2 cup brown sugar**
> **ground nutmeg for garnish**

1. Wash, stem, and drain grapes on paper towels.

2. Blend the yogurt and sour cream with a wooden spoon, and mix the grapes into the cream. Then, with just 2 or 3 stirs, stir the brown sugar into the mixture.

3. Fill 4 parfait or champagne glasses with grapes, spooning any remaining cream mixture on top. Sprinkle with a little nutmeg and chill for at least 40 minutes.

Pears Poached in Port

Save the pear poaching liquid! Use a little as a base for Port Syrup to pour over the cooked pears, and freeze the rest to add to and use the next time. I have been adding to one for four years, and it is great. If you do not want the pears to be red, poach them in apple juice and white wine, and eliminate the red food coloring.

Yield: 4 servings
Preparation and cooking time: 40 minutes

> 4 ripe Bosc, Red Bartlett, or Comice Pears with at least 1/2" stems
> 2 cups Port
> 1 cup red wine
> 1 cup apple juice
> 1 tsp. red food coloring
> 1/2 cup granulated sugar

You will need a large, deep saucepan (stock pot works) with a lid.

1. Peel pears and slice bottoms so they will stand on their own.

2. Pour Port, wine, apple juice, and food coloring into the pan, stirring to mix. Place the pears upright but not touching in the pan. Add more wine if necessary to cover up to the stems.

3. Bring liquid to low simmer, check to make sure the pears are not moving, cover the pan, and poach until just soft when pierced with a sharp knife (about 15 minutes, but watch carefully because the time depends upon the firmness of the pears, and it's never the same from batch to batch; looking doesn't hurt, and it smells wonderful).

4. With a slotted spoon, carefully remove the pears from the pan, and cool on a plate. Cooled pears may be covered tightly with plastic wrap and refrigerated for up to 2 days.

int #3: Is this pear ripe? Gently press a pear
t the top next to the stem; if it just barely
ives to the pressure, it is perfectly ripe. Like
vocados and bananas, pears ripen quickly in
brown bag.

Port Syrup
- 3/4 cup poaching liquid
- 1 cup currant jelly
- 1/4 cup Port

1. While the pears cool, transfer 1 1/2 cups of the poaching liquid into a small saucepan, and add the sugar.

2. Bring to a low boil and cook until it reduces into a syrup, about 15 minutes. Strain the syrup into a glass or plastic container, cover with plastic wrap directly touching the syrup, and cool to room temperature.

To serve: Place each pear onto a plate, and pour warm or room temperature syrup over it. Swirl Crème Fraîche (p. 282) into syrup or sprinkle chopped candied ginger over pear at the top.

I learned the hard way that pears that have been bruised or frozen in the center (outside or perhaps in the grocer's walk-in refrigerator) cannot be poached successfully. I always ask the grocer how cold the refrigerator is, and I cu into one before I buy them to make sure.

Hint #22: Swirls made in sauces add a special touch that makes you look like a pro. All you need is a plastic bottle with a 1/8" open tip lid (drug stores carry them for travel cosmetics). Suggestion: practice on a plain plate. Put the sauce into the container and squeeze swirls to your heart's content. For "bleeding hearts": squeeze dots about 1" apart on top of sauce. In one movement, pull the tip of a paring knife, skewer, or toothpick through and slightly beyond each dot. For fleur-de-lis, squeeze straight, horizontal lines across the sauce about 1" apart. Using the tip of a sharp paring knife, skewer, or toothpick, pull vertical lines through the horizontal lines, alternating from top to bottom, then from bottom to top.

Winter Fruit Compote

I know that the word "compote" brings to mind college dining halls or hospital menus, but I urge you to try this one. You will produce a beautifully colored, delicious dessert that holds refrigerated for a week.

Yield: 6 cups
Preparation and cooking time: 20 minutes

> 1/2 cup dried cranberries
> 1/2 cup golden raisins
> 1/2 cup dried apricots
> 1/2 cup dried, pitted prunes
> 1 lemon, with skin on, cut into 8 wedges
> 1 tbsp. whole cloves
> 2 cups apple juice, or 1 cup apple juice and 1 cup Marsala wine
> 1 orange, peeled and sectioned
> 1 grapefruit, peeled and sectioned
> 1 sliced pear, stem and core removed
> 1 apple, peeled, cored, and sliced
> 1/4 cup slivered blanched almonds

1. Put the dried fruits into a saucepan with the apple juice and/or wine. Bring to a boil and then transfer to a glass or other non-reactive container (See Hint #30, p. 18).

2. Poke cloves into the lemon wedges, and add them and the remaining ingredients to the compote.

3. Let flavors set up for an hour before serving.

Store tightly covered in the refrigerator. When serving, leave the lemon wedges in the compote.

Hint #15: The fastest way to get skinless citrus fruit sections is to set the fruit upright on a cutting surface, and peel it from top to bottom with a sharp knife, cutting away any of the white pith. Pick up the skinned fruit and cut into it directly alongside the separating membranes until all the sections are removed.

Sautéed Fruit with Puff Pastry

This is a good example of a delicious dessert made up from a full pantry. I needed dessert for guests, and that box of frozen puff pastry dough was there. Also serve sautéed fruit alone or over ice cream.

Yield: 4 servings
Preparation time: 30 minutes

> 1 **sheet frozen puff pastry dough***
> 2 **tbsp. unsalted butter**
> 1/2 **cup granulated sugar**
> 2 **apples, pears, peaches, nectarines, etc.,**
>   **peeled, cored and sliced**
> 2 **tbsp. Grand Marnier**
> 3/4 **cup heavy cream or orange juice**

*If you buy Pepperidge Farm® Puff Pastry, roll it out to less than its normal thickness, and it will cook more evenly.

1. Thaw puff pastry and cut it into small rectangles (2"x3").

2. Cook according to manufacturer's directions. Cool on rack. Slice pastries in half so that there is a top and bottom for each rectangle, and scoop away any uncooked dough

3. Melt butter in small sauté pan over medium heat. Sprinkle sugar evenly over melted butter and cook until sugar turns golden brown.

4. Add sliced fruit and cook until just soft.

5. Place rectangle bottoms on individual dessert plates. With a slotted spoon, divide fruit among the plates, taking care to leave sauce in the pan.

6. Add liquor and cream or orange juice to syrup and cook over medium high heat until a thick sauce has formed. Pour sauce over fruit and place tops on each dessert.

7. Sprinkle pastry and remaining plate with powdered sugar.

Options: Leave the tops for another time, and just serve the dessert open-faced. Unsweetened, softly whipped cream or ice cream is also delicious with this dessert. For lower fat content, substitute orange juice for the cream.

> **To winterize this dessert, use dried fruit and currants, which have been soaked to plump, and pears. Add almond slivers to the final sauce.**

Homemade Ice Cream Sandwiches

VARIATION: ELEGANT VERSION

A deceptively easy dessert that they won't soon forget! Try using more than one flavor of ice cream or sauce and/or piping one sauce over another in a pattern.

Yield: 4 servings
Preparation time: 30 minutes. Cooking time: 20 - 25 minutes.
Freezing time: 1 hour

> **1/2 pint honey vanilla ice cream**
> **8 oz. mascarpone cheese (Italian fresh cream cheese) or soft cream cheese**
> **1 sheet frozen puff pastry dough**
> **1 cup chocolate sauce (your favorite)**

1. With an electric mixer or in a processor, blend the ice cream with the mascarpone or cream cheese.

2. Spoon into a shallow 8 x 8" glass or non-stick pan, cover with plastic wrap, and freeze until hard.

3. Meanwhile, cut the puff pastry sheet into four, 4" squares, and bake according to manufacturer's directions. Cool to room temperature on a wire rack. Slice the puff pastry squares into tops and bottoms, and scoop out and discard any uncooked dough.

4. When you are ready to serve, warm the chocolate sauce just enough so that it will pour, a few degrees above room temperature.

To serve: Place the bottom halves onto the dessert plates. Take the ice cream out of the freezer and cut it into 4" squares. With a spatula, transfer the ice cream squares to the puff pastry bottoms. Put the tops on and drizzle chocolate sauce over each dessert. Serve immediately.

ELEGANT VERSION
>   **1/4 cup Vanilla Sauce** (p. 335)
>   **24 fresh raspberries**

Read these instructions through and get everything in place so you can work faster than the ice cream can melt.

1. Line up the dessert plates.

2. Ladle 1/4 cup chocolate sauce onto each dessert plate, covering up to the rim.

3. Make the sandwiches as described on p. 317.

4. With a small spoon or from a small pitcher, drop vanilla sauce in single drops around the outside of the sauce, about 1" apart. With the sharp point of a paring knife, draw a line through each dot, dragging the line slightly, to form a "weeping valentines."

5. Drizzle chocolate sauce over the top of each sandwich, place 6 fresh raspberries around the sauce and over the top of the sandwich, and sift powdered sugar over the plates including the rim (it will dissolve immediately when it touches the sauce). Serve at once.

Hint #22: Swirls made in sauces add a special touch that makes you look like a pro. All you need is a plastic bottle with a 1/8" open tip lid (drug stores carry them for travel cosmetics). Suggestion: practice on a plain plate. Put the sauce into the container and squeeze swirls to your heart's content. For "bleeding hearts": squeeze dots about 1" apart on top of sauce. In one movement, pull the tip of a paring knife, skewer, or toothpick through and slightly beyond each dot. For fleur-de-lis, squeeze straight, horizontal lines across the sauce about 1" apart. Using the tip of a sharp paring knife, skewer, or toothpick, pull vertical lines through the horizontal lines, alternating from top to bottom, then from bottom to top.

Bread Pudding

VARIATIONS: POUND CAKE PUDDING, CORNBREAD PUDDING, PUMPKIN BREAD PUDDING

Bread pudding transforms stale bread into ambrosia. As versatile as it is delicious, this bread custard adapts to fruit, berries, nuts, flavors, just about anything. Heat a little maple syrup and you have sauce. For me the hardest part of bread pudding is waiting until it's cool enough not to burn the roof of my mouth!

Yield: 6 servings
Preparation and cooking time: 1 1/2 hours; 20 minutes resting

1/2	cup currants or golden raisins
2	tbsp. brandy or Grand Marnier
3	slices stale bread, torn into 2" pieces
4	large eggs
3/4	cup granulated sugar
3 1/2	cups half–and–half
1	tsp. vanilla
1	tbsp. grated orange zest (optional)

Note: For a lighter pudding, use brioche; add blueberries; flavor custard with 1/4 almond extract and sprinkle slivered almonds over the top before baking; add pears or apples, peeled, cored, and thinly sliced.

Preheat oven to 375°. This cooks in a water bath, so you will need a pan for the pudding and a slightly larger pan into which it will fit.

1. Soak the currants in the brandy while you are putting together the rest of the recipe.

2. Beat eggs and sugar together until the eggs are thick and pale yellow. Mix in the half-and-half, the liquor (save the currants), vanilla, and zest if you have selected it.

3. Put the bread cubes into an 8" x 8" buttered baking pan or an 8 cup souffle dish. Pour the egg mixture over the bread, pressing the pieces down gently so that they will absorb the liquid. Let the mixture set up for 30 minutes (see box below). Sprinkle the currants over the bread pieces.

4. Set the pan in the larger pan and pour enough water into the larger pan to reach halfway up the sides of the smaller pan.

The longer it sets up, the smoother the pudding will be. For special occasions, I let it absorb for 3 - 4 hours.

5. Bake for 45 - 50 minutes or until the top is golden brown and a tester poked into the center of the pudding comes out clean.

6. Remove the pudding pan from the oven, place it on a rack and let it cool for about 30 minutes until it is cool enough to eat.

Serve all bread puddings with Vanilla Sauce (p. 335), Berry Sauce (p. 333), Lemon Sauce (p. 337), Whiskey Sauce (p. 336), or warm maple syrup.

POUND CAKE PUDDING
Substitute pound cake for bread in above recipe.

CORNBREAD PUDDING
Substitute day-old cornbread for regular bread, add 1 tsp. pure maple extract, and use golden raisins.

PUMPKIN BREAD PUDDING
Yield: 6 - 8 servings
Preparation and cooking time: 15 minutes preparation; 2 hours soaking; 45 minutes baking; 15 minutes resting

> 1 **pint half-and-half**
> 6 **large eggs**
> 1/4 **cup granulated sugar**
> 1/2 **cup brown sugar**
> 1 **cup canned pumpkin (freeze remaining for another pudding, or put it in your Stock Bag** [p. 12]**)**
> 1 **tbsp. pure vanilla extract**
> 1 **tsp. nutmeg**
> 2 **tsp. ground cinnamon**
> 4 **slices bread (or pumpkin bread, raisin bread, bran muffins, etc.)**
> 3/4 **cup golden raisins**
> 3/4 **cup chopped pecans**

Preheat oven to 400°.

1. Butter the sides and bottom of an 9" square baking pan or 3-quart casserole dish.

2. Slice bread into 1/2" slices and then break into 1" pieces.

3. Whisk together half-and-half, eggs, sugar, pumpkin, and spices, until thoroughly blended.

4. Place bread in prepared baking dish. Sprinkle raisins and pecans over bread, and pour pumpkin mixture over it. Let the mixture absorb moisture for at least 1 hour.

Follow Steps 4 and 5 above. Note that this pudding may collapse slightly as it cools.

Cranberry Pudding

This recipe may look like it's missing something; it's not. It is simple and wonderful, but sauce is essential.

Yield: 4 servings
Preparation and cooking time: 35 minutes

- 1 1/2 **cups all-purpose flour**
- 2 **tsp. baking soda**
- 1/4 **tsp. salt**
- 1/2 **cup light molasses**
- 1/3 **cup hot water**
- 2 **cups whole cranberries**
  Quick Honey Vanilla Sauce (melted honey vanilla ice cream) or Hard Sauce (p. 336)

Preheat oven to 350°.

1. Sift flour soda and salt together. Mix water and molasses and add to sifted dry ingredients. Fold in cranberries.

2. Transfer to a buttered baking dish and bake for 30 minutes. Serve warm on plates, with sauce ladled over each portion.

Rice Pudding

VARIATION: PUMPKIN RICE PUDDING

Yield: 6 servings
Preparation and cooking time, including refrigeration: 2 hours

> 1 **cup white rice, uncooked**
> 1 **quart plus 2 tbsp. milk**
> 1/2 **oz. (1 envelope) unflavored gelatin**
> 1 **tsp. kosher salt**
> 1 **cup granulated sugar**
> 1 **tsp. pure vanilla extract**
> 1 **pint whipping cream**

1. In a saucepan over medium heat, bring rice and 1 quart milk to a boil. Reduce heat and cook, stirring occasionally until rice is tender, about 20 minutes.

2. While the rice cooks, sprinkle the gelatin over 2 tbsp. cold milk and stir until softened.

3. Add softened gelatin, salt, sugar, and vanilla extract to cooked rice. Stir until well-combined, then cover with plastic wrap and refrigerate until pudding has cooled completely.

4. Whip the cream until it hold stiff peaks and fold it into the chilled pudding.

5. Serve plain, with berry sauce, or warm maple syrup.

PUMPKIN RICE PUDDING

> 1 **cup puréed pumpkin (put**
> **remaining into Stock Bag** [p. 12]**)**
> 1/2 **tsp. pumpkin pie spice**

Add the pumpkin to the rice as it is cooking. Add the spice with the vanilla. Proceed as above.

Pudding Cake

VARIATIONS: BLUEBERRY LEMON PUDDING CAKE, CHOCOLATE PUDDING CAKE

I think pudding cake is best made and served in 1-cup ramekins or baking cups. I have tried inverting them onto small plates, but that is a delicate process to pull off, and if doesn't work, it looks like it's been dropped (which is touchy to explain).

Yield: 4 - 6 servings
Preparation time: 25 - 30 minutes. Cooking time: 40 minutes

BLUEBERRY LEMON PUDDING CAKE

- 2 tbsp. unsalted butter, room temperature
- 1/2 cup granulated sugar
- 4 large egg yolks
- 1/4 cup pastry flour
- 1/4 cup lemon juice
- zest from 1 lemon, soaked in 1/2 cup boiling water for 5 minutes, drained, and chopped
- 1 cup half–and–half
- 6 egg whites
- 1 cup fresh or frozen, drained blueberries (if you are using fresh, save 3 per serving for garnish)

Preheat oven to 325°. Prepare boiling water for baking the cakes.

1. Butter baking dishes and set them into a larger pan.

2. In a mixing bowl, mix the butter and sugar with an electric beater on low speed, or with a whisk. Mix in the egg yolks and flour, and then add the zest and lemon juice, a little at a time, blending thoroughly. Add the half-and-half, and stir until blended.

3. Beat the egg whites until they are stiff.

4. Gently fold blueberries into cake batter. Then gently whisk in the beaten egg whites just until the mixtures are combined.

5. Ladle the batter into the prepared baking dishes. Set the large pan in the oven on a center rack, and pour boiling water into it to cover halfway up the baking dishes.

6. Bake for 40 minutes. Remove from the oven and let the ramekins cool in the water for about a half hour.

To serve: Dust with powdered sugar and serve slightly warm or at room temperature. If you used fresh blueberries, garnish each serving with 3 berries.

CHOCOLATE PUDDING CAKE

- **1/2 cup unsweetened cocoa powder**
- **1 tsp. instant espresso**
- **2 tbsp. rum**
- **1/3 cup boiling water**
- **1/2 tsp. instant espresso**
- **1/2 pint whipping cream**
- **3 tbsp. powdered sugar**

1. Mix the cocoa powder, 1 tsp. instant espresso, 1 tbsp. rum, and the boiling water together.

2. Follow the directions on p. 323, substituting the cocoa mixture for the lemon juice, zest, and blueberries.

3. Just before serving, dissolve 1/2 tsp. instant espresso in the remaining 1 tbsp. rum. Whip the cream. When it is almost whipped to the soft peak stage, add the rum/coffee mixture and the powdered sugar, and continue whipping until it forms soft peaks.

To serve: Put a generous dollop of whipped cream on the top of each serving.

Michigan and New Jersey produce most of the blueberries we buy in the grocery store. Wild blueberries are produced in Maine.

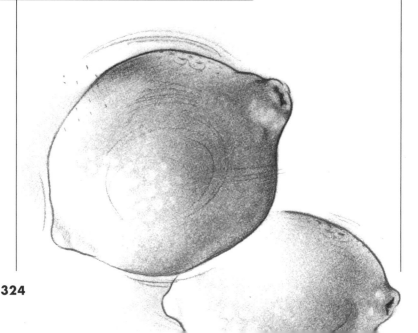

Chocolate Pan Cake

This is one recipe from the 50's that will last well beyond the year 2000, and for good reason.

Yield: 12 - 16 servings
Preparation time: 25 minutes. Baking time: 30 minutes
Cooling time: 15 minutes

3	cups cake flour
2/3	cup unsweetened cocoa
2	tsp. baking soda
2	cups granulated sugar
1	tsp. salt
2	cups cold water
1/2	cup plus 2 tbsp. corn oil
1	tbsp. vanilla
1	tbsp. white vinegar or strained lemon juice

Preheat oven to 350° and grease a 9 x 13 x 2" pan.

1. Mix together flour, cocoa, baking soda, sugar, and salt. Sift.

2. In separate bowl, mix together water, corn oil, vanilla, and vinegar or lemon juice.

3. Whisk together the wet and dry mixtures. Pour through strainer into bowl, breaking up lumps and pressing them through. Whisk again.

4. Pour into prepared pan. Tap the edge of the pan against the edge of the counter or drop from 6" to the counter several times to pop air bubbles.

5. Bake for 25 to 30 minutes, until tester inserted in center comes out clean. Cool on rack to room temperature.

> **Old cook's adage: The better the chocolate the better the cake. P.S. Chocolate chips may contain paraffin.**

Easy Chocolate Frosting

It will be as basic or elegant as the chocolate you use to make it. Add a little instant espresso and you can turn brownie mix brownies into frosted wonders!

Yield: frosting for one 2-layer cake
Preparation time: 15 minutes

> **8 oz. unsweetened cooking chocolate**
> **1 tsp. instant espresso, or 1 1/2 tsp. instant coffee, dissolved in 1 tbsp. hot water**
> **1 lb. powdered confectioners sugar**
> **1 tbsp. unsalted butter, at room temperature**
> **1/2 cup whipping cream, at room temperature or slightly hotter**
> **1 tsp. vanilla extract**
> **1/2 cup chopped nuts (optional)**

1. Melt chocolate in a double boiler over simmering water (the water *must* be touching the upper pan).

2. Put cream in a mixing bowl, and stir in dissolved coffee. Whisk in melted chocolate until completely blended.

3. *Cool to room temperature*, or place the bowl into a larger bowl containing a layer of ice cubes.

4. Whisk (or use a hand electric beater) the powdered sugar and butter into the chocolate mixture until fluffy. You may not need all the sugar, but if the frosting is too thin, refrigerate it covered until it thickens. Add vanilla and nuts if you wish.

Most recipes calling for a double boiler assume that the upper pan will be touching the water, and cooking times are based on that. (Remember, steam is hotter than water!) I curdled lots of custards because I didn't know that until a year ago.

Apple Ginger Upside-Down Cake

VARIATION: PEAR, NECTARINE, PEACH, OR PINEAPPLE

This cake has the fun of upside-down cake and tastes more interesting than plain gingerbread—a great chilly night by the fire dessert, and it only takes 20 minutes to prepare (I don't count the time it's in the oven cooking itself).

Yield: 9 x 13 x 2" pan
Preparation time: 20 minutes; **cooking time:** Bake until tester inserted into the center comes out clean, 35 - 40 minutes.

- 1 **box gingerbread mix (regular size)**
- 1 **box of Jiffy® or other small, single layer yellow cake mix**
- 1 **cup unsweetened applesauce**
- 2 **whole eggs**
- 8 **oz. orange juice**
- 2 **tbsp. molasses**
- 1 **tsp. ground ginger**
- 2 **medium or 3 small tart and juicy apples such as Macintosh, Gala, Granny Smith, etc., peeled, cored, and chopped into 1/2" pieces**
- 3 **oz. melted unsalted butter**
- 1 **cup light brown sugar, firmly packed**
- 1 **medium apple, peeled, cored, and thinly sliced**

Preheat oven to 350°.

1. Grease cake pan.

2. Cook (microwave) butter and brown sugar until the sugar melts and forms into a paste. Spread over the bottom of the pan. Place apple (or other fruit) slices, overlapping slightly, into a circular pattern where each portion of cake will be. Set aside.

3. Put cake mixes, applesauce, eggs, orange juice, molasses, and ginger into a bowl and mix until blended, approximately 2 minutes. Stir in apple (or other fruit) chunks. Pour cake batter over the apple slices in the pan.

> **Did you know unsweetened applesauce may be substituted for the oil added to cake mix? It's true.**

4. Bake for 30 - 35 minutes, until tester comes out clean and the edges have come away from the pan slightly. Remove from oven and cool on a rack for 5 - 6 minutes.

5. Run a dinner knife around the rim of the cake to ensure that the edges have separated from the pan. Place a piece of waxed paper or parchment and an inverted wire rack over the top of the cake. Invert cake pan onto the rack. If any apple slices have stuck to the bottom of the cooking pan, remove them with the cake spatula, and place them back onto the cake carefully. Replace any topping also.

6. After the cake has cooled about 20 minutes, slide the cake onto a serving plate, carefully taking off the waxed or parchment paper as you make the transfer. Serve warm or at room temperature with whipped cream or Quick Honey Vanilla Sauce (p. 335).

PEAR, NECTARINE, PEACH, OR PINEAPPLE CAKE
Substitute desired fruit wherever recipe calls for apples.

Lemon Soufflé

VARIATIONS: RHUBARB SOUFFLÉ, BERRY SOUFFLÉ

This is the first molded dessert I ever made for guests (I used little individual ring molds that turned up years later in the sandbox). Now I make it in a glass bowl, serve it at the table, and cover each serving with fresh berries or Frozen Berry Sauce (p. 333).

Yield: 6 servings
Preparation and cooking time: 4 hours, including set-up time

3/4	cup cold water
1	envelope unflavored gelatin
3/4	cup granulated sugar or honey
1/4	tsp. kosher salt
	juice from one lemon (about 1/4 cup)
	zest from one lemon
2	egg whites at room temperature
1 1/2	cups sour cream, or 1 cup ricotta and 1/2 cup sour cream
1	cup whipping cream

1. Soften gelatin in water. Place in non-reactive saucepan and add sugar, salt, lemon juice, and zest. Cook over medium heat, stirring constantly, until gelatin dissolves.

2. Transfer to mixing bowl and chill until partially set.

3. Beat egg whites until soft peaks form.

4. If using ricotta, process with sour cream. Whip cream until stiff.

5. Fold sour cream mixture into partially jelled mixture. Fold in egg whites and then whipped cream. Put into a large serving bowl or prepared molds, cover with plastic wrap and chill until set, at least 6 hours.

Serve with fresh berries, warm berries with currant jelly, or Frozen Berry Sauce (p. 333).

RHUBARB SOUFFLÉ
3 cups chopped rhubarb cooked with 1 cup granulated sugar, making 1 cup rhubarb sauce

STRAWBERRY, RASPBERRY, OR BLUEBERRY SOUFFLÉ
2 cups berries, puréed

This soufflé makes a great bottom filling for fresh berry tarts.

Substitute rhubarb sauce or berry purée for the lemon juice and proceed with recipe.

Lemon Bars

This recipe came from Kathy Murphy, an inspired baker and meticulous cook. She also developed the Nordy Bar, an ingenious chocolate chip bar cookie that has drawn thousands of chocolate lovers to Nordstrom cafes and espresso bars.

Yield: 36, 2" bars
Preparation time: 1 hour

Crust

2	cups all-purpose flour
1/2	cup powdered sugar
1	cup softened unsalted butter

Filling

4	eggs, slightly beaten, room temperature
4	tbsp. all-purpose flour
6	tbsp. fresh lemon juice
1	tbsp. chopped lemon zest
2	cups granulated sugar
1	tsp. baking powder

Preheat oven to 350°.

Crust
1. Combine all crust ingredients. Press into a 16" x 11" pan.
2. Bake 18 minutes.

Filling
1. While crust is baking, combine remaining ingredients and mix well. Pour over baked crust and return to oven for 20 - 25 minutes. Remove from oven and cool on a baking rack for 10 minutes.
2. While still warm, sprinkle with powdered sugar and loosen the edges around the pan.
3. When it is completely cool, cut into bars and remove from the pan with a spatula.

These bars freeze well (a new application of powdered sugar after thawing), and they will keep in an air-tight container for 4 - 5 days.

Oatmeal Fruit Bars

These bars are crispy when they are very fresh. They soften if they are wrapped in plastic wrap or stored in an air-tight container. Both ways are good.

Yield: about 24
Preparation time: 15 minutes. Baking time: 35 minutes
Cooling time: 45 minutes

Crust

1 3/4	cups sifted all-purpose flour
1/2	tsp. kosher salt
1/4	tsp. nutmeg
1	cup brown sugar, firmly packed
1 3/4	cups old-fashioned oatmeal (not instant)
1/2	lb. unsalted butter, melted
1/2	cup sliced almonds, coarsely chopped (for apricot and date only)

Fillings

BERRY BARS

1/2	cup raspberry jam
1/2	cup blackberry or strawberry jam
2	tsp. finely grated lemon zest
1	tbsp. lemon juice

APRICOT BARS

1	cup apricot jam
1	tsp. orange juice concentrate
1	tsp. lemon juice
2	tsp. finely grated orange or lemon zest
1/2	tsp almond extract

DATE ALMOND BARS

2	cups chopped, sugared dates
3/4	cup orange juice
2	tsp. orange zest
1/4	tsp. almond extract

1. Line bottom and sides of 9" x 9" pan with foil, with enough hangover to lift cooled bars out of pan. Brush foil with melted butter.

2. Mix flour, salt, nutmeg, and sugar in a mixing bowl. Mix the oatmeal (and almonds if using). Add melted butter and stir until completely mixed.

3. Remove 1 cup+ of the crust mixture and set it aside for the topping. Press remainder smoothly over the bottom of the prepared pan to make an even layer.

4. Blend filling ingredients and spread evenly over crust.° Sprinkle reserved crust mixture evenly over filling, pressing gently into smooth, even layer.

5. Bake in preheated 350° oven for 40 minutes. Cool in the pan for 45 minutes, then cover the pan with a rack or a cookie sheet and invert. Carefully remove the foil and invert again— *this is a touchy process, be gentle.*

6. Cool completely, and then chill until firm enough to cut easily into bars.

°For Date Bars, mix filling ingredients and cook over medium low heat until dates are softened, then purée in a food processor.

Berry Sauce

VARIATION: WHOLE BLUEBERRY SAUCE

I keep this sauce in the freezer year round, so I will have instant, spectacular dessert sauce for ice cream, fresh or poached pear, pound cake, or just me and a spoon about 10 p.m.

Yield: 1 1/2 cups
Preparation time: 5 minutes

> 1 **8 - 10 oz. package frozen raspberries, blueberries, blackberries, etc., or a mixture without sugar, or 1 quart fresh berries, cleaned, stems and hulls removed**
> 1/2 **cup (approximately) superfine granulated sugar**
> 1 **tsp. fresh lemon juice**

1. If berries are frozen, thaw partially.
2. Purée berries in a processor or blender. Strain through a fine mesh strainer to capture seeds, then stir in sugar until completely dissolved.
3. Taste. If it has no tartness (because berries were slightly flavorless) add about 1 tsp. lemon juice. Add more sugar if you wish.

WHOLE BLUEBERRY SAUCE

> 2 **pints fresh blueberries, or 2 packages (12 oz. each) frozen blueberries (frozen separately, no sugar) thawed in packages**
> 1/2 **cup superfine granulated sugar**
> 1 **tbsp. fresh lemon juice**

1. Place half the berries into the bowl of the processor or a blender. Drain the remaining berries in a strainer and save the juice.
2. Put the strained juice, the sugar, and the lemon juice into the processor or blender with the berries and purée until the sauce is completely smooth.
3. Add reserved whole berries to the sauce and serve.

Did you know that blueberries are indigenous to North America?

Fresh Fruit Sauce

This sauce freezes beautifully, so it's available all winter long.

Yield: 1 quart
Preparation time: for raw fruit, 15 - 20 minutes
Cooking time: 6 - 8 minutes

> **6 - 7 cups peeled, pitted, cored, and sliced fresh fruit (apples and bananas don't work)**
> **juice of 1/2 lemon**
> **1 - 2 cups granulated sugar, depending upon the sweetness of the fruit**

For rhubarb or cranberry, you may need more sugar. For cranberry, also add 2 tbsp. orange juice concentrate.

1. Process prepared fruit into a coarse purée. Transfer to a saucepan, add lemon juice and 1 cup of sugar.

2. Bring to a low boil and simmer, stirring constantly, until the sugar has dissolved, less than 10 minutes.

3. Taste and add more sugar according to your preference.

4. Transfer to a non-reactive container, put plastic wrap directly onto the sauce, cover, and refrigerate until you are ready to serve. Serve cold or at room temperature over ice cream, cheesecake, or fresh fruit.

I thaw the frozen sauce in the microwave.

Vanilla Sauce

This is an incredibly simple sauce to make. Try it over ginger-bread, Bread Pudding (p. 319), fresh berries, Apple Pie (p. 302), Crisps (p. 309), etc.

Yield: 1 pint
Preparation and cooking time: 15 minutes

> 1/4 **cup granulated sugar, or brown sugar**
> 1 **tbsp. all-purpose flour**
> 1 **pint half-and-half**
> 1 1/2 **tsp. vanilla extract**

Note: To flavor this sauce other ways, add additional flavoring such as:

> 1 **tsp. *pure maple* extract (imitation tastes terrible in this sauce)**
> 1 **tbsp. brandy or dark rum**
> 1/2 **tsp. almond extract**
> 2 **tsp. Grand Marnier**

1. Mix sugar and flour in a saucepan. Add half-and-half slowly, whisking continually to avoid lumps.

2. Bring mixture to a low boil and simmer until sauce thickens and flour taste dissipates.

3. Remove from heat and add vanilla or other flavoring.

It may be stored in a glass container, tightly covered and refrigerated for up to 10 days.

An even simpler, quicker version is Quick Honey Vanilla Sauce, which is honey vanilla ice cream melted in the microwave!

Whiskey Sauce

This is one of my favorite sauces for Bread Pudding (p. 319), or Rice Pudding (p. 322). It's also a wonderful boost for plain old vanilla ice cream.

Yield: 1 1/2 cups
Preparation time: 10 minutes

> 1/2 **cup unsalted butter**
> 1/2 **cup firmly packed golden brown sugar**
> 1/2 **cup sugar**
>   1 **egg**
>   3 **tbsp. whiskey or dark rum**

1. Melt butter with sugars in heavy saucepan over low heat, until sugar is dissolved.

2. Whisk egg in small bowl. Add some of the hot mixture, then return it to saucepan and whisk until smooth. Do not boil.

3. Stir in whiskey and vanilla. Cool to room temperature and serve.

This sauce will last, covered tightly and refrigerated, for 2 weeks.

Hard Sauce

I cannot remember a family Thanksgiving table without a big bowl of this elixir. My normally well-balanced brother-in-law, Dave, has been known to eat an entire pint all by himself, with one arm protectively surrounding the bowl.

Yield: 1 pint
Preparation time: 10 minutes plus 2 hours to chill

> 1 **pound butter, room temperature**
> 1 **pound powdered sugar**
> 1 1/2 **tsp. pure vanilla extract**
> 1 **tbsp. + 1 tsp. brandy**
> 1/4 **tsp. ground nutmeg**

The word "hard" in the title actually refers to the liquor included.

1. Cream butter and powdered sugar in a mixing bowl. Stir in vanilla and brandy.

2. Transfer to a serving bowl, sprinkle the top with nutmeg, cover with plastic wrap and refrigerate until it sets up hard.

Quick Ginger Sauce

For a delicious, quick dessert, sauté peeled orange sections and banana slices in a little butter for 3 - 5 minutes, put them on a serving plate, and ladle ginger sauce over them.

Yield: 1/2 pint
Preparation and cooking time: less than 10 minutes

> **1 half-pint jar ginger preserves**
> **1/2 tsp. lime juice**

1. Put ginger preserves into a small saucepan over medium heat.
2. Add lime juice and heat until sauce is thin enough to be poured, about 5 minutes.

Lemon Whipped Cream Sauce

This somehow seems to lighten traditional whipped cream. It is especially good over fresh berries.

Yield: 2 cups
Preparation time: 10 minutes

> **1 tsp. lemon zest**
> **1 cup whipping cream**
> **1 tbsp. lemon juice**
> **1/4 cup powder sugar**

1. Boil the lemon zest in 1 cup water for 2 - 3 minutes (microwave: 1/2 cup water for 1 minute). Strain.
2. Whip cream to soft peak stage. Add lemon juice and powdered sugar during the final minute of whipping, then fold in zest.

This is also wonderful over pound cake, Bread Pudding (p. 319), and lots of other things.

Apricot, Lemon, or Lime Cream

I put this sauce together one night as a desperation sauce for unexpected guests. Now it's an old standby.

Yield: 1 1/2 pints
Preparation time: 10 minutes

> 1 **cup apricot preserves, lemon curd, or lime curd**
> 1 **tbsp. apricot liqueur, Grand Marnier, or brandy**
> 1 **cup heavy whipping cream**
> 2 **tbsp. sour cream**
> 1/4 **cup powdered sugar**

1. Mix liqueur with preserves or curd until thoroughly blended.
2. Pour cream into a chilled bowl. Beat to soft peak stage, add the powdered sugar and sour cream and continue beating until the cream is whipped into firm peaks.
3. Fold the fruit mixture into the whipped cream.

The preserves or curd make the sauce hold, refrigerated for 24 hours, but not longer.

- **The quality of preserves or curd make or break this sauce!**
- **The term "fold" means that the mixing is rolled with the flat side of a spatula or wooden spoon, gently and as little as possible, so the air won't be pushed from the whipped cream. This should take no more than 3 folds.**

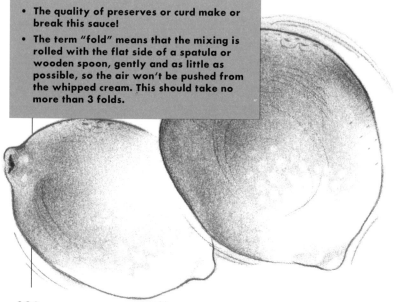

Resources for Hard-To-Find Ingredients

Your local grocer and produce manager

Get to know your grocer! Your grocer is a knowledgeable resource, waiting to be consulted. Don't hesitate to ask for help locating specialty produce, spices, flours, pastas. Many grocers can and will order specific items for you.

Commercial restaurant supply companies

Many restaurant suppliers are open to the public, and though usually a little more dusty than a trip to your local kitchen shop, they can be a terrific source for pots, pans and specialty baking supplies.

Asian Markets

Most large cities have at least one authentic Asian market where you will find many spices, rice noodles, jasmine rice, teas, dried chili peppers, dried mushrooms, and fermented black beans.

Gourmet America   CATALOG AVAILABLE
350 Lincoln St.
Hingham, MA 02043
800-352-1352 (Monday through Friday, 8:00 a.m. to 5:00 p.m. EST)

Importers of all manner of gourmet foods. Vinegars, oils, spices—including Patak's Garam Masala Curry Paste®, imported chocolate, other specialty items. Wholesale only, they will refer you to a distributor in your area or send you a catalog to use a a resource guide.

King Arthur Flour Baker's Catalog   CATALOG AVAILABLE
P.O. Box 876
Norwich, VT 05055-0876
800-827-6836 (Monday through Friday, 8:30 a.m. to 8:00 p.m. EST)

Flours, specialty baking supplies, and cooking equipment. Orders shipped within 48 hours via UPS, parcel post, or Federal Express. Master Card, Visa, American Express, Discover, check, or money order.

Penzeys Spice House   CATALOG AVAILABLE
P.O. Box 1448
Waukesha, WI 53187
414-574-0277
Fax 414-574-0278 (Monday through Friday, 9:00 a.m. to 5:00 p.m., Saturdays
(9:00 a.m. to 3:00 p.m. CST)

Purveyors of highest quality spices, including varietal chili peppers, curries—
garam masala, rare saffron from Kashmir, India. Spices are ground in small
batches to preserve their freshness, and always shipped within two weeks of
grinding. No preservatives. Competitive with grocery store brands even at the
smallest sizes, and well worth the extra trouble. They accept Master Card, Visa,
check, or money orders. Free 36-page catalog available. Orders shipped via
UPS within a week.

Sur La Table   CATALOG AVAILABLE
410 Terry Avenue N.
Seattle, WA 98109-5229
800-243-0852
Fax 206-682-1026 (8:00 a.m. to 5:00 p.m. PST for customer service, orders
taken 24 hours a day)

Cookbooks, kitchen equipment, tools, appliances, knives, every gadget in the
world, and specialty baking supplies, including such hard-to-find items as
reusable parchment paper. Master Card, Visa, American Express, Discover,
checks, or money orders. Orders shipped within 48 hours by Federal Express,
UPS, or parcel post.

Index

Index

Index

Index

Index

Index

Trademark Acknowledgments

All possible efforts have been made to acknowledge the specific products and give correct trademark credit to the manufacturers.

Acea® Garlic Slicer, made in Italy; **Beano®** is a registered trademark of AKPharma Inc., Pleasantville, New Jersey 08232; **Bisquick®** is a registered trademark of General Mills, Inc., Minneapolis, Minnesota 55440; **Chef Boyardee®** is a registered trademark of ©American Home Foods, Madison, New Jersey 07940; **Garam Masala Curry Paste®** is a registered trademark of Pakak (Spices) Ltd.; **Hellmann's®** and **Best Foods®** are registered trademarks of CPC International, Inc., Englewood Cliffs, New Jersey 07632-9976; **Jiffy®** is a registered trademark of Chelsea Milling Co., Chelsea, Michigan 48118; **Krusteaz®** is a registered trademark of Continental Mills, Inc., Box 88176, Seattle, Washington 98138; **Minute Tapioca®** is a registered trademark of Kraft, Inc., Glenview, Illinois 60025; **Pepperidge Farm®** is a registered trademark of Pepperidge Farm, Inc., Norwalk, Connecticut 06856; **Pickapeppa™** is a trademark of Pickapeppa Co. Ltd.; **Tupperware®** is a registered trademark of Dart Industries, Inc.